THE ECONOMICS OF SEA TRANSPORT AND INTERNATIONAL TRADE

Institute of Chartered Shipbrokers

THE ECONOMICS OF SEA TRANSPORT AND INTERNATIONAL TRADE

Published by the

Institute of Chartered Shipbrokers
85 Gracechurch Street, London, EC3V 0AA
United Kingdom

Telephone: +44 20 7623 1111
Email: books@ics.org.uk
www.ics.org.uk

First published 2013
ISBN 978-1-908833-18-1
©Institute of Chartered Shipbrokers 2013

Terms of use

While the advice given in this document 'Economics of Sea Transport and International Trade' had been developed using the best information currently available, it is intended purely as guidance to be used at the user's own risk. No responsibility is accepted by the Institute of Chartered Shipbrokers (ICS), the membership of ICS or by any person, firm, corporation or organisation (who or which has been in any way concerned with furnishing of information or data, the compilation or any translation, publishing, supply or sale of the document) for the accuracy of any information or advice given in the document or any omission from the document or for any consequence whatsoever resulting directly or indirectly from compliance with or adoption of guidance contained in the document even if caused by a failure to exercise reasonable care.

Printed and bound in the UK by CPI Group UK, Croydon CR0 4YY
Artwork Production by Phil McAllister (philmacallisterdesign.com)
Front Cover Image: Portpictures.nl
Front cover design by Mark Clubb (www.theclubb.co.uk)

Institute of Chartered Shipbrokers

Acknowledgements

First and foremost we would like to thank Julian Bray, editor of TradeWinds, for his support and encouragement in the revision of this book. We must also acknowledge the contribution of several industry professionals, but special thanks are due to Bridget Hogan and Fernando Dominguez-Iniguez.

Also special thanks to Simon Sharp for his efforts to improve the contents of the book.

The illustrations have been sourced from across the industry but with particular thanks to the World Trade Organisation, UNCTAD, the World Bank and BP for their statistical data. Without whose assistance much of this book would have been impossible.

Foreword

By Julian Bray,

Editor-in-Chief, TradeWinds

While working as a young business reporter working for the Reuters news agency, I was once take aside for some advice by one of the grizzled old hands on the newsdesk who had heard I had a little specialist knowledge of maritime markets.

"Son," he said, "just remember, all of human life is in shipping –heroes, rogues, billionaires, bankrupts, triumphs and tragedies – so there's always a great story to be told."

It was a sage comment that has stayed with me down the years. And since all of human life is in shipping, then at its centre, at its heart, is maritime economics.

Despite the maritime world being a generally convivial place, where people often put down roots which last a lifetime, it is always important to remember that first and foremost shipping is a business. And as in all business, to perform at one's best a working knowledge of economics is vital.

Economic factors such as scarcity of resources and demand for services are fundamental drivers not just of the ebb and flow of freight rates. They influence shipbuilding capacity, labour supply and finance availability, to mention just a few.

Knowledge of the basic forces that affect price and availability should give confidence to support decisions fuelled by experience and the need to seize the right opportunity.

However, never forget that economics has been burdened for over 150 years with Thomas Carlyle's label 'the dismal science'.

Despite their detailed professional knowledge, few economists predicted the severity of the global financial crisis that took hold in 2007, and that they continue to struggle to accurately forecast economic prospects to this day.

Nevertheless the study of maritime economics is a great asset. It will help everyone who is involved in shipping - from those working in finance departments, to those more focused on operations – to take better informed decisions, which will provide a platform for a successful career, whatever direction you choose.

About the editors

Andrew Lansdale – Technical Editor

The Institute's Technical Editor comes from a naval family. His father served in capital ships in the Royal Navy. Andrew Lansdale served aboard the three-masted training ship HMS Worcester before going to sea, serving as a Cadet and Deck Officer in the British Merchant Navy. He came ashore and started in the Shipbroking sector of the shipping industry. He passed the Institute examinations in October 1972.

He has worked in Dry Cargo Chartering and in Tanker Chartering as well as in Ship Management and in Shipping Research. He has plied his trade in London, in Tokyo and in Hong Kong.

Ten years ago, he turned to journalism and has worked as Markets Editor for Fairplay and as a freelance journalist for Lloyd's List and TradeWinds. He was presented with the News Journalist of the Year Award in 2006.

In July 2012, he completed 50 years of service in the shipping industry. He has been a blood donor for many years, but when trying to renew his donations, was told that his blood was now too salty. Apart from writing, his hobbies include navigating his small sailing yacht around the south coast of England. He is rear-commodore of the Old Worcester's Yacht Club.

Jurgen Verreet – Technical Reviewer

Born and raised in a small village on the edge of the Port of Antwerp and with a grandfather who had been employed most of his life as a 'buildrager', a career in shipping seemed almost predetermined. After graduating with a Masters in Ancient History, faith caught up and returned him to his home town.

Jurgen Verreet started his maritime career in 2004 as a contract manager in the Department of Port Dues at the Antwerp Port Authority. While at the Port of Antwerp, Jurgen completed a master in Maritime Business with great distinction.

In 2007 he exchanged his native Belgium for the bustling City of London to take up a job at IHS Fairplay, the former Lloyd's Register – Fairplay, as an analyst. After which he promptly enrolled for the courses of the Institute of Chartered Shipbrokers to further improve his understanding of the shipping world. In 2010, Jurgen successfully completed the professional qualification of the Institute of Chartered Shipbrokers.

Jurgen resides with his partner in a quiet Kentish town along the river Thames.

Contents

Acknowledgements   i
Foreword   ii

Chapter 1: The basic tool kit

1.1	A definition of economics and maritime economics	2
1.2	Factors of production	2
1.3	Utility and price	3
1.4	Opportunity cost	5
1.5	The price mechanism	6
1.6	Dynamic adjustment	14
1.7	Conclusion	14

Chapter 2: Demand for shipping

2	Introduction	16
2.1	An economic analysis of the demand for shipping	16
2.2	Distance and the concept of tonne/miles	23
2.3	Derived demand for shipping	25
2.4	Elasticity of demand	25
2.5	Derived demand elasticity	32
2.6	Conclusion	33

Chapter 3: The supply of shipping services

3	Introduction	36
3.1	A broad perspective	36
3.2	A framework for analysing the supply of shipping services	36
3.3	Trends in the world merchant fleet, 1970-2010	41
3.4	Factors affecting the short-run supply of shipping services	49
3.5	Productivity trends and supply conditions	52
3.6	Surplus tonnage and the concept of the active fleet	54
3.7	Segmented supply	56
3.8	Relating theory to empirical evidence	57
3.9	Measuring supply responsiveness: the concept of elasticity of supply	59
3.10	Conclusion	61

Chapter 4: Shipping cost analysis and economies of scale

4	Introduction	64
4.1	An outline of basic cost concepts	64
4.2	The conventional analysis of vessel operating costs	69
4.3	Specific factors affecting the relationship between costs and shipping output	70
4.4	Long-run vessel costs: economies of scale and optimal ship size	75
4.5	The effect of different fiscal regimes on costs	81
4.6	The effect of flag of registry on costs	82
4.7	Costs and quality: the problem of sub-standard ships	84
4.8	The effect of demand and inventory on optimal ship size	85
4.9	Trends in ship size and the concept of the optimum size of vessel	86
4.10	Conclusion	91

Institute of Chartered Shipbrokers

Chapter 5: Competitive shipping markets: dry bulk cargo

5	Introduction	94
5.1	Definition of the dry cargo sector	94
5.2	Market characteristics	96
5.3	Dry bulk market demand structure and trends over the past 25 years	97
5.4	An analysis of the cost structure of tramp ship operators	99
5.5	The use of break-even analysis in determining minimum freight rates	101
5.6	Modelling the dry cargo market	103
5.7	Determining the equilibrium freight rate	107
5.8	Confronting the model with the evidence	108
5.9	Dynamic considerations	114
5.10	Conclusion	115
	Appendix	116

Chapter 6: Competitive shipping markets: tankers

6.1	Seaborne trade in crude oil and oil products	118
6.2	Changes in the tanker fleet	131
6.3	The relationship between tanker and dry cargo markets	134
6.4	The structure of the tanker market	135
6.5	Segmented supply	139
6.6	Modelling demand	139
6.7	Modelling supply	140
6.8	The market model	141
6.9	Fluctuations in market freight rates	143
6.10	Environmental issues	143
6.11	Conclusion	144

Chapter 7: The liner trades

7	Introduction	146
7.1	Definition of a liner shipping service	146
7.2	Ship types serving in the liner trades	149
7.3	The nature of demand for deep-sea liner services	153
7.4	The container revolution	154
7.5	Pricing behaviour in the liner and tramp trades	155
7.6	The conference system: key institutional element or historic throwback?	157
7.7	Price discrimination in the liner trades	161
7.8	The conference paradox	162
7.9	Developments in the liner trades	166
7.10	The european commission and the liner trades	167
7.11	Conclusion	169
	Appendix 1	170
	Appendix 2	171

Contents

Chapter 8: Ports, sea canals and waterways

8	Introduction	176
8.1	Definition of ports and harbours	176
8.2	The function of ports	177
8.3	Port costs and ships' time	178
8.4	Port cost structure	183
8.5	The aims or principles of port tariffs	186
8.6	Port privatisation: ownership and efficiency	187
8.7	Port competition	188
8.8	Ports in the logistics supply chain	188
8.9	Sea canals and inland waterways	189
8.10	Conclusion	192

Chapter 9: Shipping and international trade

9	Introduction	194
9.1	The growth and pattern of world trade	194
9.2	Trade and economic growth	200
9.3	Types of trade flows: intra-industry trade and inter-industry trade	204
9.4	Trade growth and the demand for shipping services	205
9.5	Economic models of trade flows	205
9.6	The benefits and costs of free trade	215
9.7	Free trade versus protectionism	216
9.8	Methods of protection	218
9.9	Transport costs and international trade	223
9.10	Developing free international trade: the role of the world trade organisation	225
9.11	Conclusion	225

Chapter 10: The balance of payments and exchange rates

10	Introduction	228
10.1	Definition of the balance of payments	229
10.2	The structure of the balance of payments	229
10.3	Exchange rates and the balance of payments	241
10.4	Dealing with a balance of payments deficit: fixed exchange rates	243
10.5	Dealing with a balance of payments deficit: floating exchange rates	245
10.6	Exchange rates and shipping	245
10.7	Conclusion	246

Chapter 1
. . . .
The basic tool kit

Bartering was first recorded in Egypt over 4,500 years ago. In the past, people have used many different things as money. Among them salt, cocoa beans, grain, cows, shark's teeth and precious stones.

1.1 A DEFINITION OF ECONOMICS AND MARITIME ECONOMICS

There are numerous definitions in economics all of which agree that the subject contains three elements:

1 Scarcity;
2 demand;
3 choice.

The economic challenge is that there is a scarcity of resources to meet the limitless demand. This scarcity means considerable care must be taken in choosing the way resources are to be employed. Since resources can be used in many ways, the question that needs to be asked is:

What is the best use of these resources to meet demand?

As some authors refer to economics as the science of choice, others a 'dismal' science because its essential problem is scarcity. To attempt a tentative definition, economics is a study of the allocation of scarce resources that have alternative uses to satisfy demand.

Maritime economics is the application of economic analysis to all the functions involved in moving goods and people by sea. As one author put it *'Maritime Economics is a field of study concerned with the manner in which scarce productive resources are used to bridge the spatial separation of international trading countries most effectively'* (McConville J (1999) Economics of Maritime Transport). Such a definition serves to illustrate how broad the subject is and how imprecise are its boundaries.

1.2 FACTORS OF PRODUCTION

Scarcity arises from the shortage of resources. Economists call resources 'factors of production'. Resources have to be understood to mean not just raw materials, but also services, infrastructure, capital, work force and anything else needed to produce goods. All factors of production are combined together in an economy to produce a range of goods and services to satisfy demand.

The factors of production are generally divided into:

- land;
- labour;
- capital;
- enterprise.

Land. The term land includes all natural resources; which have been termed gifts of nature. In this context natural resources include mineral deposits such as oil, coal or iron ore, agricultural land, forests and building sites. Hence it comprises both the space required for production and specific raw materials. These resources are in limited quantities at any given time. Land, therefore, can be defined precisely as the limited source of raw materials and the area in which production can be organised.

Labour. This is the fundamental factor of production, being the human physical effort, skill and intellectual power that people apply to the production of goods and services. Labour, therefore, may be defined as the people's physical and mental contribution to production.

The quantity and quality of labour will vary from nation to nation. It will depend on such things as the age profile of the population, the availability of educational opportunities and the political, social and cultural structure of particular societies. In a similar way to land, labour will be limited in both quality and quantity at any given time.

Capital. Capital or physical capital is the stock of all material goods or material resources used in production. It is a characteristic of capital goods that they are not usually wanted for their own sake, but rather for the contribution they make to production. It is the stock of machinery, equipment, buildings, roads, coal mines, oil wells, ships and so on. Capital is created by the use of resources to increase the value or productivity of land and labour resources. In economics capital is not to be confused with money, it may be expressed in terms of money but that is simply a measure or indication of value. Money produces nothing. Furthermore, capital is not to be confused with such things as shares, bonds or debentures. Buying and selling such items simply changes the ownership of capital; it does not create any. They are securities, not productive capital.

Enterprise. As production processes have become more and more complex, the need for better organisation is more and more apparent. Enterprise combines the previous three factors into one working production process. Without it, production might not be possible. The entrepreneur provides the structure for production and brings together the needed raw materials, labour and capital.

The total stock of the factors of production, or resources, determines what an economy can produce. Each country has varying totals of resources. This must be seen against the fact that very few productive processes require a strictly fixed proportion of each factor. The proportions of factors of production used in a particular process usually depends upon which factors are most abundant such as the cheapest. Take, for example, the building of a large sea canal in North America. There, massive amounts of capital will be involved, while in China it will more likely be built using large amounts of labour, the least expensive resource.

1.3 UTILITY AND PRICE

Resources are used in production to create what economists call utility. This is attributed to any commodity capable of creating human satisfaction. In a broad sense it is the power of goods or services to give pleasure, satisfaction or what is termed 'real need' fulfilment. It is a purely subjective idea incapable of direct measurement. The objective of the process of production is to increase the amount of goods and services available to satisfy human desire, that is, to create utility. When you buy something, and say it is value for money, what you are really saying is that the utility you have obtained from the goods or services purchased was worth at least the price you paid. If instead, you feel that something is a bargain, what you are saying is that you value this product more than the price that you paid for it; you would have been prepared to pay more, but you did not need to. A bargain therefore illustrates the difference between price, what you have to pay for a product, and utility, what you subjectively feel that the product is worth to you.

Shipping and the maritime industry as a whole is an important element in the process of creating utility. It is involved in creating utility in a number of ways.

For example, place utility: the accessibility of goods at a certain place, such as potatoes shipped from Egypt to a vegetable shop in a small town in Holland, and

Time utility: the accessibility of goods at a certain time. For example, heating oil from West Africa or the Middle East in the storage tank of a small house in Northern Norway in mid-winter.

Other forms of utility are also contributed to by shipping or transport, such as the act of providing a service. It is also important in the import and export of goods or the act of exchange. Therefore shipping is a major factor in creating utility. In other words, creating the entire amount of satisfaction obtained from consuming various amounts of a commodity in a given time period and place.

1.3.1 Real and nominal prices

To be able to compare any information a common standard is needed. In economics the results are often values and can be compared on face value; however, if a comparison is made in monetary terms over different periods the face value (or nominal value) will lead to wrong conclusions.

Nominal values do not take changes in price into consideration. Because of inflation the most recent values will often be the highest but will not necessarily be the largest if we compensate for inflation. The values obtained after corrections for inflations are known as real values.

To be able to calculate the nominal value (N) of a commodity, we require the price (P) for a unit of that commodity and the quantity (Q).

$$N_i = P_i \times Q_i$$

The calculation of the real value is a bit more complex as we will need a price index for every year we are comparing. For the rest the calculation is rather simple as we just divide the nominal value in a specific year (t) by the price index of the same year (Pt).

$$R_i^t = N_i^t / p^t = (P_i^t \times Q_i^t)/P^t$$

For example, the graph and table below represents the nominal value and real value for a tonne of coal from 1995 - 2012.

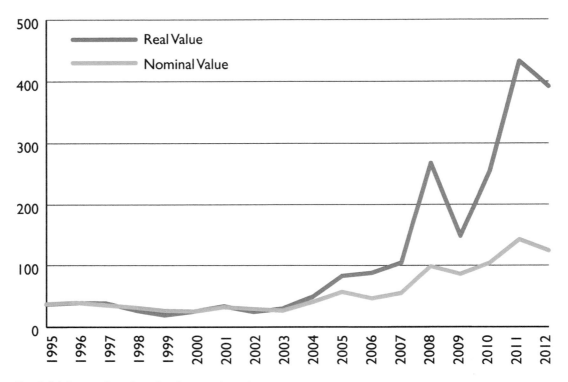

Fig 1.1 Nominal and real value coal trade

As can be seen clearly from the table and graph above, the nominal value and real values vary quite a bit due to compounding inflation. The real value allows us to compare the price of a tonne of coal over different years and draw conclusions on the change in value of the commodity.

For instance, if we compare the nominal value for a tonne of coal between 2007 and 2011, the price seems to have nearly tripled. The real value tells us that the price actually more than quadrupled. In real money terms this means that a company had to pay 4 times more for a tonne of coal in 2011 than in 2007.

Year	Price per tonne	Index	Nominal Value	Real Value
1995	37.1	0.9829	37.1	36.47
1996	39.37	0.9879	39.37	38.89
1997	35.23	1.0854	35.23	38.24
1998	31.4	0.8581	31.4	26.94
1999	26.1	0.7282	26.1	19.01
2000	25.1	1	25.1	25.1
2001	32.1	1.0406	32.1	33.4
2002	29.1	0.8415	29.1	24.49
2003	26.68	1.1142	26.68	29.73
2004	40.45	1.2071	40.45	48.83
2005	56.83	1.4546	56.83	82.66
2006	46.27	1.8957	46.27	87.71
2007	54.95	1.8972	54.95	104.25
2008	98.3	2.7231	98.3	267.68
2009	85.71	1.7196	85.71	147.39
2010	103.93	2.4503	103.93	254.66
2011	141.94	3.0506	141.94	433
2012	124.18	3.158	124.18	392.16

Table 1.1 Nominal value and real value for a tonne of coal from 1995 - 2012

1.4   OPPORTUNITY COST

Scarcity of resources for production and insatiable demand forces the making of choices. Every time a choice is made something must be foregone or sacrificed.

For example:

In an economy which can only produce two goods, ships or cotton, shipbuilding will use a certain amount of the available factors of production. Which means that they cannot be used in the production of cotton. So an amount of cotton that could have been produced has been foregone. Now let us assume that cotton is the best alternative to ships using the same amount of the factors of production available. The opportunity foregone or sacrificed by the use of resources in one way rather than another is the central idea of cost in economics.

Opportunity or alternative cost doctrine defines the utility of what has been produced, in our example ships, by measuring the utility of the best alternative production given up which is cotton. Put simply, the cost of producing a unit of Y is the utility of the unit of X that as a result must be given up.

Case Study: Factors of production:

A shipowner ordering a new ship at a shipyard will need to have money to pay for this new build. Hence it will be using one factor of production: Capital.

To build the ship, the shipyard will need the facilities to build the ship (more Capital). Further, all the buildings and slipways in the shipyard physically exist which mean they use other factor of production: Land.

Apart of the physical buildings, the shipyard will also need manpower to construct the ship. This constitutes another factor of production: Labour.

The modern vessels of today are a complicated piece of machinery and its construction requires a high level of expertise and coordination of many components. A careful planning of the work process requires coordination and management (Enterprise).

1.5 THE PRICE MECHANISM

The price mechanism is a central feature of price theory or how prices are set. The two basic components of the price mechanism are demand and supply. These are governed by what are known as economic laws and confirm a general tendency in everyday activity. The law of demand states: *'the demand for goods or services falls when the price increases, and rises when the price decreases, all other things being equal'.* To put it another way, demand and price are inversely related.

The law of supply states: *'the higher the price the greater the quantity supplied by the producer, the lower the price the smaller the quantity the producer will supply, all other things being equal'.* In other words, the supply of goods increases or decreases in relation to the increase or decrease of the price, so price and quantity supplied are directly related.

The phrase 'other things being equal' is used to isolate or concentrate on particular effects, as it is impossible to study all economic changes at the same time. In the present case, it is only possible to concentrate on the relationship between supply and demand of a commodity and its price or price changes by assuming all other influences remain unchanged. It isolates the effect of any changes that are being examined by holding all other relevant factors constant.

Having looked at the basic law of the two sides of a price mechanism, each side will now be considered in more detail.

1.5.1 Demand

The concept of demand in economics is not just need, desire or want. It is all these things backed up by a willingness and ability to pay the price. This is known as effective demand, but is generally referred to simply as demand. It expresses the quantity of a commodity which consumers are prepared to buy over a range of prices. The two factors of primary interest are the price and quantity demanded.

Let us take as an example the international cruise market. A demand schedule can be drawn up which records how much consumers, in this case potential passengers, are prepared to pay for a cruise at different prices. See Table 1.2.

Column 1	Column 2	Column 3	Column 4
Price of Cruise ($)	Quantity Demanded (passenger trips) (D)	New Higher Level of Demand (passenger trips) (D1)	New Lower Level of Demand (passenger trips) (D2)
15,000	9,000	10,000	7,000
14,000	10,000	12,000	8,000
13,000	12,000	15,000	10,000
12,000	15,000	18,000	12,000
10,000	20,000	22,000	15,000
9,000	25,000	27,000	16,000

Table 1.2 Market Demand Schedule for Cruises

The schedule serves to illustrate the law of demand. As price falls in column one, the quantity demanded increases in column two, and vice versa. Columns three and four will be discussed further in this section.

At any price, for example, $14,000, there is a definite quantity demanded of 10,000. The schedule gives the different quantities demanded at six selected price levels. The information given in the market demand schedule can be represented as in figure 1.2.

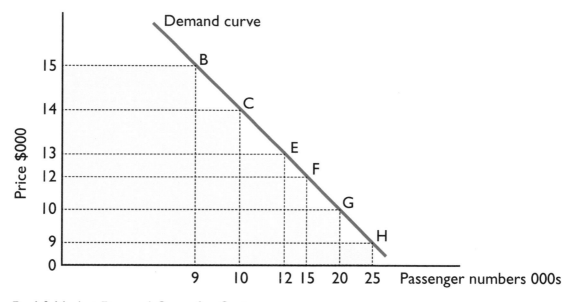

Fig 1.2 Market Demand Curve for Cruises

The vertical axis shows the possible prices. The horizontal axis shows the quantity of the commodity that can be demanded. It should be noted that normally price is shown on the vertical axis and quantity on the horizontal axis. The negative slope for the demand curve, down to the right, reflects the demand and price/quantity relationships. In other words, the negative slope illustrates that a reduction in price of cruises leads to an increase in the quantity demanded. Similarly, an increase in the price results in a fall in the quantity demanded.

It has already been shown that the higher the price the lower the quantity demanded, and vice versa. Other factors have to be assumed to remain constant. The other factors which will affect the levels of demand are:

Income. Normally it is expected that any change in income will create a change in demand. If people have more money to spend they will buy more, if the money they have to spend falls they will buy less. Historically, an increase in income has been a factor raising the demand for cruise trips.

Taste. This term is used in economics to represent all other factors which influence demand. There can be many influences on taste and it can change quite suddenly. For example, a serious disaster involving a cruise vessel would change demand levels in one direction while a successful publicity campaign could change it in another.

1.5.1.1 Prices of other commodities

The prices of commodities are often interrelated and a change in the price of one commodity might well influence the level of demand for another commodity. This relationship exists in respect of complementary goods and substitutes.

The price of complements: Items of goods are a complement if consumers purchase them jointly with another product such as milk and tea, milk and coffee, sugar and tea. In the present example assume a cruise ship entails an air flight before joining the vessel. A change in air fares would have a positive or negative effect on the demand for cruise trips.

The price of substitutes: An item of goods is a substitute if consumers purchase it instead of another product. Simply put, when the price increases for one item, the demand increases for the substitute item. Hence the price of any commodity which has many substitutes is very sensitive to change. For example if the prices of other comparable forms of holiday were to change this would have an impact on the cruise market.

If it is assumed that there is a rise in income, this would create an increase in demand, all other things being equal. This is shown in column three of the Table 1.3, and the effect would be to shift the demand curve to the right as shown below, from D to D1.

On the other hand, a reduction in income would cause the opposite effect, a fall in the number of trips demanded at any possible price, all other things being equal. This is shown in column four of Table 1.3, and the corresponding leftward shift of the demand curve is shown in Figure 1.3, from D to D2.

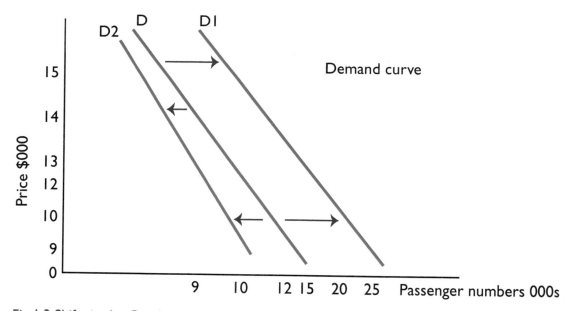

Fig 1.3 Shifts in the Conditions of Demand

There are two distinct movements in demand.

a. A movement along the curve in any direction known as **changes in the quantity demanded.**

b. A shift of the whole curve bodily to the left or the right is known as a shift in **conditions of demand**.

1.5.2 Supply

This refers to the quantity of a product that will be offered on the market at a given price during a particular time period. The law of supply states that more of a commodity will be supplied at a higher price than at a lower one. It is important to note here that the supply schedule derived in this section is based upon the assumption that the market is a perfectly competitive one. While accepting that the cruise industry does not fit this model perfectly, it is still a useful model to develop because it is one of the few shipping markets that impinges directly upon the final consumer.

A supply schedule is a table showing the different quantities the sellers are willing to offer on the market at various prices at a given time.

Column 1	Column 2	Column 3	Column 4
Price per Passenger Trip	Quantity Supplied Passenger Trips	Increase in Quantity Supplied Passenger Trips	Decrease in Quantity Supplied Passenger Trips
($)	(S)	(S1)	(S2)
15,000	25,000	27,000	21,000
14,000	20,000	22,000	17,000
13,000	18,000	20,000	15,000
12,000	15,000	18,000	12,000
10,000	12,000	15,000	10,000
9,000	10,000	12,000	8,000

Table 1.3 Market Supply Schedule for Cruises

In a similar way to demand, the supply schedule serves to illustrate the law of supply. As price increases in column 1 the producers (which are the cruise companies) increase the numbers of trips offered, as shown in column 2. At each price there are related quantities supplied, for example, at a price of $13,000, 18,000 passenger voyages or trips are supplied. Once again a graph can be constructed for supply. As usual the vertical axis indicates price and the horizontal axis indicates quantity offered.

The positive slope of the supply curve, upward to the right, reflects the law of supply and the direct relationship of price to quantity. In other words the positive slope illustrates that an increase in the price of a cruise leads to an increase in the quantity supplied, all other things being equal. Similarly, a fall in the price means a fall in the quantity offered. Alternative price quantity combinations are represented by the various points of the supply curve. For example, at price $9,000 per trip the quantity supplied is 10,000 trips, point H on the curve.

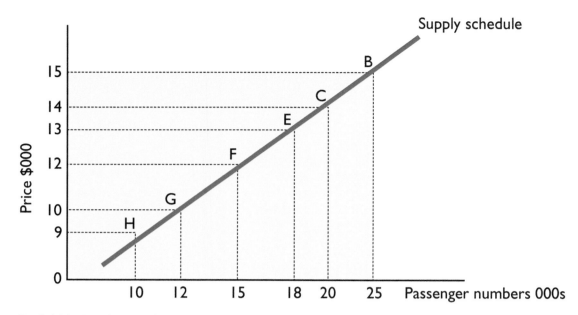

Fig 1.4 Market Supply Curve for Cruises

At point E the price has increased to $13,000 and the quantity offered to 18,000 trips, while at point B the price is $15,000 and 25,000 trips are offered. As with demand the supply schedule is based on the assumption that during the period under consideration the assumptions underlying the schedule remain constant. The factors affecting supply are:

1. Costs of the factors of production: Changes in the costs of production would influence the quantity supplied at any particular price. A major modification in crew costs would have an impact on the cost of operating a ship and hence on the amount of cruises offered.

2. Changes in the method of production: New inventions or technologies can reduce costs of production and so change producers' or suppliers' attitudes to price. In the cruise market a break-through in engine or hull design would result in a lowering of the price.

3. Inventory or stock levels: If there is a substantial amount of tonnage laid up or under- utilised, owners of vessels might accept lower prices for their cruises. They might offer discounts, or special offers such as two travelling for the price of one.

4. Expectations of future price: If there is an expectation of a rise in price, owners or the suppliers may be reluctant to sell tickets for their next cruise in the hope that the expected market price rise comes through.

To return to the cruise example, if it is assumed there has been a substantial fall in bunker prices, affecting the costs of production, this would create an increase in supply, all things being equal. This is shown in column three of the Table 1.3 and the effect would be to shift the supply curve to the right as shown below:

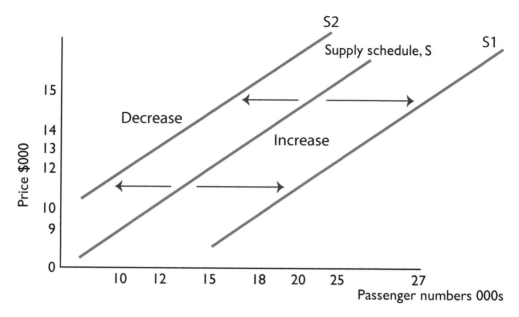

Fig 1.5 Alterations in Supply Conditions

As can be seen, the supply curve (S) has moved as a whole to the right, to S1. In this new situation, 12,000 trips are supplied at the price of $9,000 and 15,000 trips are offered if the price is $10,000, and so on, up to the point where 27,000 trips are offered at the price of $15,000. Joining these points up on a graph generates the new supply schedule S1.

Column four of Table 1.3 showed the effect of a fall in quantity supplied at any possible price, and is shown as S2 in Figure 1.5. This schedule shows the fact that supply will be less at any possible price, compared to the original schedule S.

This brings us to two different and distinct movements in supply.

a. A movement along the curve in any direction is known as **changes in the quantity supplied**.

b. A shift of the whole curve bodily to the left or the right is known as **change in conditions of supply**.

1.5.3 The basic market model, bringing demand and supply together

Up until now each side of the market, in this case the imaginary cruise market, has been analysed separately.

Neither demand nor supply can by themselves decide the market price of any product nor the quantity of the product sold. This is because individually, demand and supply only indicate consumers' and producers' intentions. The next stage is to bring the intentions into reality, so demand and supply must be combined in a single schedule as below:

Column 1	Column 2	Column 3	Column 4	Column 5	Column 6
Price of Cruise for Passenger ($)	Quantity Demand for Passenger Trips (D)	Quantity Supplied of Passenger Trips (S)	Passenger	Trips	Market Pressure on Price
			Shortage	Surplus	
15,000	9,000	25,000		14,000	Downward
14,000	10,000	20,000		10,000	Downward
13,000	12,000	18,000		6,000	Downward
12,000	15,000	15,000	0	0	Equilibrium
10,000	20,000	12,000	8,000		Upward
9,000	25,000	10,000	15,000		Upward

Table 1.4 Cruise Market: Demand and Supply Equilibrium

It will be recognised that the above is based on the demand and supply schedules used earlier in this chapter. Such schedules refer of course to a particular time period.

Column one is a list of prices a cruise passenger could be asked to pay. Column two is the quantity passengers would demand at those different price levels. Column three is the quantity cruise operators would offer at different price levels. Columns four and five highlight the differences between the two earlier columns of demand and supply. At the higher prices there is a positive difference or an excess of quantity supplied. At the lower prices of $10,000 and $9,000 there is a negative difference or an excess of demand. But at the price of $12,000 the intention of passengers and the cruise operators are exactly matched. A price where there is neither an excess of supply nor demand is known as the equilibrium price or the market clearing price. This is the point where the opposing forces of demand and supply are in perfect balance and there is no net tendency for market prices to change. To put it another way, a point where the quantity demanded of a commodity equals the quantity supplied, causing market clearance. Once obtained there will be a tendency for the equilibrium point to persist. Changes will only occur if the basic conditions of either demand or supply, or both, are disturbed. For instance if any of the factors which have been held constant actually change. The above schedule includes the two criteria of price and quantity and therefore can be represented in a market model as in figure 1.6.

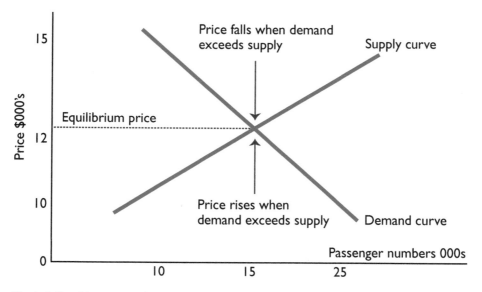

Fig 1.6 Equilibrium in the Passenger Cruise Market

The individual demand curve and supply curve are brought together in a market model. The demand curve shows the passengers' intentions or plans to purchase at each level or price following the law of demand. As prices fall, the quantity demanded increases. The curve slopes downwards from left to right. The supply curve shows the quantity cruise operators plan to sell at each level of price. Once again the law of supply is in evidence. The producers offer more at a higher price. The supply curve moves upwards from left to right. Only at an equilibrium price of $12,000 are the intentions of the passengers and cruise operators exactly meshed together. At a price above $12,000 there is a surplus and market pressures force prices to fall. Suppliers will withdraw from the market. At prices below the equilibrium value, there is a shortage, and market pressure develops for the price to rise. The quantity demanded will fall, while the quantity supplied will increase, reducing the excess of demand over supply. The excess demand disappears at $12,000.

In the following diagram the above argument is represented in a different form.

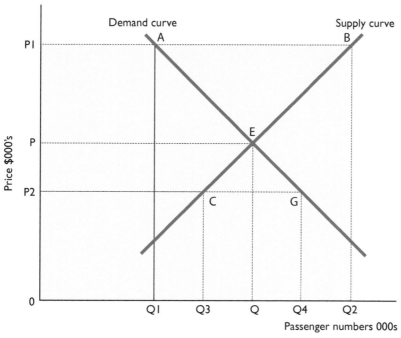

Fig 1.7 Simplified Model of Cruise Market

In the model, equilibrium price is P with quantity Q. At the higher price P1, quantity demanded stands at Q1 and quantity supplied is Q2. Therefore there is an excess of quantity supplied over the quantity demanded at price P1, which creates downward pressure on the price, forcing it towards equilibrium price P. Comparing P to P1, less is supplied but more is consumed. These two processes both help to eliminate the excess supply that exists.

At the lower price P2 the quantity supplied would be Q3, while buyers wish to purchase Q4. This means that at price P2, there is an excess of quantity demanded over the quantity supplied. A shortage exists at price P2, and pressure will be built up to force the price up, to return to market equilibrium P.

1.6 DYNAMIC ADJUSTMENT

The model described above is the simplest possible model of competitive market price determination. It is a static model, in that the effects of shifts in supply and demand on the model are not really considered. Indeed, there is an assumption that all transactions that take place in the market do so only at the equilibrium price, such as the price P in Figure 1.6. No transactions are permitted to take place at disequilibrium prices.

While a useful model in many ways, it also has some drawbacks. Perhaps the most significant is the failure to allow for the fact that there may be a considerable period of time for the required adjustments in supply to take place. For example, the shipping markets went through a crisis of severe overcapacity of tonnage in the early 1980s. This problem did not resolve itself for several years. The market model described above would therefore have to be modified to allow for this problem.

1.7 CONCLUSION

This chapter has been aimed at providing students with knowledge of some of the basic concepts of economics. The key concepts of opportunity cost, utility and price have been discussed. Secondly, a model of demand and supply and price determination in a competitive market was developed. It is very important that all readers grasp these basic concepts, and the analysis of demand and supply, because they will be heavily used in the following chapters.

Chapter 2
. . . .
Demand for shipping

The first record of a coin is by Croesus, King of Lydia (now part of Turkey)

2 INTRODUCTION

Demand for shipping, like that for all forms of freight and passenger transport, results from the final consumer's demand for goods. It is not a direct demand but a derived demand. Shipping is a factor that is not in demand for its own sake but is derived from the demand for the goods that are being transported. This discussion does not include any consideration of the cruise trade. This demand is closely related to the growth in world income, particularly that of the developed world, which is the major influence on the level of seaborne trade. The average distance of hauls, costs of transportation, and other factors, particularly international crises, have an important impact on the levels of derived demand for shipping. In this chapter empirical evidence of trends in the level of seaborne trade, and factors influencing it, will be related to a theoretical analysis of demand.

2.1 AN ECONOMIC ANALYSIS OF THE DEMAND FOR SHIPPING

The demand for shipping is dependent upon the amount of international trade generated between countries. Seaborne trade accounts for the bulk of international movements. About 75% of the world trade volume is carried by sea. The level of demand is dependent on a number of factors, the most important of which are:

- The level of world economic activity and particularly that of countries which are members of the Organisation for Economic Co-operation (OECD), i.e. the developed market economies;
- the volume of seaborne trade generated and its major components;
- distance over which the cargo is hauled;
- external factors and events.

These factors will be examined individually in the light of their importance in an economic analysis of shipping demand.

World economic activity. This is a major factor in the level of demand for seaborne trade. In the long run it is dependent upon elements such as the level of world population and changes in standards of living. In the short run, a diversity of elements can be and are important. One study of the relative contributions of economic growth, trade liberalisation and transport cost reduction found that 70% of the observed increase in world trade was solely due to simple economic growth in the relevant economies.

The best guides to changes and trends in the economy of the world or that of individual countries are Gross Domestic Product (GDP) and Gross National Product (GNP).

GDP is a measure of the total flow of goods and services produced by the economy, normally calculated on an annual basis. It is obtained by adding together the value of output, that is final consumption, investment goods, government consumption and investment and exports less imports, at current market prices. It measures the level of economic activity within the national frontiers of a country. It is gross because no allowance is made for the depreciation of capital goods and labour used in the production of those services. This explains why it is often referred to as Gross Domestic Value Added.

GNP is the annual total of the goods and services produced in a country's economy, valued at current market prices. It includes incomes accrued from investments abroad less incomes earned by foreigners in the domestic economy. It is gross domestic product plus net foreign investment earnings earned on overseas assets owned by that country's residents. It is national because it is a measure of all resources controlled by its citizens, irrespective of the physical location of those resources. For example, UK net earnings from assets in the USA are included in GNP figures, but are not in GDP figures.

Case Study: Price mechanism for demand and supply

When there are several vessels available to carry one cargo (there is excess supply), the freight rate will be low as shipowners compete by lowering the cost for the charterer, i.e. the freight rate.

In the reverse case, when there are several cargos for one vessel (excess demand) the freight rate will be higher as charterers try to insure transport for their cargo by offering higher rates.

In the shipping industry, however, it is important to keep in mind that these prices can have long term effects. When shipowners observe the first case in a systematic way, they will order fewer ships in an effort to limit the supply of shipping capacity and over time push rates higher. At low prices, production (shipping capacity) gets limited.

In a converse way, if shipowners find themselves systematically in the second case, high freight rates will encourage owners to order more ships and increase shipping capacity. Over time this will stabilise and possibly reduce rates. At higher prices, production gets increased.

GNP and GDP are measured in two different ways. When valued at current market prices, the year to year variation in value can be as much to do with changes in the price at which outputs are valued, rather than changes in the volume of output. A good example is the case of Zimbabwe in 2007. With a reported inflation rate of 3,000% per year, GDP in nominal terms will increase by 3,000%. This does not reflect the underlying performance of the economy, because all of this growth is generated by an increase in prices. A better indicator of changes in volume is obtained when GDP and GNP are measured at constant prices, which simply means measuring, for example, the value of UK GDP in 2004, 2005 and 2006 in 2004 prices. This means that any change in output between 2004 and 2006 would reflect changes in volume only, not changes in prices. Economists refer to this as real term measurement. Prices, used as the basis for this process, are quite arbitrary. Often the base is changed every 5 years or so. Thus 2007 UK GDP measured in 2005 prices means that the growth in GDP when using these figures would reflect the change in the volume of economic activity between 2005 and 2007. This is useful because volume changes in economic activity are better related to changes in physical activities, such as seaborne trade, than changes in the nominal or current prices series that incorporates changes in both volume and value.

In this chapter the main indicators of growth in all countries of the world, GDP or GNP, are simply added together and so a crude indicator of the level of international activity is obtained. Rather than examining the whole world, most analysis of shipping demand is concentrated on the OECD. This is an economic organisation whose members consist of Scandinavia, most of Europe including Turkey, North America, Japan, South Korea, Australia and New Zealand. Despite the absence of such economic powers as Russia and Central Europe, as well as the dynamic economies of Asia, such as Taiwan and Singapore, China and India, the OECD still exerts a massive influence within the international economy. This is because it includes virtually all the industrially-developed countries which account for a very large percentage of world output and international trade. It has been estimated that OECD countries account for somewhere in the region of 80% of world international production, 70% of world exports by value and some 65% by value of the world's inter-regional dry cargo trade, as well as consuming approximately 55% of oil production. This is the primary reason for concentrating on the OECD. In recent years, two non-OECD countries have figured significantly in their influence on shipping markets, namely China and India. OECD data, while still very important, now has to be widened to include such countries when examining the prospects of future economic growth and the implications for seaborne trade.

The second reason is that statistical and other information on the OECD is more easily obtainable and comparatively more reliable. Since 2000, economic growth and world trade have grown considerably, notwithstanding the events of September 11th 2001. In fact, western economies have grown relatively rapidly, along with the additional impetus from China, which has grown at 10% per year since 1995. India's growth has also reached 6-7% per year, and the combination of high growth in these economies with reasonable growth in the OECD countries led to prosperous shipping markets in the period 2002–2006.

2.1.1 Seaborne trade

Seaborne trade dominates international trade. It has been estimated that approximately 75% of world trade by weight moves by sea, but when measured in terms of value the share falls to approximately 65%. The total volume of trade has nearly doubled in the period 1980–2005. Against the background of this increase were changes, in particular commodities' contribution to trade. Crude oil and oil products declined from 44% to 34% of the total. Iron ore movements in percentage terms were unchanged at 9%. The most remarkable difference is in coal, which doubled in importance from 5% to 10%. The 2005 shares are shown in Figure 2.1.

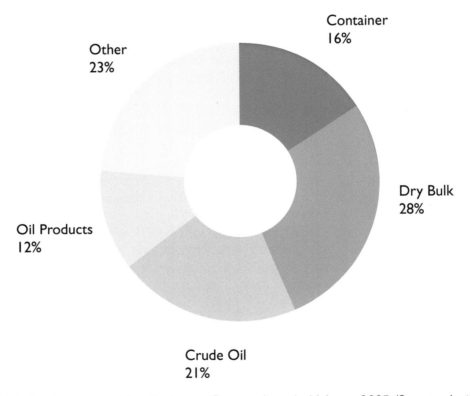

Fig 2.1 Market Shares of Major Seaborne Commodities by Volume, 2005 (Source: derived from Table 2.1)

Note: Shares based on tonnes data

Table 2.1 provides detailed information on the development of shipping movements over the period 1980-2005, measured in millions of tonnes of cargo.

Year	Crude oil	Oil products	Iron ore	Coal	Grain	Other dry cargo	Total trade	% change over prev. year
1980	1320	276	314	188	198	1310	3606	-2.9
1981	1170	267	303	210	206	1305	3461	-4.0
1982	993	285	273	208	200	1240	3199	-7.6
1983	930	282	257	197	199	1225	3090	-3.4
1984	930	297	306	232	207	1320	3292	6.5
1985	871	288	321	272	181	1360	3293	0.0
1986	958	305	311	276	165	1370	3385	2.8
1987	970	313	319	283	186	1390	3461	2.2
1988	1042	325	348	304	196	1460	3675	6.2
1989	1120	340	362	321	192	1525	3860	5.0
1990	1190	336	347	342	192	1570	3977	3.0
1991	1247	326	358	369	200	1610	4110	3.3
1992	1313	335	334	371	208	1660	4221	2.7
1993	1356	358	354	367	194	1710	4339	2.8
1994	1403	368	383	383	184	1785	4506	3.8
1995	1415	381	402	423	196	1870	4687	4.0
1996	1466	404	391	435	193	1970	4859	3.7
1997	1519	410	430	460	203	2070	5092	4.8
1998	1524	402	417	473	196	2050	5062	-0.6
1999	1480	410	410	480	210	2110	5100	0.8
2000	1669	498	474	523	210	2415	5866	n.a.
2001	1672	497	478	571	212	2376	5891	0.4
2002	1647	497	511	578	245	2405	5948	1.0
2003	1690	533	540	610	240	2491	6188	4.0
2004	1770	546	590	650	250	2855	6758	9.2
2005	1877	565	645	682	274	2986	7129	5.5
2006	1814	517	711	755	262	2924	6983	
Average Growth Rates								
1980/99	0.6	2.1	1.4	5.1	0.3	2.5	1.8	1.6
1990/99	2.5	2.2	1.9	3.8	1.0	3.3	2.8	2.8
2001/05	2.4	2.6	6.4	5.5	5.6	5.6	2.3	4.0

Table 2.1 Development of World Seaborne Trade 1980 – 2005 (Source: 1965-1999, Fearnleys Review, various issues. 2000 on, UNCTAD Maritime Review, various issues. Break in series in 1999-2000.)

The acceleration and deceleration in world trade over the last twenty-five years broadly mirrors the experience of the level of economic activity. This is reflected fairly closely in the demand for shipping. What occurred was an extremely sluggish first few years of the decade, apart from 1984, until the last years of the decade. The early 1990s saw the beginnings of a recovery of world seaborne trade, especially in the oil sector, where cargo volumes exceeded figures last seen in the mid-1970s. Dry cargo has grown more steadily over the period, but note that growth did slow down in 1991-2, but the lowest growth years were in the late 1990s. In the period 2000-2005, dry bulk cargoes in particular, but also oil, grew in volume, with oil reaching levels last seen in the late 1970s. Any practical economic analysis or forecast undertaken into the demand for seaborne trade needs to include the important individual components evident in the Table 2.1. These were as follows:

- the volume of oil movements;
- iron ore and coal shipments, and in particular their relationship to steel production;
- movements in grain;
- changes in other general cargoes;
- freight rates;
- other factors.

To look at each component individually:

Oil Movements: The change in the price of oil was the main influence on changes in volume throughout the decades. Looking at the price movement using official Saudi Arabian light oil in dollars per barrel at January 1st and July 1st of each year, the price rose from $18 in mid 1979 to a long-standing peak of $34 through 1982 and much of 1983. The impact of these prices is clearly indicated in the substantial decline in oil movements in the early years of the decade. Such price levels encouraged importing countries to curtail their consumption and seek oil substitutes and stimulated the opening of new fields closer to the market. This dramatic rise in oil prices was matched by an equally dramatic decline beginning in early 1986 and continuing, at a very low pace, until 1990. During much of this period official prices varied in the region of $17.5 to $18 per barrel. The low level of price, combined with exchange fluctuations favouring consumer countries and the de-regulation of import controls on petroleum and petroleum products, served to encourage oil movements from 1986 onwards.

Iraq's invasion of Kuwait in August 1990 led to a sharp increase in the world price of oil, but other oil exporting countries, particularly Saudi-Arabia, boosted production to offset the loss of Kuwaiti oil. Prices soon came down again, reaching levels that were similar to the pre-1973 crisis values, when adjusted for inflation. World crude oil prices stabilised at around $16 per barrel in the years 1994-95. There were some decreases in the supply at the end of the decade and into the year 2000 which caused oil prices to increase substantially to over $30 per barrel.

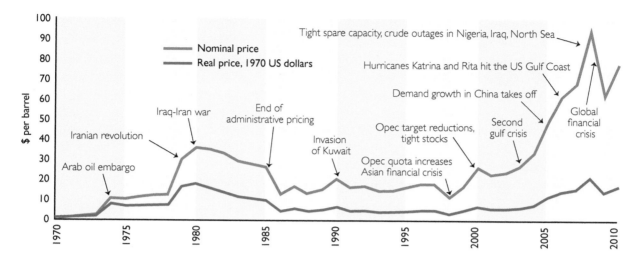

Fig 2.2 Nominal Spot Price of Crude Oil, 1972 – 2006 ($/bbl) (Source: BP Worldwide Review of Energy 2007. available at www.bp.com)

Notes: 1. Price is Arab Light, 1972-1985; 1986-2006 Dubai dated 2. Price is nominal per barrel. Nominal means measured in that year's prices. No adjustment made for changing value of the dollar over time.

Oil prices have risen dramatically in the past few years, following the crisis of September 11 2001. Figure 2.2 shows that the annual average price of spot crude oil, which itself hides large daily fluctuations, rose to around $60 per barrel in 2006. In historical terms, this is a very high figure. But in real terms, the price was still well below the equivalent values recorded in the 1977-1981 period. This may explain the fact that high oil prices have not, as yet, triggered the same kind of reaction as occurred in the 1980s. In late 2007, oil prices again accelerated, reaching $147 a barrel early in 2008, before falling back in August to around $120 a barrel. The price of oil continued to fall for most of 2009 only to rebound sharply in 2010.

In 2008 real term prices were the highest ever and have led to significant shifts in motoring behaviour as retail prices increased. The financial crisis caused by the sub-prime mortgage crisis, triggered a full blown recession in most Western countries. Nevertheless, the prevailing level of oil prices reflects the fact that the industry demand levels are running close to present refinery capacity production limits. The high oil price will trigger both greater efforts at exploring and extracting oil, as well as greater efforts at economising on its use. Increased awareness of climate change and the role of hydrocarbons in CO_2 emissions, means that there may be a long term decline in the intensity of use of oil products, but at present oil demand is high and projected to keep rising further as Brazil, Russia, India and China (the BRIC-countries) develop.

Iron ore and coal shipments. The trend in demand for steel and steel products is closely associated with other bulk cargoes. This makes demand for steel of considerable importance to the shipping industry, as it means not only an increase in the movement of crude steel, but also in iron ore, coking coal, steam coal and other bulk products necessary for its production.

During the period under consideration the steel industry underwent several important structural changes. To simplify a complex situation, production by the advanced steelmakers of Europe, America and Japan remained comparatively static. Capacity expanded rapidly in the semi-industrialised nations such as South Korea, Taiwan and Brazil. There was also additional expansion in the Eastern Block including China. China increased its steel production from about 60m tonnes per year to 90m tonnes over the period 1990-1995, an increase of 50%. The volume of seaborne movement in iron ore and coal followed the crude steel production and economic levels of activity fairly closely during the 1980s. It showed serious contractions in the volume of seaborne movements in the first half of the decade. In the second half, both sectors improved, growing steadily during this period. The upward trend continued in the 1990s, with iron ore exports reaching 402m tonnes in 1995, with both Australia and Brazil recording significant increases over this period. By 2005 iron ore exports had reached 645m tonnes, an increase of 60% over the 10 year period.

The coal trade has also experienced significant expansion in the 1990s, from 340m tonnes in 1990 to 480m tonnes in 1999. Australia especially increased its exports in this period. Coal trade expansion has continued, with export volumes rising to 680m tonnes in 2005. These changes have clear implications for the pattern of seaborne trade in coal. The growth was especially driven by the continued increase in Chinese steel production. It grew from 127m tonnes in 2000 to a spectacular 695.5m tonnes in 2011. As result China produces nearly 4 times the total production of the European Union. Also the Indian economy has begun to grow rapidly after moving away from protectionist policies. Its steel production reached 72.2m tonnes in 2011.

The effect on shipping demand has been palpable. Iron ore and coal shipments from Australia, Brazil and South Africa have increased rapidly, creating boom market conditions for the dry bulk sector.

The data presented in Tables 2.1 and 2.2 show that demand for these commodities has grown rapidly in the period 2004-6. Coal tonne/mile demand has grown by over 10% a year for the period 2004-6, with iron ore growing in a similar fashion. Again, China and India are the principal reasons for this tremendous expansion. It was claimed that in 2007 China was opening new coal-fired power stations at the rate of two a week. Some of the coal needed will have to be imported. With China being the world's largest steel producer and with continued growth, prospects for iron ore imports are favourable. China imports the largest share of iron ore in seaborne trades. Although it is the largest steel producer in the world, it imports relatively little coal; 177m tonnes compared with 621m tonnes of iron ore in 2010. The largest importer of coal remains Japan at 187m tonnes.

Grain. There are numerous definitions of grain and coarse grain. Generally in maritime transport both cargoes are based on several types of grain such as wheat, barley, oats, rye, sorghum and soya beans. Rice is usually bagged and so excluded from this analysis. Grain is a significant factor in demand for bulk dry cargo tonnage.

In the longer term, changes in the standard of diet and the growth in world population are major factors, as is the use of grain as animal feed. The balance of demand and supply is in the main covered by the production of North America. Here two points should be made.

Firstly, against the level of total growth in grain production the percentage volume movement in seaborne trade appears to be at first sight insignificant. According to figures from the International Grain Council the estimated world production of grain from June 2010 to July 2011 was 2,157.3m tonnes but the total trade of grain in the same period was limited to 242.8m tonnes.

Secondly, while the long run or 10-year figures may indicate smooth movements, short run experience is totally different. To state the obvious, grain production is influenced largely by weather conditions and varies from year to year.

The subsidised farming arrangements in the EU and the USA have led to accusations that the trade in agricultural products is heavily distorted and has lowered the world price of grain, to the detriment of farmers in developing countries. This debate has been central to the Doha round of negotiations at the World Trade Organisation. The Doha round has dragged on since 2001, and is still not completed. The last meeting in 2008 failed on the removal of agricultural subsidies. It is the case that world trade in grain, and in other agricultural products, is still subject to trade barriers that have long since been removed from other commodities. The failure of the grain trade to grow rapidly in the past 10 years may be due to this fact. But it is still the case that wars, famines and crop failures due to exceptional weather conditions are still factors in explaining the year to year variations in grain trading that occurs. Such changes have generated significant shifts in the trading pattern of vessels engaged in grain transportation.

The production of ethanol and biofuels in the USA swallows 25% of that country's grain crop. Enough grain to feed 350m people per year was pumped into transport vehicles in 2010. This effort to reduce America's reliance on foreign oil imports has also altered trading patterns in the grain trade.

Other general cargoes. This term includes such things as the lesser bulk cargoes, general merchandise and unitised cargoes. The latter has seen multiple changes, especially the vast increase in containerisation. The liner trade's growth has been spectacular in the past 10 years, encouraged by the steady expansion in world trade. The role of China, as a major manufacturer of finished goods, in driving the growth of the container trade cannot be over-emphasised. The growing globalisation of production has been assisted by the development of the liner industry. Containerised traffic has been given a significant boost by greater trade liberalisation and by economic growth. It is estimated that the liberalisation of trade has contributed about 20% to growth in the liner industry. The largest factor contributing to the success of the liner industry is still economic growth, hence the current problems the liner market is facing since the economic downturn following the financial crisis.

Freight rates and external factors. Freight rates are included here to complete the analysis. They will be discussed in some detail below and in later chapters. Empirical evidence has shown that the lowering of freight rates in real terms over the period 1950–1988 has made a small but significant contribution to the growth of world trade. At the level of individual trading companies, such prices are seen as key to their success.

External factors. These include natural phenomena, changes in technology and political events. For example, any major breakthrough in railways, aircraft or pipelines would have a serious impact on shipping demand. A more obvious and immediate impact would be political events, the most profound being wars, which change demand criteria overnight.

Finally, natural events, especially natural disasters, such as droughts which have an impact on grain harvests or frosts on coffee crops, result in alterations in the demand for shipping. The Boxing Day tsunami that struck Indonesia, India and Sri Lanka in 2004 disrupted shipping and affected rates in the region. The Japanese earthquake and tsunami in March 2011 shut down all but one of Japan's 54 nuclear plants, closing out 30% of the country's power production. This has been replaced by fossil fuels such as coal and natural gas, causing an increase in coal and LNG demand at a time when rates in these sectors were under pressure.

2.2 DISTANCE AND THE CONCEPT OF TONNE/MILES

It has already been argued that the demand for shipping space is largely determined by the level of economic activity, which is closely related to the quantity and nature of the commodities offered in seaborne trade. This is based on the number of tonnes of cargo transported. The other important factor is shipping distance. One tonne of wheat to Liverpool from Australia via the Cape will generate three times the demand for tonnage as the same tonne of wheat from Canada. Therefore, a far more satisfactory measure of demand is the weight in tonnage multiplied by the distance that the tonne has travelled. This is known as tonne/miles.

For example:

8 tonnes of cargo are carried 500 nautical miles. The tonne/miles will be $8 \times 500 = 4,000$ tonne/miles.

The central importance of distance can be illustrated by the fact that between the late 1940s and the oil crisis of the mid 1970s the annual rate of growth of total tonnage was 8% while in total tonne/miles it was 12%. During the period the average distance moved increased steadily and exceeded that of capacity.

The reasons for this are not hard to find:

- the expansion of oil exports from the Persian Gulf;
- the importance of the closure of the Suez Canal;
- the rapid economic growth of Japan with its lack of raw materials;
- the establishment of new mineral resources in Australia and South Africa.

Figure 2.3 presents the trend changes in seaborne tonne/miles over the period 1965 - 2005. It is clear that the oil sector has behaved quite differently from dry cargo markets, and this will be explored in more detail in later chapters. It is only since the mid-1990s that oil transportation began to exceed demand levels which had peaked in 1980, whereas dry cargo has broadly risen year-on-year, albeit with differing growth rates.

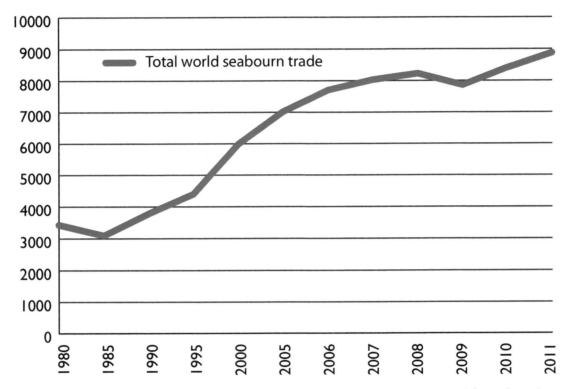

Fig 2.3 Development of World Seaborne Trade, 1965 - 2005 (Source: Derived from Fearnleys Reviews, 1965-2000, UNCTAD Maritime Reviews 2000–2005)

Table 2.3 indicates the trends in the major bulk trades between 1965 and 2005 in terms of tonne/miles. This differs from data measured in tonnes of cargo to the extent that demand is affected both by changes in the cargo volumes and by changes in the average distance that the cargo is carried, or average haul.

In tonne/mile terms, total trade has risen from 16,654 billion in 1980 to nearly double, 29,045 billion, in 25 years. This is a substantial increase, but it is clear from Figure 2.3 that dry cargo and oil have behaved in different ways over this period.

Crude oil trades experienced dramatic declines in demand in tonne/mile terms over the period 1980–1985. In terms of tonne/miles, demand only reached the 1980 level in the early years of the new millennium. This shows just how long it can take for a shipping market to recover if its recession is severe. Some of the decline in the early 1980s was due to a shift in production to sources nearer to large markets, such as the North Sea, Alaska and Mexico. With the peaking of North Sea oil production in the late 1990s, oil production has again begun to shift towards the Middle East, West Africa and the Caspian Sea. The increased share of Middle East oil in world production raises the average length of voyage for crude oil and increases tonne/mile demand still further. Oil products have increased by approximately 220%, from the level observed in 1980, partly helped by a lack of refinery capacity in Asia, demand being met by increased shipments from Middle East refineries in larger product tankers.

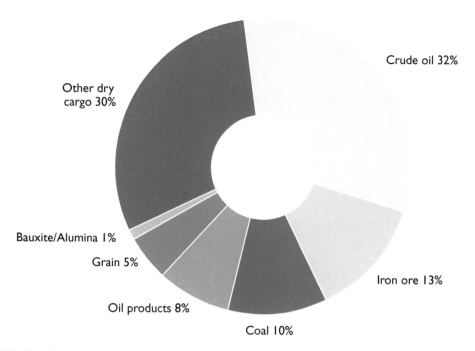

Fig 2.4 Market Share of Principal Cargoes, 2005 (Source: Derived from Table 2.1 data. Note: Shares based on tonne/mile data in billion tonne-miles)

2.3 DERIVED DEMAND FOR SHIPPING

In chapter 1 it was argued that normal effective demand was an expression of the quantity that consumers are prepared to buy over a range of products, supported by the ability to pay. This discussion examined the case of an imaginary cruise market where the consumers' objective was to have an enjoyable holiday, including in it a sea voyage back to the original point of embarkation. Sea cruises are the exception and not to be confused with the pure transport activity of the rest of the shipping industry. Demand for shipping is an indirect demand. Shipping is seen as an element in the process of production, demanded not for its own sake but for the contribution it makes to the production of final consumer goods and services.

We illustrate the concept of derived demand with examples;

- the demand from the final consumers for petrol to fill their car or motor cycle in Singapore. This is related to the earlier derived demand for tankers to convey the oil from the producer in Kuwait to the refinery and then to the distribution point;

- the demand for a cup of coffee at the end of a meal in a restaurant in Glasgow is part of a derived demand for tonnage to transport coffee from Brazil to the United Kingdom.

This is the essential difference from the cruise passenger market, whose final demand was a satisfactory holiday on a cruise ship. To re-state the definition, the derived demand for a factor like shipping is dependent on the ultimate demand for the final consumer product. The derived demand for dry cargo tonnage in conveying wheat comes directly from the final consumer's demand for bread. Students will have perceived that the theoretical economic concept of derived demand underlies much of the previous discussion of the importance of the relationship between increased economic activity and the level of international seaborne trade.

2.4 ELASTICITY OF DEMAND

Many company executives either knowingly or unknowingly use the concept of price elasticity of demand without ever being aware of the fact. Consider the managing director of an imaginary

Year	Crude Oil	Oil Products	Iron ore	Coal	Grain	Other Cargo	Total Trade	Annual %change
1980	8219	1020	1651	957	1087	3720	16654	-5.1
1981	7193	1000	1558	1124	1131	3710	15716	-5.6
1982	5212	1070	1443	1094	1120	3560	13499	-14.1
1983	4478	1080	1320	1057	1135	3510	12580	-6.8
1984	4508	1140	1631	1270	1157	3720	13426	6.7
1985	4007	1150	1675	1479	1004	3750	13065	-2.7
1986	4640	1265	1699	1558	914	3780	13856	5.9
1987	4671	1345	1761	1622	1061	3840	14300	3.2
1988	5065	1445	1950	1682	1117	4040	15299	7.0
1989	5736	1540	2012	1752	1095	4250	16385	7.1
1990	6261	1560	1978	1849	1073	4400	17121	4.5
1991	6757	1530	2008	1999	1069	4510	17873	4.4
1992	6977	1620	1896	2001	1091	4650	18235	2.0
1993	7251	1775	2001	1949	1038	4840	18854	3.4
1994	7330	1860	2165	2014	992	5100	19461	3.2
1995	7225	1945	2287	2176	1160	5395	20188	3.7
1996	7495	2040	2227	2217	1126	5705	20678	2.4
1997	7830	2050	2444	2332	1169	6000	21825	5.5
1998	7793	1970	2306	2419	1064	5940	21492	-1.5
1999	7500	2010	2220	2430	1170	6150	21480	-0.1
2000	8180	2085	2545	2509	1244	6790	23693	n.a.
2001	8074	2105	2575	2552	1322	6930	23885	0.8
2002	7848	2050	2731	2549	1241	7395	24155	1.1
2003	8390	2190	3025	2810	1273	7810	25862	7.1
2004	8910	2325	3415	2965	1325	8335	27635	6.9
2005	9270	2435	3720	3140	1380	8730	29045	5.1
2006	9516	2635	4120	3372	1436	9608	30687	
Average Growth Rate								
1980/99	-0.5	3.6	1.6	5.0	0.4	2.7	1.3	
1990/99	2.0	2.9	1.3	3.1	1.0	3.8	2.6	
2001/05	2.6	3.2	8.0	4.7	2.2	5.2	4.2	

Table 2.3 Seaborne Trade Volume in Tonne-miles – Transport Performance (source: Fearnleys Review, various issues, UNCTAD Maritime Review, 2000 on. Note: Line indicates break in series)

ferry company that is losing money. The central problem is what will happen to passenger revenues when fares are lowered. There are three possibilities to be considered.

The situation could be that, with a lowering of fares, more passengers travel by ferry and the total revenue increases. Total revenue is defined as price multiplied by quantity, which in this case is identical to the product of the fare charged multiplied by the number of passengers.

(1) Price (£) (P)	(2) Ferry Passengers Demand (000)(Q)	(3) Total Revenue (TR) (£000) (P x Q)	(4) Marginal Revenue (MR (£000) (1)	(5) % Change in Price (2)	(6) % Change in Quantity (2)	(7) Arc Elasticity (col 6/col5) (3)	(8) Point Elasticity (4)
200	0	0	200	-	-	-	-
180	1	180	160	-10.5	200.0	-19.0	-9.0
160	2	320	120	-11.8	66.7	-5.70	-4.0
140	3	420	80	-13.3	40.0	-3.00	-2.3
120	4	480	40	-15.4	28.6	-1.90	-1.5
100	5	500	0	-0.01	1.01	-1.01	-1.0
80	6	480	-40	-21.5	18.7	-0.87	-0.7
60	7	420	-80	-28.6	15.4	-0.53	-0.4
40	8	320	-120	-40.0	13.3	-0.33	-0.3
20	9	180	-160	-66.7	11.8	-0.18	-0.1

Table 2.4 Price Elasticity of Demand for a Ferry Service. (Daily trip numbers)

Notes: 1. Marginal Revenue, column 4, is defined as the derivative of the demand function P = 200 – 20Q, used to calculate the figures in the first two columns. Total Revenue is the product of price times quantity.

2. Percentage changes are here defined relative to the average of the initial and final values for the change. For example, the 10.5% fall in price is derived from −20/((200+180)/2) = −20/190 = −10.5%.

3. The Arc elasticity is measured as the ratio of the percentage change in quantity demand divided by the percentage change in prices, as defined in note 2.

4. Point elasticity is defined as the ratio (P/Q)*dQ/dP, which in this case is P/Q*(−0.05), as dQ/dP = 1/(dP/dQ) =1/(−20) = −0.05.

The lowering of fares leaves the number of passengers unchanged; this would also serve to reduce total revenue.

The lowering of fares increases the number of passengers travelling with the company, but total revenues actually decline as the increase in the number of passengers is more than offset by the fall in the average fare that each passenger pays.

An important point arises from the above analysis. The importance of being able to forecast the effect on demand of a change in price, and whether or not the passengers have substitute modes of travel that they can easily utilise is crucial. The central point here is the responsiveness of buyers to a change in price. This is known as the price elasticity of demand, or simply elasticity of demand. In general terms, elasticity can be defined as a measure of the responsiveness of one variable to a change in another.

In the ferry service example the degree of responsiveness of passenger traffic is measured with regard to changes in fares. The ferry situation is set out in Table 2.3 from which a number of observations can be made.

An important fare in the table is that of £100. Lowering fares has the effect of raising both the quantity of ferry trips demanded by consumers, and the ferry company's total revenue, until the price is reduced from £120 to £100. Further reductions beyond that point cause total revenue to contract, even though the number of ferry trips continues to increase. It can be seen that marginal revenue changes from a positive to a negative. Any reduction below the £100 fare, for example to £80 or £60, causes a fall in total revenues, even though passenger numbers still rise. The percentage increase in quantity demanded is now smaller than the percentage fall in fares and therefore total revenue or price times quantity falls. It reduces from £500,000 at a fare of £100 to £420,000 at a fare of £60. The table highlights the importance of the relationship between percentage changes in the number of passengers and the percentage changes in fares and the effect this will have on total revenue.

It has already been pointed out that when the price falls below £100, further decreases in price lead to a fall in revenues. You will note that at this point, the arc elasticity changes from being greater than unity to becoming smaller than unity. In fact, total revenues are maximised and cannot be made any larger at the price of £100 per ticket. This point of maximum revenue always corresponds to the own price elasticity having unit value. You will also note that marginal revenue switches from being positive at prices greater than £100, goes through zero at the price of £100, and becomes increasingly negative as prices fall below the £100 mark. This is no accident. It can be shown, in general terms, that marginal revenues, total revenues and elasticity values are all related, and are essentially different aspects of the same fundamental relationship derived when demand functions are linear in price and quantity.

Column 8 Table 2.3 provides a different measure of price elasticity of demand, known as point elasticity or marginal elasticity. This is the most accurate conceptual measure, as it is defined in terms of a very, very, small percentage change in price and the associated percentage change in quantity demanded that it brings about.

The above results are laid out in Table 2.4.

If Demand is	Symbolically	Means That	When Price falls	May Imply Presence of
Price Elastic	$E_d > 1$	% change in Q > % change in P	Total revenues **rise**	Substitute products
Unit Price Elastic	$E_d = 1$	% change in Q = % change in P	Total revenues remain **unchanged**	
Price Inelastic	$E_d < 1$	% change in Q < % change in P	Total revenues **fall**	Few or no close substitutes
Perfectly Price Inelastic	$E_d = 0$	% change in Q = zero	Total revenues **fall** by the percentage **fall** in price	No substitutes at all

Table 2.5 Elasticity of Demand and Total Revenue

Q stands for quantity demanded. P stands for unit price.

Note: Values are calculated ignoring the sign of the price elasticity. If the signs are included, the inequalities would have to be reversed.

Consider the importance of elasticity, not in the case of a passenger ferry but, as an example, in relation to dry cargo freights. A simple model can be constructed around a group of dry cargo shipowners who need to be able to calculate what effect the fall in freight rates would have on their total revenue.

Let us consider three different situations:

Situation 1 Elasticity >1 (Elastic)

Original freight rate per ton	= $10 (F$_1$)
Number of tonnes which shippers demanded	= 9000 (Q$_1$)
Total revenue is	= $90,000 (OF$_1$ Q$_1$)
Freight rate contracts to	= $8 (F$_2$)
Number of tonnes shippers' demand increases to	= 15000 (Q$_2$)
Total revenue increases to	= £120,000 (OF$_2$ Q$_2$) E$_2$

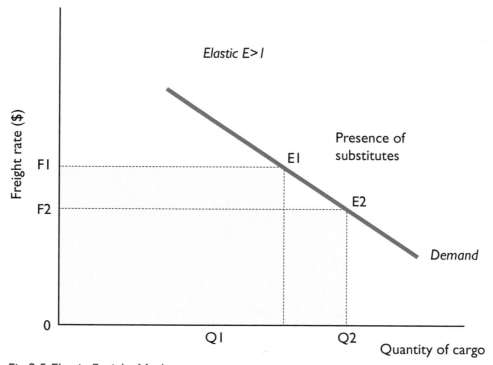

Fig 2.5 Elastic Freight Market

Total revenue area $OF_1 E_1 Q_1$ < area $OF_2 E_2 Q_2$.

In this situation, despite the contraction in the freight rate, shippers receive an increase in the amount of total revenue.

In terms of arc elasticity, the calculated value of the above example is found as follows:

% change in Q = (15000 - 9000) / ((15000 + 9000)/2) = 6000/12000 = +1/2

% change in P = ($8 − $10) / (($8 + $10)/2) = -2/9.

Elasticity = (1/2) / (-2/9) = (1/2)*(-9/2) = -9/4 = -2.25.

This is an Elastic value, as it exceeds unity (ignoring sign).

Situation 2 Elasticity <1 (Inelastic)

Original freight rate	= $6 ($F_1$)
Number of tonnes which shippers demanded	= 20,000 (Q_1)
Total revenue is	= $120,000 ($OF_1 Q_1$)
Freight rate contracts to	= $4 ($F_2$)
Number of tonnes shippers' demand increases to	= 25,000 (Q_2)
Total revenue contracts to	= $100,000 ($OF_2 Q_2$)

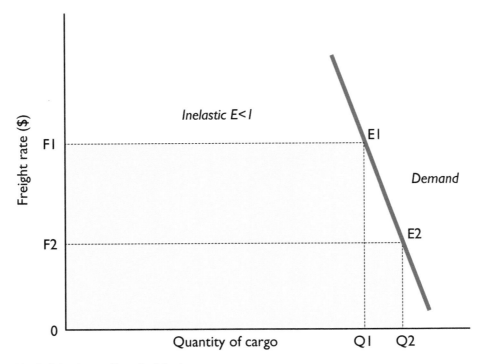

Fig 2.6 Inelastic Freight Market

Total revenue area $OF_1 E_1 Q_1$ > area $OF_2 E_2 Q_2$.

In this situation a fall in the freight rate has resulted in a contraction in total revenue despite the fact that an inelastic demand implies that there are no, or few, substitutes available.

In terms of arc elasticity, the calculated value of the above example is found as follows:

% change in Q = (25000 - 20000) / ((25000 + 20000)/2) = 5000/22500 = 50/225 = 2/9

% change in P = ($4 –$6) / (($4+$6)/2) = -2/5.

Elasticity = (2/9) / (-2/5) = (2/9)*(-5/2) = -0.556.

This is an Inelastic value, as it is less than unity (ignoring sign).

Situation 3 Elasticity = 1 (Unity)

Original freight rate	= $8 (F1)
Number of tonnes shippers' demanded	= 15,000 (Q1)
Total revenue is	= $120,000 (OF1 E1 Q1)
Freight rate contracts to	= $6 (F2)
Number of tonnes shippers' demand increases to	= 20,000 (Q2)
Total revenue remains the same at	= $120,000 (OF2 E2 Q2)

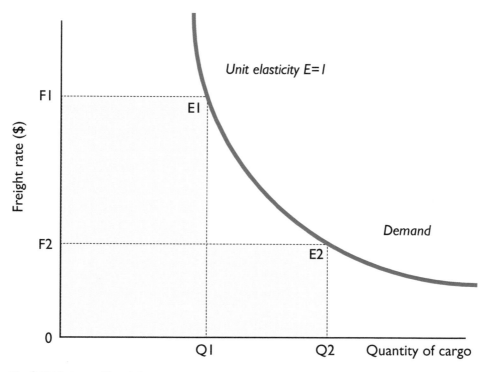

Fig 2.7 Unitary Elasticity

Total revenue area $OF_1 E_1 Q_1$ = area $OF_2 E_2 Q_2$.

In terms of arc elasticity, the calculated value of the above example is found as follows:

% change in Q = (20000 - 15000)/((20000 + 15000)/2) = 5000/17500 = 50/175 = 2/7.

% change in P = ($6 – $8)/(($6 + $8)/2) = -2/7.

Elasticity =(2/7)/(-2/7) = -1.0.

This is a unit elasticity value, as it is exactly unity (ignoring sign).

Finally, it should be pointed out that the concept of elasticity does not just apply to price alone. Any variable that is measurable, and affects the demand for goods and services, can be measured in elasticity form. For example, income elasticities can be computed to determine the likely responsiveness of demand to changes in economic activity, or real incomes. Similarly, the impact of changes in the prices of substitute products can be measured. This is known as cross elasticity, for example, the effect of a 10% rise in the price of crude oil on the demand for coal, given that oil and coal are alternative forms of energy for power stations. Estimating elasticities and using them in projections is one of the more useful tools in the economist's tool kit.

2.5   DERIVED DEMAND ELASTICITY

You will have noted that in the above discussion that demand was for the final or ultimate consumers, as in the case of ferry passengers. This was done to develop the discussion of elasticity in a logical way. What was overlooked or ignored was that all freight shipping is an intermediate part of a process of production and the demand for shipping, like the demand for raw materials or intermediate goods, is a derived demand. The demand is derived from the consumer's demand for the final product.

Derived demand has a particular set of rules relating to its elasticity. These rules, which are known as the Marshall Rules after Alfred Marshall, a 19th century English economist, have been adapted and modified to relate them to the derived demand for shipping and the factors which govern its elasticity in the short term.

Rule 1 There are few, if any, substitutes for shipping. The argument here is that most products in international trade require transportation by sea, for which there is not a close substitute.

Rule 2 Although there may be alternative sources of the product supplied, these too will normally require transportation by sea. Again it is a case of there being no substitutes. For example, while coffee from Africa could be an alternative to coffee from South America, from the point of view of the European consumer all will require sea transport. Again it is a case of there being no substitutes.

Rule 3 Freight rates are a small proportion of final cost. In terms of the value of cargo carried, freight rates are a small, often insignificant, proportion of the total cost, hence a relatively large increase in freight rates makes relatively little difference to the price of the product to the final ultimate consumer. The following table illustrates this point.

Decade	Developing Africa	Developing Oceania	Developing America	Developing Asia	Developed World	World
1980s	12.3%	11.6%	8.3%	8.9%	7.4%	9.7%
1990s	12.1%	12.0%	8.3%	8.4%	7.3%	9.62%
2000s	10.6%	9.5%	8.2%	7.4%	6.4%	8.42%

Table 2.5 (Source UNCTAD)

This table serves to confirm the general conclusion that freight rates are relatively minor proportions of the value of the final or finished commodity.

Rule 4 The elasticity of demand for the final product will be an important factor in the elasticity of the derived demand for shipping. The lower or higher the price of elasticity of the final product, the lower or higher will be the price of elasticity for shipping. Since many goods transported by sea have a low elasticity, this will be reflected in the low elasticity of demand for shipping. A simplified model of the whole idea can be put into the following words:

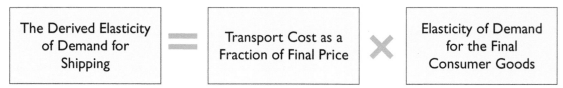

The model combines the ideas of lack of substitution and confirms that, in general, the derived demand for cargo shipping will be inelastic. Given that on average, freight constitutes only one tenth of the import value of a commodity, it follows that a 30% rise in the freight rate will only increase the import cost by 3%. From the Marshall rules, it follows that even if the own price elasticity of demand for the imported commodity is high; the derived demand elasticity of freight will almost certainly be very price inelastic. Indeed, for crude oil, it can plausibly be argued that the freight rate elasticity is close to zero.

2.6 CONCLUSION

This chapter has been aimed at relating the theory of derived demand to the experience of the shipping industry over the last few decades. International trade was looked at both in the widest sense, and in terms of specific trades. These make up the essential components of shipping demand and assist in analysing not only what has happened, but are part of creating expectations about what will happen.

Chapter 3
. . . .
The supply of
shipping services

*The world's smallest coin weighed only .002 grams
and was from Nepal.*

3 INTRODUCTION

In this chapter we will introduce the idea of the supply of shipping services. The first part of the chapter provides a broad perspective on supply and trends in the world merchant fleet are examined. Further, the concepts of supply are reviewed and related to the data analysed previously. Finally, the concept of supply elasticity is discussed.

3.1 A BROAD PERSPECTIVE

In the long run, one would expect to observe a correlation between the volume of world seaborne trade, measured in either tonne/miles per time period or cargo tonnes moved per year, and the stock of vessels employed in that activity.

It has already been observed that cargo volumes rose, peaked, declined and rose again, as world trade and economic activity recovered from the recessionary period of the late 1970s/ early 1980s It moved into strong growth in the period 2002-2007. If the fleet size is affected by market forces these changes in demand for shipping services should be reflected in long term trends in the size of the merchant fleet.

But analysing the behaviour of shipping supply is a much more complex task. There is a need to be able to identify how shipowners and operators respond to changes in demand that might occur on a very short term basis, as well as considering the longer term view. To do this, a clear framework within which to examine the many different facets of supply behaviour is required, along with an analysis of how supply can be adjusted to changes in demand.

Having outlined a suitable framework, the statistical evidence concerning the world merchant shipping fleet is reviewed, and then a simple theoretical model of short and long term supply responses to changing market conditions is constructed.

It is important to note that, for the purpose of this analysis, there is an assumption that in effect there is only one market for shipping services. This is of course completely false. There are many distinct market sectors within the shipping industry. Although the assumption is false, it is nevertheless a useful one to make at this point. To a certain extent it can be defended. Despite the existence of market segments, there is strong evidence that in the longer term at least, those markets are all inter-related, so that they tend to move in sympathy with each other.

3.2 A FRAMEWORK FOR ANALYSING THE SUPPLY OF SHIPPING SERVICES

3.2.1 Measuring output

To define supply properly, one needs to clarify what the shipping industry actually produces. For example, one should examine what is the output of a unit of shipping service. There are, in fact two possible answers to this question, as was touched on earlier in respect of demand.

First, shipping produces the act of moving cargo around the world from port to port and from terminal to terminal. Adding up the tonnes of cargo moved per time period such as per day, per week or per year gives a picture of activity generated by the working fleet. It should be noted that output is measured in volume terms, and not by cargo value. It is volume that determines how much carrying capacity is required, rather than its value. Cargo volume is generally measured in cargo tonnes, which can be related to the deadweight tonnage or carrying capacity of a ship.

Second, shipping produces nothing if ships do not move. This obvious point means that output can be measured in terms of the movement of one tonne of cargo over distance in a given period of time. This measurement is called the tonne/mile, the product of the volume of cargo tonnes and the distance it travels in a given period of time. Therefore, a fully laden 250,000-tonne capacity tanker carrying crude oil from the Arabian Gulf to Rotterdam via the Cape of Good Hope, will generate 11,169 nautical miles x 250,000 tonnes of cargo = 2,792,250,000 or nearly 2.8 billion tonne/miles.

The distinction between the two measures of output is important for two reasons. First, changes in a route composition of demand can generate changes in the demand for tonne/miles, even if the cargo volume appears unchanged. Consider the following example:

Case A			
Cargo Volume Generated	Route Distance	Time Taken (days)	tonne/miles
100	22,238	93.1	1,116,900
100	10,348	43.1	517,400
200			1,634,300

Case B			
Cargo Volume Generated	Route Distance	Time Taken (days)	tonne/miles
150	22,238	93.1	1,675,350
50	10,348	43.1	258,700
200			1,934,050

Table 3.1 Effect of a Change in Route Volumes on tonne/miles Produced

By simply switching cargo volume from one route to another but keeping the total constant at 200 tonnes, an increase in tonne/miles has been generated.

3.2.2 A schematic representation of the supply of shipping

The supply of shipping services can be altered in two principal ways; first by altering the stock of vessels and second by altering the way that the existing stock of vessels is employed.

3.2.2.1 Altering the stock of vessels

Before data on the stock of shipping is examined, it may be helpful to lay out schematically the different ways in which shipowners can alter the output that is produced by ships, whether measured in terms of tonne/miles or tonnes of cargo. Table 3.1 illustrates the different ways of altering the present stock of vessels. This would be equivalent to the economist's concept of the 'long run' period; the period in which the capital stock tied up in a firm or industry can be varied. Such changes alter the long run level of output supply. This is because the items identified in the figure take a considerable period of time to implement. Newbuild merchant ships need to be designed, constructed and commissioned before coming into service, and this can take two years or more. The boom years of 2004 – 2006 led to deliveries extending much further into the future, in some cases up to four years as order-books expanded. Scrapping a vessel takes less time, but if the ship is still committed to trade it may not necessarily happen quickly.

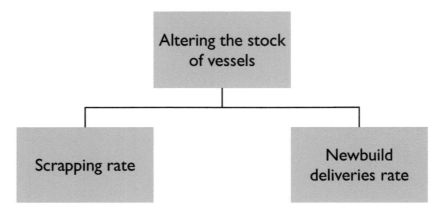

Fig 3.1 Altering the Stock of Vessels

The net change in the tonnage supply is clearly the result of the relative sizes of these two factors. In good times, deliveries will be at a high rate, and scrapping rates will be low. But in bad times, the flow of deliveries will falter, while the level of scrapping will tend to increase. This will be seen in the data presented later in the chapter. It is worth mentioning here that the tonnage supply can fall even if there are some deliveries: it is the difference between the two that alters the stock.

Formally, the above statement can be written as:

$$S_{t+1} = D_t - scR_t + S_t$$

where:

S is the stock at the beginning of the next period,
D_t is the volume of newbuildings delivered during the period,
scR_t is the tonnage scrapped

It is clear that the difference $S_{t+1} - S_t$ measures the fleet change over the period and is equal to the difference between the rate of delivery and the rate of scrapping.

Case Study: Opportunity Cost:

An entrepreneur has $500 million to invest and she faces two possible options: to invest in one ultra large ore carrier of 350,000 MT or to invest the money in a financial fund with a set return of 3%.

After careful consideration of the markets, the entrepreneur decides to invest in a new ship and, therefore, becomes a shipowner.

When the shipowner does her cost calculation for the new vessel, she will need to consider all the costs of running the vessel but also the compensation that she wants to obtain for its investment. This compensation needs to be at least the money she could have earned by depositing the money into the fund with fixed return. Otherwise, she should have been better off by not buying the ship and keep the money in the financial fund with a fixed return.

In our example this means that the shipowner should obtain $15 million in one year to compensate for the forgone opportunity (i.e. interest from the fund).

In the daily running cost of the ship she should include an opportunity cost of about $41,000 or an opportunity cost of $ 0.1174/tonne/day.

3.2.2.2 Altering the way that the existing stock of vessels is used

Figure 3.2 illustrates the principal ways in which the output from a given stock of vessels can be varied even if the present stock is unchanged. Imagine, for the moment, that no new ships are delivered and none is scrapped or lost. It may appear that the supply of shipping services is therefore fixed, but this is an incorrect assumption.

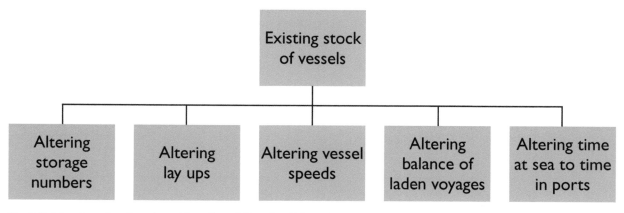

Fig 3.2 Altering the Supply with a Fixed Stock of Vessels

As can be seen from Figure 3.2, there is a number of ways in which the availability of the shipping stock can be varied, even when the numbers remain unchanged.

One method is to convert vessels to alternative use, such as a floating storage facility. This was unheard of 25 years ago, but during the period of overcapacity a number of different methods of using that capacity were developed. Large tankers have been adapted for use as floating oil stores. Large bulk carriers can be used to store grain, acting as floating silos. It is worth drawing attention to the fact that such a decision is not always readily reversible as the ship may suffer significant corrosion or other long-term damage. There may also have been some degree of conversion which would reduce their ability to be re-employed at sea. Nevertheless, this is a method of reducing tonnage supply. Once a stock of storage vessels exists, it can be added to or reduced over time.

The second method of altering the active tonnage supply is by laying up vessels. The ship is usually put in a safe anchorage, a skeleton crew retained to keep up essential maintenance, and is left unemployed. In parts of the world there are special areas, such as Scottish lochs, where ships are left for considerable periods with a company providing management and maintenance services. It should be clear that there are in fact additional costs to be met when preparing a vessel for lay-up; and there are costs involved in making them fully operational again. But these costs are relatively small compared with the large losses than might be experienced if the vessel trades at very low rates for any sustained period of time. Shipowners will have due regard for the present and future state of the market when deciding on lay-up.

When demand conditions are very poor and the outlook does not look promising for the next few years, one would expect to see a rise in the proportion of the merchant fleet that is laid up. When demand improves, these vessels can be re-activated fairly rapidly and tonnage supply expanded quickly. Once all available vessels are back in the active fleet there is no possibility of further increases in supply from this source.

The third method of altering the short-term supply of cargo tonnes or tonne/miles per year or per day is by changing the speed of vessels. By altering speed downwards, journey times can be increased, so the same fleet size can generate a smaller throughput of cargo volume moved in a given period of time. This practice is commonly referred to as slow steaming. The range of speed variation that is possible depends upon the technical design of a ship's main engines. It is limited at the top end by maximum engine revs and at the lower end by considerations of engine efficiency and balance. There is usually a range of speeds that are available, although the ship is often designed and optimised for a particular speed.

Fourth, it may be possible to alter the amount of cargo throughput generated by the fleet overall by altering the proportion of laden to ballast voyages. Many seaborne trades are 'unbalanced', in the sense that cargo volumes delivered in one direction may well be larger than flows in the opposite direction. An extreme case exists in the tanker trade, where most journeys are laden in only one direction. This implies that 50% of the potential cargo carrying space is wasted. If a backhaul cargo can be found, cargo throughput can be increased without any alteration in the tonnage supply.

But it should be noted that the ability to achieve improvements in this area is driven by the nature of demand conditions, rather than supply. As demand patterns change, with new sources of production coming on-stream or new sources of consumption becoming more significant, supply has to respond. The changing utilisation of the fleet reflects these changes. The ship manager must always be on the look-out for new ways of utilising vessels.

Finally, altering the proportion of time that vessels spend in port relative to time spent at sea can affect supply. If port turnaround times are reduced, ships can sail more frequently in a given time period and produce a larger output. If they lengthen, or if significant port congestion occurs, shipping supply is reduced. If the proportion of trade on long haul trades rises relative to short haul routes, the ship tonnage supply can be used more efficiently, as it can spend more of its time at sea. Again, this factor is partly driven by elements outside the shipowners' control. Generally speaking, ports are operated independently of shipowners, so decisions affecting port efficiency and organisation are made free of influence by owners.

Ways in which the tonnage supply can be manipulated are covered in more detail in 3.3.

3.2.3   Supply in the very long run

So far, a number of ways in which the supply of shipping can be altered have been discussed.

Section 3.2.2.2 discussed what could be done even when the availability of vessels was unchanged, a position that economists would describe as 'the short run'.

In 3.2.1.1 we considered how supply is altered when the stock is allowed to change, which is defined as the long run. In both these cases, economic theory still keeps certain elements fixed, at least in theory. These factors are the level of technology available to the suppliers, and the prices of the inputs used in providing those services.

The level of technology

This phrase is the economist's shorthand to describe the prevailing set of technical know-how, organisational knowledge and management structures that are currently available to the industry. Technical progress is the name given to the idea that, over time, new things are discovered. These new ideas are implemented to improve the products and services produced. New, stronger steels can be employed to reduce weight without reducing tensile strength. New engine designs generate the same power output from a smaller engine with lower fuel consumption. New ways of organising cargoes, from pallets to containers, reduce port time. Some of these changes occur suddenly, others are gradual, but incessant. They all add up to the ability to deliver more output with less input. The most dramatic example of this process in shipping was the container revolution; each container vessel could generate the equivalent output of 2-3 general cargo vessels of equivalent size, so output can be maintained with less input.

Changes in the price of inputs

Supply can be influenced by alterations in the cost of key inputs such as an increase in bunker fuel costs. One way of offsetting this is to reduce the speed of the vessel. This leads to lower fuel consumption, but it also leads to lower output, given our discussion above. One might expect to observe, in those trades where it is feasible to do so, a reduction in vessel speeds when fuel prices are high, and a restoration of speed when prices fall again. The proviso is key; in liner trades, keeping to a timetable is important and the option of changing speed is not always available. So suppliers have to find other methods of insuring themselves against fluctuations of the bunker fuel price.

To summarise, the supply of shipping services can be varied in many different ways. In the short run, the principal means of doing this is to alter the proportion of the fleet that is laid up, or where possible, to alter the vessel speeds. In the longer run, the tonnage supply can be altered by delivering newbuilds or scrapping some of the present units. Finally, in the very long run, the efficiency of supply can be altered by technology change and input price movements.

3.3 TRENDS IN THE WORLD MERCHANT FLEET, 1970-2010

Defining the World's merchant fleet is not an easy task. First, one must establish the smallest size of vessel that should be included. Lloyd's Register of Ships uses 100 gross tons (gt), but other industry analysts use different criteria. For example bulk market analysts use 10,000-dwt as the minimum size of vessel that fits into this category. Second, the United States has a fleet of vessels held in reserve for strategic purposes. There are also vessels that trade exclusively on the US and Canadian Great Lakes. Often these are excluded from the analyses of the world fleet since they are effectively limited in their purpose or their scope of operations. However, Lloyd's Register of Ships, published by IHS Fairplay, includes them.

Table 3.2 illustrates the development of the World Fleet, as defined by IHS Fairplay, over the period 1970-2010. The table shows the merchant fleet in both gross tons and deadweight tonnes, and the annual percentage change in those categories. These two measures reflect slightly different aspects of a vessel's carrying ability, as noted earlier. Both measures will be referred to in the following discussion.

The annual growth rates are:

3.41% per year for gt
3.19% per year for deadweight.

Such a growth rate will quadruple the total availability of the world fleet over 40 years as shown by the table.

Although the long-run trends of capacity and demand growth appear to be quite closely related, short term variations tell quite a different story. The strongest growth rates of the period are to be found in the period 1971-1977 and between 2002 and 2008. The growth rate for the former period averaged around 7.5% per year for the period in gt terms, and more than 9% for deadweight. In the period 2002-2008 the average is over 4% per year. The high recent growth rates suggest that market conditions have been good for shipowners since 2002. But market conditions have changed radically since late 2008, following the financial crisis and the economic downturn and recessions for many Western countries.

In the 1980s the tonnage supply actually declined. In 1982, a peak of 423m gt was reached. Deadweight actually peaked in 1983 at 690m, followed by several years of decline. The newbuild rate of delivery was lower than the scrapping loss rate in this period, which was one of crisis, both in shipping and shipbuilding. This process continued throughout the 1980s, coming to an end in 1989, a year of recovery. The average annual growth rate in the period 1980-1989 was -0.21% for gt and -0.91% for dwt. This generated a cumulatively significant decline in tonnage supply by the end of the decade. In contrast, the 1990s were years of relatively steady expansion. Growth rates recovered to around 3% per year in the 1990s, and have risen more rapidly since 2001. This can be interpreted as the first boom of the world shipping markets since the 1970s.

The process of rapid expansion, overcapacity, decline, and recovery has been tied to the cyclical fashion of most shipping markets.

The greatest increase in capacity occurred in 1970-75, where three factors were at work. First, trade had boomed in the late 1960s, and continued to do so until October 1973 when the Arab-Israeli conflict triggered a 400% increase in the price of crude oil.

The boom in trade led to optimistic expectations about the future and large numbers of vessel orders were placed. Second, the closure of the Suez Canal in 1967, following the six-day war between Egypt and Israel, had generated a large increase in demand for tankers. Coupled with this was a significant increase in tanker sizes and in the size of large bulk carriers from 1970 onwards. A huge wave of optimism engulfed the shipping world. In 1973 for example, the total number of orders for new tankers was equivalent to about 20% of the existing world tanker stock. This rather fanciful view of the market was shattered by the rise in the price of crude oil. The effect was to slow down the growth of all major world economies, and so the growth of world trade. Large increases in the tonnage supply arrived at the time when demand growth faltered, a combination that generated depression in the shipping markets for some years.

But ships are long-lived assets; they have technical lives of 30 years or more. A few bad years can always be expected. Owners and operators found ways of matching supply to demand, as discussed earlier, but scrapping was and is still seen as a 'last resort'.

Year	Mn GRT	Growth	Mn DWT	Growth
1970	227.5		338.8	
1971	247.2	7.97	376.2	9.94
1972	268.3	7.86	414.1	9.15
1973	289.9	7.45	452.5	8.49
1974	311.3	6.87	494	8.4
1975	342.3	9.06	553.4	10.73
1976	372	7.98	608.3	9.03
1977	393.7	5.51	648.8	6.24
1978	406	3.03	670.4	3.22
1979	413	1.69	681.5	1.63
1980	419.9	1.64	672.1	-1.4
1981	420.8	0.21	679.7	1.12
1982	424.7	0.92	686	0.92
1983	422.6	-0.5	690	0.58
1984	418.7	-0.93	681.5	-1.25
1985	416.3	-0.58	668.1	-2.01
1986	404.9	-2.82	654.3	-2.11
1987	403.5	-0.35	632.2	-3.5
1988	399.5	-1	625	-1.15
1989	404.9	1.33	620.7	-0.69
1990	426	4.95	630	1.48
1991	436.3	2.36	651.3	3.27
1992	445.2	2	674.4	3.43
1993	457.9	2.77	683.6	1.35
1994	475.9	3.78	699.7	2.3
1995	490.7	3.02	719.2	2.71
1996	507.9	3.39	731.9	1.74
1997	522.2	2.74	755.3	3.1
1998	532.2	1.88	772.8	2.26
1999	546.7	2.65	785.3	1.59
2000	543.6	-0.57	793.8	1.07
2001	558.1	2.6	802.8	1.12
2002	584.8	4.57	822	2.34
2003	600.2	2.57	841.7	2.34
2004	619.6	3.13	863.7	2.55
2005	633.8	2.24	907.5	4.83
2006	729.1	13.07	965	5.96
2007	778.9	6.39	1042.3	7.42
2008	833.4	6.54	1117.8	6.75
2009	853.3	2.33	1192.3	6.25
2010	933	8.54	1276.1	6.57
Average Growth		**3.41**		**3.19**

Table 3.2 Development of the World Merchant Fleet 1970 - 2006 (Sources: UNCTAD Maritime Review 1989, 1993, 2006; Lloyd's Register-Fairplay Statistical Tables 1995 N.B. Estimates are Mid-Year until 1992. Lloyd's Register-Fairplay data has been adjusted to end-year measures from 1992 on. Dwt data for 1993 to 1995 is inconsistent with earlier series, hence the gap in percentage growth. Gt data from IsL for 1996 on).

Trade demand began to pick up in the late 1980s, and has recovered steadily since. Trade volumes only recovered to 1970s levels in the beginning of 1983 as fleet statistics show. The world fleet exceeded the 1983 peak in deadweight terms in the same period. The world merchant fleet has continued to grow ever since. The full impact of the current slowdown in the world economy is still unknown, but a decline in newbuild orders is already apparent.

One final point worth noting from Table 3.2 is the implication of the different rates of growth of gt and dwt on a year to year basis. Vessels such as bulk carriers and tankers have a much larger carrying capacity when expressed in deadweight terms than when expressed in gross tonnage. Other vessel types have a closer correlation. The expansion in the early 1970s is accompanied by dwt growth rates that are higher than those of gross tonnage. This is the period in which the average size of tankers and bulk carriers grew rapidly, and it is this fact that explains the difference. In later years, the difference has not been so marked.

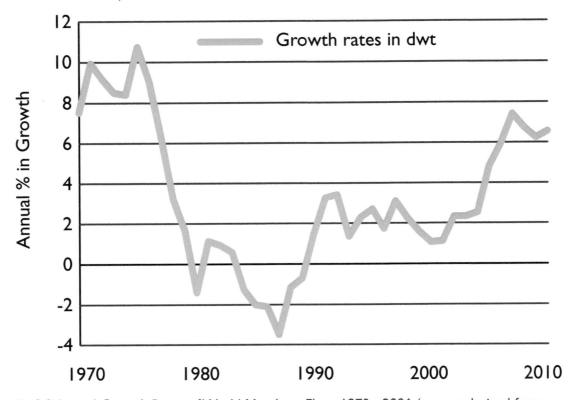

Fig 3.3 Annual Growth Rates of World Merchant Fleet, 1970 - 2006 (source: derived from Table 3.2)

Figure 3.3 shows the variability that exists in the growth rate of the world merchant fleet, when measured in terms of dwt growth. Given that the trend average over the past thirty-five years is 3%, it is clear that the fleet grew faster than trend in the early 1970s, declined in the early 1980s, recovered in the 1990s and has experienced a 'boom' in 2004-2008. The boom in shipping can be clearly seen in the higher than average growth rates in 2006 and 2007, reaching levels last seen in the 1970s.

3.3.1 Newbuild trends

It has been shown that the change in fleet size is given by the net position of newbuild and scrapping rates. Table 3.3 shows trends in newbuilds by vessel types for the period 1980-2010 expressed as a percentage of the existing fleet. The rate of deliveries is strongly affected by expectations about the future, conditioned by market knowledge at that time. The individual figures are not in themselves terribly useful, as year-to-year variations can be quite large. The series begins very low in 1980 at just over 2.5% and climbs to over 3.5% by 1990.

Year	1980	1985	1990	1997	1998	1999	2000	2001	2002	2003	2004	2005	2006	2007	2008	2009	2010
Tankers No.	99	72	81	69	120	161	154	112	182	281	294	315	329	372	437	1562	743
DWT	7	3.9	8.7	7.5	12.6	19.1	20.8	14.4	23.4	29.4	27	29	24.7	29.6	33.7	50.07	45.03
Bulk Carrier No.	135	339	119	299	217	195	188	310	226	161	266	308	307	312	355	1057	985
DWT	4.7	14.7	96	18.8	11.6	13	13	21	14.1	11.2	19.8	23.2	25.1	24.5	28.9	33.93	79.55
General Cargo No.																88	350
DWT																2.78	3.27
Container Ships No.																549	260
DWT																17.62	16.47
Other Ships No.	552	539	523	699	704	589	1202	1048	1131	1265	1262	1341	1762	2098	2207	402	1410
DWT	4.4	5.7	4	10.5	11.1	8.8	10.5	9.8	11.5	8.6	7.9	16.8	21.3	27.8	19.7	12.91	5.43
Total No.	786	950	723	1067	1041	945	1544	1470	1539	1707	1822	1964	2398	2782	2999	3658	3748
DWT	18	25	23	36.8	35.3	40.5	44.4	45.2	49	49.2	49.4	70.5	71.1	81.9	82.3	117.3	149.75
World Fleet %	2.64	3.67	3.71	5.03	4.67	5.24	5.65	5.69	6.1	5.99	5.87	8.16	7.83	8.49	7.9	10.49	12.56
World Fleet	672.14	668.14	629.98	755.3	772.8	785.33	793.77	802.77	822.01	841.73	863.67	907.47	965	1042.33	1117.78	1192.32	1276.14
World Fleet (Year-1)	681.5	681.54	620.73	731.87	755.3	772.8	785.33	793.77	802.77	822.01	841.73	863.67	907.47	965	1042.33	1117.79	1192.32
Average % World Fleet	6.45																

Table 3.3 Developments in Newbuild Deliveries Selected Years, 1980-2006 (Sources: UNCTAD Maritime Reviews, 1988, 1993, 1995, 2003, 2006, ISL Monthly Shipping Statistics, various issues).

Notes:
1. % World Fleet defined as Delivery dwt divided by dwt of the World Fleet in the previous year (from Table 3.1)
2. Dwt measured in millions. 'No.' measures numbers of vessels
3. Separate Container ship figures not available for years prior to 1992
4. 'other ships' are passenger ships from 1996 onwards a – vessels of more than 10,000-dwt

Note that this statistic allows for the fact that the absolute amount of available tonnage was falling at the time. It is clear that confidence in the future of shipping had reached a low ebb in the 1980s, and very small numbers of vessels were being delivered.

It should be explained at this stage that ship capacity is measured in three main ways. A ship's deadweight tonnage (dwt) is the total weight of cargo, bunkers, water and extra items usually expressed in metric tons, which it can lift when loaded in salt water to maximum draught under winter, summer or tropical loadlines. Gross tonnage (gt) measures the internal volume of all enclosed spaces in the ship and is equal to the tonnage below the tonnage deck plus the tonnage of all enclosed spaces above deck. Net register tonnage (nrt) is the residual tonnage after various allowances for propelling power, crew spaces and navigation spaces etc. Gt is often used as a basis for payments, such as to P&I clubs, whilst NRT is used to assess port and terminal dues. Dwt is the best measure of cargo capacity. (Source B N Metaxas, The Economics of Tramp Shipping, Athlone Press, 1971, pages 13-19.)

The numbers show clearly that the 1980s and the first part of the 1990s were a slow period in shipping with a steady but low growth in the amount of new deliveries. It is from 2000 that the market seems to be picking up speed and more ships are being delivered. Especially from 2005 the growth measures around or above 8%.

The very high delivery percentages for 2009 and 2010 of over 10 and 12% respectively, can be explained by delays between the order being placed and the actual delivery of the ship. When orders rise rapidly, the shipyards inevitably build up a back-log and one sees the time elapsed between order and delivery increase.

The cyclical pattern of the shipping industry is clearly brought out in Table 3.3, as the numbers and dwt delivered declined in the1980s. Recovery took place in the early 1990s; by 1997 deliveries were greater than those in 1980 in terms of numbers, and twice as high in terms of dwt. Bulk carrier deliveries were significantly higher after 2001. In the period 2005-2006, deliveries reached 70m dwt or 8% of the world fleet. The 2,398 vessels delivered in 2006 were over three times the numbers delivered in 1990. The expansion of deliveries continues as shipyards are working through their order books, built up during the boom in 2005–2008. This gives clear evidence of the cyclical nature of the shipping market.

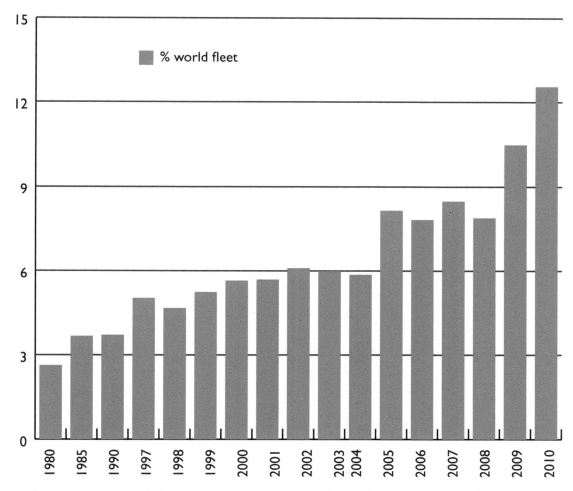

Fig 3. 4 Development of Deliveries, Selected Years 1980 - 2006 (source: derived from Table 3.3).

The annual average rate of delivery, expressed as a percentage of the existing fleet, is 6.45%. It is clear that, since 2000, this has been exceeded every year, which again provides evidence of the recovery of world shipping and the optimism of owners in the early part of the new millennium.

3.3.2 Scrapping trends

Data on the behaviour of scrapping in the last decade is shown in Table 3.4 and Figure 3.5. These figures do not include losses. The table presents information on the numbers and dwt of the basic vessel types that have been scrapped over the past decade, and shows the total dwt scrapped per year.

In the volume scrapped we can clearly see again the same trend as before, with very low scrap levels between 2005 and 2008. From the data for 2009 and 2010 it is clear that as the recession deepened more vessels were send to scrap yards in an attempt to reduce over-capacity.

An intelligent question is 'when is the best time to scrap a vessel'? This is not an easy question to answer, as it depends on each specific vessel's particular circumstances. But economists make a distinction that is very useful in considering the answer. They distinguish between the economic life and the technical life of any asset.

An asset's economic life is, as its name implies, determined by economic conditions. Essentially, an asset has reached the end of its economic life when a replacement for it can be operated at a lower overall unit (or average) cost than the present one. At that point, it is worthwhile for an asset's owner to replace the existing asset with a new one. There are usually two principal drivers that determine the critical point. The first is the rate of depreciation of the capital tied up in the existing asset; the second is the level of operating cost required to maintain and operate it. Put crudely, the former tends to decline with vessel age, while the latter rises.

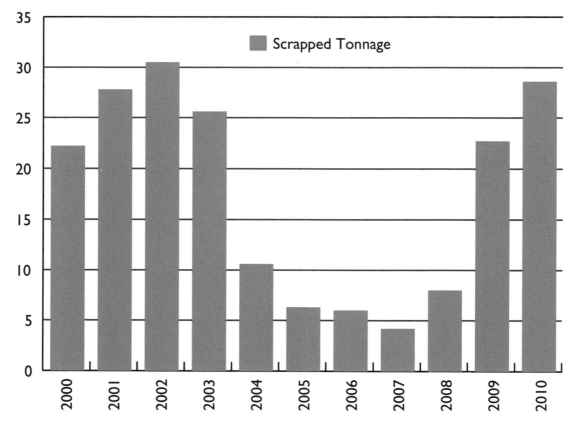

Fig 3.5 Scrapping Rates of World Merchant Fleet, 1985 - 2010 (source: derived from Table 3.4)

Apart from cost considerations, the profitability of the vessel also affects the scrapping decision. With tight market conditions and high rates, it becomes feasible to extend the economic life of vessels, providing they are still compliant with existing regulations. The low scrapping rates of bulk carriers between 2004 and 2008 reflected the buoyant markets they faced. Even old and high operating cost vessels can be profitable in such a market.

Year	2000	2001	2002	2003	2004	2005	2006	2007	2008	2009	2010
Tankers	13.5	15.7	18.1	18.4	7.8	4.5	2.7	2.2	3.6	4.3	14.3
Bulk Carriers	4.6	8.1	5.9	3.3	0.5	0.9	1.3	0.1	3.1	5.1	5.3
Container Ship										5.1	2.2
General Cargo										2.2	2.2
Others	4.1	4	6.5	3.9	2.3	0.9	2	1.9	1.3	6	4.6
Total	**22.2**	**27.8**	**30.5**	**25.6**	**10.6**	**6.3**	**6**	**4.2**	**8**	**22.7**	**28.6**

Table 3.4 Scrapping Rates, 1985 - 2006 (source: Tutorship Manual, 1985- 1999, IsL Monthly shipping statistics, various issues, 2000 on).

Notes:
1. Dwt measured in millions
2. ships greater than 300-gt included
3. column sums will not add to total because certain ship types omitted.

Also regulation can have a large influence on limiting the economical life span of a ship. A good example is the introduction of double hull requirements for tankers.

At some point, it becomes worthwhile to replace an older vessel with a newer one. Newer vessels will have advances in engine design and automotive technology, with lower fuel consumption and so on. Older vessels have the advantage of being fully depreciated, but with higher operating costs. The owner has to balance these two aspects.

This economic life of a ship may well be around 15-20 years, but many passenger vessels have lives considerably in excess of this, particularly cruise vessels. It is remarkable to note that according to the UNCTAD report on shipping the average age for a scrapped vessel in 2010 was 29½ years.

The vessel's technical life may well be considerably more. Essentially, it is the maximum length of life that it is possible to extract from the vessel. Since most parts of a vessel can be repaired/replaced, this could be 30-40 years or more. But such repairs become increasingly expensive as a vessel ages. Furthermore, legislative changes may make the design technically obsolete. The crucial point is that scrapping is usually determined by the economic life, rather than the technical life, of a vessel.

3.4 FACTORS AFFECTING THE SHORT-RUN SUPPLY OF SHIPPING SERVICES

The previous section examined data relating to the elements for altering the tonnage supply of vessels. Attention is now turned to the trends in factors that affect that supply, even when the stock of ships might be fixed.

3.4.1 Use of vessels for storage

Certain vessel types can readily be turned into storage facilities. The obvious ones are the use of crude oil tankers for oil storage, and bulk carriers for grain storage. In 2010 the UK Government considered anew a proposal that some vessels might be modified and used as floating prisons, to deal with the overcrowding in jails.

Using ships as floating storage devices does have a cost, however. The vessel will suffer increased corrosion, and it is a relatively expensive way of storing something compared to dedicated ground based equivalents. But if land is scarce, and therefore expensive, and ships are oversupplied, and therefore relatively cheap, it may be feasible. Japan in fact holds a strategic stockpile of crude oil in just such a fashion. Useable land is very scarce in Japan. BP regularly monitors the numbers of tankers used in this way, and classifies them into semi-permanent, and temporary. In 1985 6.5% of the tanker stock was employed in this way; by 1993 the figure had fallen to 3.5%. In September 2010 it was reported only 57 tankers were involved in floating storage.

These tankers are not necessarily immediately available to move cargoes, as they may be hired out on long term storage contracts. Nevertheless, they are still a potential source of extra supply if demand grows more rapidly than anticipated.

3.4.2 Laying up/reactivating vessels

A vessel that temporarily stops trading is said to be laid-up. This happens when the shipowner or manager can no longer justify trading at the prevailing levels of freight rates and demand conditions and, presumably, sees no sign of any future improvement. By laying-up, some of the operational costs of a vessel are avoided. Provided that engines and other sensitive equipment are maintained in good condition, there is no damage or deterioration of the vessel. The basic idea is simple. The vessel is brought back into trading when rates recover and market conditions improve, so that the vessel can trade as a going concern.

Essentially, this can be viewed as an investment decision by the operator or owner. On the one hand, the owner can carry on trading, presumably at a loss. If they carry on trading at unprofitable rates, a series of losses will be generated over a number of trading periods.

On the other hand, certain expenses are incurred in the act of laying up. Against this is the reduction in losses which would have been incurred if the vessel continued to trade. While the cost of capital has to be met, other operational costs are clearly avoided in lay-up. The owner has to evaluate the net cost or benefit of deciding one way or the other. The decision is clearly influenced by two principal factors:

1. The expectations that the owner holds of the future levels of freight rates.

2. The actual cost of running the vessel as a going concern.

If the owner runs a high operating cost vessel, and has very pessimistic expectations about the future levels of rates, then lay-up may be considered.

Lay-ups vary over time, and are a good barometer of market conditions. They are best expressed as a percentage of the world fleet, in the same way that many countries publish their statistics on unemployed labour. The absolute number is affected by trends in the labour force, so using percentages compensates for this. In fact most published shipping data concentrates on the absolute numbers of vessels and dwt, and this can be misleading.

During the economical crisis of the 1980s lay-ups reached 12% of the fleet, then declined during the late 1990s to very low levels. Note the difference in behaviour of tankers from other vessel types. In 1982 tanker lay-ups soared to 18% but fell sharply during the following decade.

Year	Tankers		Dry Bulk		General Cargo		Containers	
	mn DWT	% Fleet	mn DWT	% Fleet	mn DWT	% Fleet	mn DWT	% Fleet
1990	40.9	15.4	19.4	8.2	2.1	3.3	0.5	1.3
1997	17.0	5.8	10.3	3.9	1.7	2.7	0.0	0.0
1998	17.3	5.9	5.8	2.3	1.6	2.6	0.0	0.0
1999	14.0	5.0	7.9	3.2	1.8	3.0	0.0	0.0
2000	13.5	4.8	3.8	1.5	1.1	1.8	0.0	0.0
2001	17.9	6.4	2.9	1.1	0.7	1.2	0.0	0.0
2002	19.1	7.1	2.2	0.9	0.4	0.7	0.0	0.0
2003	6.0	2.1	3.6	1.2	0.7	1.6	0.0	0.0
2004	3.4	1.1	2.1	0.6	0.7	1.6	0.0	0.0
2005	4.5	1.4	2.0	0.6	0.7	1.6	0.0	0.0

Table 3.5 Lay-Up Rates, selected years, 1990 – 2005 (source: UNCTAD Review of Maritime Transport, various issues)

Note: Data relates to vessels over 100-gt. data for large vessels, eg over 10,000-dwt, will generate different values.

Ship types other than tankers experienced very low levels of lay-ups, even in 1990. Since 1997, all ship types have experienced improving market conditions, with rates falling to very low levels after 2000. For tankers of more than 10,000-dwt, unemployment rate has been virtually zero since the late 1990s. It should be clear from this that different market sectors may face different market conditions, even if they are often treated as a complete whole. The period 2000-2005 was unprecedented in the existence of sustained high levels of employment in all the principal ship type segments listed, especially for the larger size vessels where lay-ups were virtually nil. It is safe to assume that since the economic downturn from late 2008 more ships have again gone into lay-up.

It is worth noting here that in the tanker sector there is a further consideration to bear in mind when an owner looks at lay-up. Oil tankers gain oil company and oil traders' approvals while they are trading and being regularly inspected. Some high-profile oil pollution incidents have been linked to poorly-performing vessels. Since then charterers have insisted that tankers wishing to be employed by them must be of high quality both in performance and operationally in the management structure. A tanker that proceeds to lay-up will cease trading and will lose the valuable approvals it has earned. When market conditions improve an owner will find it very difficult to find employment for its ships until new approvals are gained.

3.4.3 Variations in vessel speed

It was pointed out earlier that output can be increased by the simple device of making vessels go faster or slower. The range of speeds that can be used depends on engine design; as noted earlier the limits are given by the maximum speed of the vessel and the speed below which the engines can be damaged or the vessel loses steerage way.

This range can still be important however. Small changes, if applied to every vessel in a fleet, can bring about significant alterations in its cargo carrying capability.

Following the collapse of oil demand in the mid 1970s and the four-fold increase in the price of bunker fuel, a large number of tankers started to slow-steam. Prior to 1973, most tankers ran at their design speed, usually around 14 knots. By 1975-6 a large proportion of tankers were sailing at 10 knots, effectively reducing their cargo moving capacity by about 20% since half of the journey was in ballast. This practice has also been widely adopted by major container lines to reduce supply following the recent recession in many Western countries and increasing bunker costs.

This is a very effective way of reducing the tonnage supply in the short term, as well as being a sensible response to the rise in fuel input prices. This change can happen very quickly, provided of course that the fleet starts at full employment and a negative shock is experienced. Once a portion of the fleet is slow-steaming, changes in output can be generated by speeding up again. But if the new, lower vessel speed is in fact optimal for the higher fuel price, it may need a very large increase in demand to generate this result.

In the years 2005 and 2006, a number of container operators have suggested that it might be more economic to operate their service by reducing service speed from 24 to 18 knots, and compensating for the lost service by adding an extra ship into the trade. In other words, they are suggesting that the fuel savings from operating, say 6 vessels on a container service at a lower speed is greater than the capital and operating cost of employing one less vessel to maintain the same frequency of service i.e. operating 5 vessels at 24 knots. This would only be sensible if fuel prices are very high.

3.4.4 Variations in port time

Short run supply can also be altered by varying the proportion of time that a vessel spends in port. A vessel that reduces port and idle time to a minimum will produce a higher volume of output in the same time period than one that does not. When demand is low relative to existing capacity, port turnaround times and waiting times may lengthen; the productivity of the system, output relative to total input, will fall and rise accordingly.

One way in which time in port is affected is by changing the composition of demand. When long distance routes become more important in a trade, vessels employed in that trade will spend proportionately more of their time at sea, and the overall productiveness of the fleet can rise. When the opposite happens productivity will be reduced, as ships will spend a greater proportion of their time in port.

It might be argued that such alterations are not strictly in the control of the shipowner/operator, as they depend upon the port or terminal operator. But many terminal operations are now controlled by shipping companies themselves. For example, oil terminals are often controlled by the oil companies who also operate their own vessels, and Maersk, the largest container operator in the world, has a dedicated division which operates its own terminals. The difference in objectives may not be as marked as it might appear.

3.5 PRODUCTIVITY TRENDS AND SUPPLY CONDITIONS

Table 3.6 provides details of some simple measures of productivity of the world merchant fleet. Before the table is discussed in detail, it should be pointed out that these productivity measures are the result of the interaction of the present level of demand and the current stock position; they should not be taken as simply measuring the efficiency of supply on its own.

One should recall that changes in fuel input prices can affect a vessel's service speed. If demand remained unchanged, the optimal vessel's speed would tend to be reduced, in markets where this is feasible, and output per dwt will fall. So some of the reduction that occurs can be linked to this change; it does not imply a fall in efficiency. In fact, it is an optimal response. If the price of fuel goes in the other direction, one might expect the trend to be reversed.

Table 3.6 therefore needs to be interpreted with some care. Ideally, one should compare years in which demand levels, fleet sizes and fuel prices are all similar before one makes any comparisons. These remarks notwithstanding, the broad trend of the figures are still worth commenting upon.

Firstly, ship productivity appeared to be lower than it was in 1970, when expressed in terms of tons of cargo carried per dwt. The 1970 figure was only surpassed in 2006 as similar boom conditions existed. 1970 was a boom year, and a year in which capacity was stretched to meet prevailing demand. The years from 2006 to 2009 appear to present similar conditions to those that existed in 1970. The parallel can be drawn even further and also the bust following the boom in 1970 has occurred for the boom of the period following 2006.

Year	Tanker			Bulk carrier		
	Fleet	Cargo	Tons per dwt	Fleet	Cargo	Tons per dwt
1970	148	1442	9.74	72	448	6.22
1980	339	1871	5.52	186	796	4.28
1990	246	1755	7.13	235	968	4.12
2000	282	2163	7.67	276	1288	4.67
2006	354	2698	7.62	346	1836	5.31
2007	383	2747	7.17	368	1957	5.32
2008	408	2742	6.72	391	2059	5.27
2009	418	2642	6.32	418	2094	5.01
2010	450	2752	6.12	457	2333	5.11

Year	General cargo + rest			Total		
	Fleet	Cargo	Tons per dwt	Fleet	Cargo	Tons per dwt
1970	106	676	6.38	326	2566	7.87
1980	158	1037	6.56	683	3704	5.42
1990	179	1285	7.18	660	4008	6.07
2000	240	2532	10.55	798	5983	7.5
2006	260	3166	12.18	960	7700	8.02
2007	292	3330	11.4	1043	8034	7.7
2008	319	3428	10.75	1118	8229	7.36
2009	355	3122	8.79	1191	7858	6.6
2010	284	3323	11.7	1191	8408	7.06

Table 3.6 Productivity of the World Merchant Fleet 1970 - 2006 (source: UNCTAD Maritime Transport Reviews, 1987, 1990, 1995, 2003, 2006).

3.6   SURPLUS TONNAGE AND THE CONCEPT OF THE ACTIVE FLEET

Shipping economists have produced estimates of the tonnage that is surplus to demand requirements in a particular year. They do this by allowing for those vessels that are idle, laid-up or slow-steaming. This is a crude way of measuring the degree of slack in the system: in a sense it measures the amount of spare capacity that is readily available to meet unexpected increases in demand. The data is shown in Table 3.7 and Figure 3.7. The key statistic to note is the measure of the surplus tonnage measured as a proportion of the world fleet. Since the high of 1990, unemployment of ships has steadily dropped and remained around the 1-2% mark. It saw a rise in 2008 but dropped again to just over 1% in 2009 and 2010. This is probably caused by increased scrapping and continued slow-steaming.

It seems unlikely that the percentage of unemployment of ships will ever drop to zero. Underlying this calculation is the implicit assumption that somehow, the volume of demand in any one year must match the volume of shipping capacity supplied. Since demand has to be forecast, it seems extremely unlikely that this would ever occur. Now consider the cost of always being short of capacity. The inability to move cargoes in sufficient volumes in the right time periods would generate large losses of sales further up the supply chain, while having some surplus means that unexpected variations in demand can usually be met.

An analogy might be useful here. The 'normal' level of output from a factory is not 100% of capacity; it is usually set at 85-90%. The spare can be used to meet unexplained variations in demand. Remember, also, that the output of shipping cannot be stored. Once lost, it is lost forever. In a sense, a surplus of ships is one way of creating an inventory of available extra ship output if it is needed.

Of course, this argument can be taken too far. As ships represent a capital investment, too many idle ships means too much capital tied up in non-income earning assets; so there is probably some range which is optimal, balancing the cost of lost output against the cost of idle capital.

There is one final point to note about this concept; the amount of surplus tonnage may well be affected by the underlying unit costs of labour, capital and fuel. It has already been noted that slow-steaming is related to high fuel prices, and it may be that slow steaming is an optimal response. To assume that vessel speeds are constant, and compute the required tonnage balance accordingly, might well be a mistake.

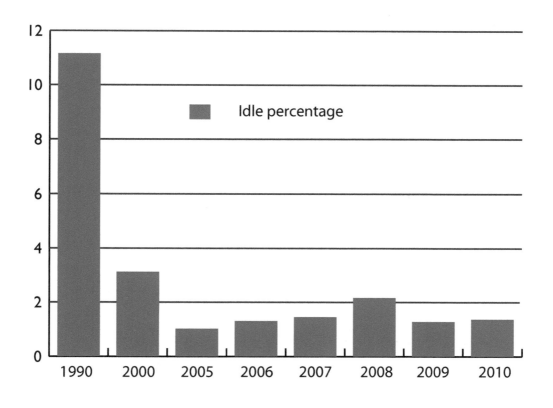

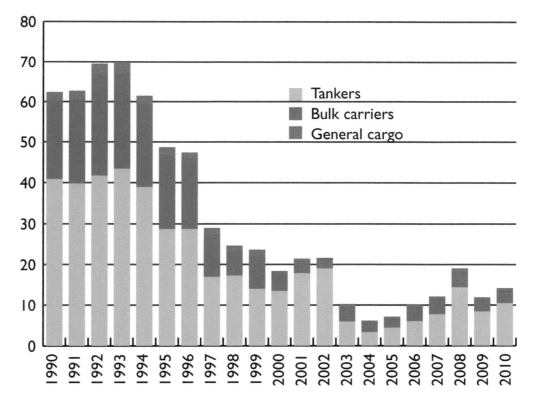

Fig 3.7 World Fleet utilisation, 1970 - 2005 (Source: derived from Table 3.6).

Year	World Fleet	Surplus Tonnage	Active Fleet	% Unemployed
1970	360.2	0.7	359.5	0.2
1975	546.3	46.3	500.0	9.3
1980	680.2	97.1	585.1	16.6
1985	664.8	161.5	503.3	32.1
1986	639.1	108.0	531.1	20.3
1987	632.3	101.1	531.2	19.0
1988	627.9	83.4	544.5	15.3
1989	638.0	62.3	575.7	10.8
1990	658.4	63.7	594.7	10.7
1991	683.5	64.2	619.3	10.4
1992	694.7	71.7	623.0	11.5
1993	710.6	72.0	638.6	11.3
1994	719.8	63.4	656.4	9.7
1995	734.9	50.8	684.1	7.4
1996	758.2	48.8	709.4	6.9
1997	775.9	29.0	746.9	3.9
1998	788.7	24.7	764.0	3.2
1999	799.0	23.7	775.3	3.1
2000	808.4	18.4	790.0	2.3
2001	825.6	21.5	804.1	2.7
2002	844.2	21.7	822.5	2.6
2003	857.0	10.3	846.7	1.2
2004	895.8	6.2	889.6	0.7
2005	960.0	7.2	952.8	0.8

Table 3.7 Lay-Up Rates of the World Fleet, Selected Years, 1970 - 2005 (Source: UNCTAD Maritime Review,1987, 2000, 2006)

3.7 SEGMENTED SUPPLY

Until this point the data for the world merchant fleet has been examined as a whole and, apart from the comments about the tanker market, it has been assumed that conditions are similar in all sectors. While this is a convenient simplification, it may give the reader a false impression; quite significant differences exist in market supply behaviour between the shipping sectors. Essentially the world's shipping fleet can be divided into eight broad categories:

1. vessels employed in serving the wet trades;

2. vessels employed in the dry bulk trades;

3. vessels employed in the unitised trades such as container ships;

4. vessels employed in non-unitized liner trades such as general cargo;

5. vessels employed in the short sea trades, such as short sea ferries;

6. vessels employed in the cruise trade;

7. specialised or dedicated vessels such as offshore supply ships and drilling rigs.

Since certain vessels are better adapted to certain trades, and not to others, local demand conditions can generate quite different supply behaviour between the segments. Most of the surplus tonnage referred to above is in fact concentrated in the tanker market. For example in 2002 over 88% of the surplus tonnage of that year was situated in the tanker market. In the same year the bulk and general cargo market had a surplus of 13.49% and 3.26% respectively. But by 2006 the percentages had changed to 60.4% for tankers, 33.66% for bulk and 5.94% for general cargo. This illustrates the point that while the markets appear to be tied together by common long term trends, there are often quite important variations from this trend in the shorter term.

3.8 RELATING THEORY TO EMPIRICAL EVIDENCE

To relate the empirical evidence presented to the theoretical framework of supply and demand is one way to make sense of the changes in the shipping market.

Demand has already been discussed, but the supply curve of shipping services has yet to be defined. To do this, a distinction will be made between the short-run, which is defined as the period in which the tonnage supply of vessels is unchanging, and the long-run, in which the supply is allowed to alter.

3.8.1 The short run supply of shipping output

It might be imagined that, since the stock of vessel tonnage has been held fixed, there can be no variation in the supply of output. But of course this is incorrect for the reasons discussed earlier. If output is measured in terms of tonne/miles of cargo moved per time period (a day, a month or a year) then output can be varied, literally from zero with all ships idle, to a maximum value, determined by the present fleet size, its productivity and vessels' speeds.

Imagine for a moment, that all the necessary information needed to work out each vessel's cost per tonne/mile of cargo was available. One could rank these in order of low cost to high cost. Then supply could be permitted to increase.

The cheapest way to increase supply would then be to use the low cost vessels first, as this is the most profitable. Now imagine raising rates a little when many more vessels will become profitable to operate. This process can continue until all vessels are utilised. Once they are all in use, the only way of producing more output is to make them go faster, but this requires higher rates still as fuel consumption is increased. At some point, all possibilities are exhausted and, no matter how much further the rate is increased, there is no possibility of supplying more tonne/miles of output from the given tonnage supply.

The general idea can be illustrated with the supply curve drawn in Figure 3.8. It has been drawn as a broad, backward L - shaped curve. This is because for much of its range, the availability of a large stock of under-utilised vessels means that tonne/mile supply can be increased rapidly in response to a small increase in rates. But when demand approaches full capacity, further increases in rates do nothing to stimulate short term supply increases. They do act as a signal to encourage further investment in shipping.

When the rate, expressed as dollars per tonne/mile of cargo carried, rises from $1 to $1.50, there is a considerable expansion in supply. But when the rate rises again, to $2, there is not such a further increase in the quantity supplied.

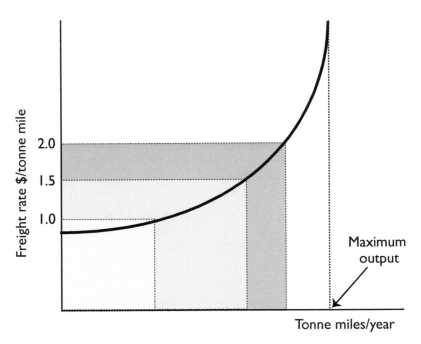

Fig 3.8 Hypothetical Supply Curve for Shipping Output, Derived from a Fixed Stock of Ships.

3.8.2 The Long Run Supply of Shipping Output

In the longer term, the supply of tonnage will increase if deliveries exceed scrapping and losses, or reduce if the reverse is the case. The new vessels will be more efficient, and hopefully, cheaper to run than the scrapped ones. This will make the entire schedule shift to the right in the case of an expansion, or to the left in the case of a contraction.

The shift is unlikely to be parallel; the efficiency gain is, on average, likely to be no more than 2-3% per year, so the 'flat' section of the supply schedule will not shift down by much. The real difference lies in the vertical section, which can shift out to the right quite sharply if, for example, increases are 10% of the existing fleet size. Such a situation is shown in Figure 3.9.

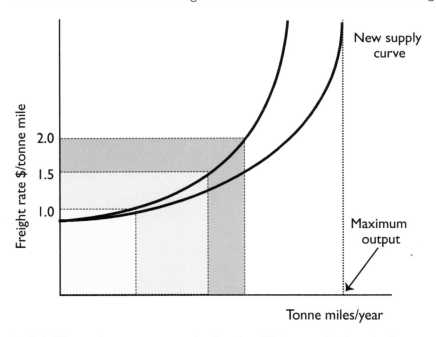

Fig 3.9 Effect of an increase in the Stock of Ships on the Supply Curve

The model of supply that has now been constructed will be combined with assumptions about demand and used to analyse the behaviour of major bulk markets in the following chapters. It is very important that one grasps the concept of the supply curve, because it has already been implicitly used when the empirical evidence was discussed in earlier sections.

Case Study: Elasticity of demand

As we have seen before, as prices rise demand drops. Elasticity is the measure commonly used to expresses the strength of the change in demand with each prise increase (or decrease).

For example, the elasticity of demand of cars is estimated to be around -1.2. This means that for every 1% increase in price demand drops 1.2%. With that elasticity, if we assume a situation where the price for cars is £10,000 and the demand 100,000, an increase to a price of £11,000 (10% higher) will bring a reduction in demand for cars to 88,000 (12% lower).

3.9 MEASURING SUPPLY RESPONSIVENESS: THE CONCEPT OF ELASTICITY OF SUPPLY

It was pointed out that the response of supply to a change in demand conditions, as measured by an increase in the freight rate, differs depending upon the amount of slack in the system. Just as the responsiveness of demand to a change in price, or the freight rate, can be formally measured, so too can the responsiveness of supply.

The formal definition of supply elasticity is:

$$\text{Own Price Elasticity of Supply} = \frac{\text{\% change in the supply of shipping services}}{\text{\% change in price (freight rate)}}$$

The number that is obtained from this calculation is expected to be positive or zero, but never negative.

It will be positive if the supply of tonne/miles or cargo tonnes moved per unit time period increases with an increase in the freight rate.

It will be zero if, despite the increase in the freight rate, there is no observable increase in tons of cargo moved or tonne/miles performed.

Examples:

If the freight rate was to rise from $10 per ton of cargo moved to $12, a 20% increase in price, and cargo tonnage lifted rose from 48,000 to 56,000, a 16.6% increase, then the elasticity of supply would be about 0.83, or inelastic, because the number is less than unity.

If, on the other hand, the same rise in the freight rate were to bring forth an increase in cargo liftings from 48,000 cargo tonnes to 96,000, a 100% increase, the computed elasticity would be 100/20 = +5, which is very elastic.

Figures 3.8 and 3.9 illustrate both types of responses. A very price-elastic supply curve appears relatively flat and nearly parallel to the axis that measures output. A highly inelastic supply schedule has an almost vertical appearance, being almost parallel to the price or vertical axis. The short-run supply of shipping possesses both of these properties over different ranges of supply output.

3.9.1   Supply elasticity and time

The above discussion implies that the responsiveness of supply to changes in freight rates is influenced by the time period allowed for that response. By permitting the stock of vessels to alter, supply is more flexible than it is in the period when the stock of vessels is fixed.

One extreme case of this is to imagine how the shipping markets respond in an even shorter time frame. Supply might even be perfectly inelastic, for instance having a supply price elasticity of zero. Suppose a charterer wants a vessel to transport a particular cargo at very short notice from a particular port. It must be moved within 24 hours for example. Contacts with brokers establish that there is only one vessel available for this cargo in the time available. If the shipowner knows this, he or she can extract the maximum price that the charterer is prepared to pay. But 24 hours later, other vessels arrive in the area, free of contract. This immediately shifts the balance towards the charterer as vessel owners compete for the business. This potential to exploit the market is thus very transient, given the mobility of vessels. Nevertheless, the supply responsiveness is more or less zero in the first 24 hours, but getting progressively larger as more time for greater supply reaction is allowed.

This idea is illustrated in the simple model below

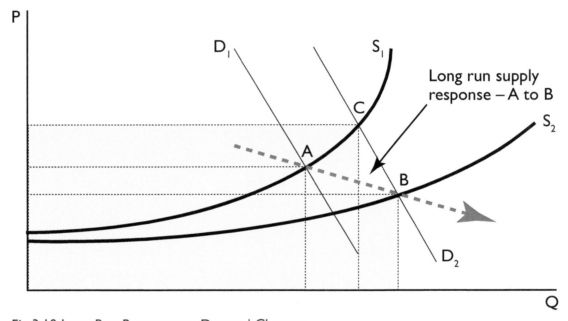

Fig 3.10 Long-Run Response to Demand Changes

In Figure 3.10, demand increases from D_1 to D_2. The initial response is given by the interaction with the short run supply curve S_1 and price rises to point C. This induces greater profits and increases in ship ordering and then deliveries of new ships. Higher deliveries mean an increase in the fleet size. Our short run model assumes the stock is fixed, so the short run supply curve shifts out to the right. If demand remains at D_2, prices now fall to B. The overall change in induced supply is therefore the move from A to B, which implies a smaller price change and larger quantity change than the move from A to C. But this means that the long run supply elasticity must be higher than the short run supply elasticity; because of the definition of elasticity the percentage change in price will be lower, and the percentage change in quantity will be higher in the long run compared to the short run.

3.9.2 Empirical evidence

Beenstock and Vergottis' masterly study of the world tanker and dry cargo markets, Econometric Modelling of World Shipping (1993), estimated that the short run supply elasticity of tonne/miles with respect to the freight rate was 0.24 for tankers, a number which implies an inelastic response. They pointed out that this number would be much greater when large numbers of laid up vessels were present. This finding is consistent with the shape of the short run supply curve of shipping services shown in Figures 3.8 and 3.9 above.

They also found that the long run elasticity with respect to the stock of ships was unity, in other words, in the long term a broadly proportional response of supply tonnage to long term trends in demand is to be observed.

3.10 CONCLUSION

This chapter has analysed the basic idea of the supply of shipping services. Data on supply trends over the last decades was analysed and the idea of a supply curve for shipping was introduced. Finally, the term, 'own-price elasticity' of supply was introduced.

Chapter 4

Shipping cost analysis and economies of scale

The world's heaviest coin was from Sweden and weighed 43 pounds 7 $\frac{1}{4}$ oz.

4 INTRODUCTION

This chapter discusses the important area of ship costs. One common theme that occurs in shipping is the role of economies of scale in influencing important commercial decisions, such as the most suitable size of ship to use. The determinant and structure of shipping costs is the focal point of this chapter.

4.1 AN OUTLINE OF BASIC COST CONCEPTS

Economic theory discusses cost determinants with specific reference to a company type which produces just one type of output. In the shipping business, the output can be measured either by:

- the volume of tonnes of cargo moved per day, per trip or per year, or;
- the volume of tonne/miles produced by the vessel per day, per trip or per year.

The nature of the cargo carried is really immaterial to cost analysis; the focus is on measuring either the total cost of moving a given quantity of output, or on the average total cost. This is the total cost divided by the volume of cargo carried. The latter is sometimes referred to as unit cost, or average cost.

Costs measured per tonne of cargo are very useful, since the freight rate is usually expressed in dollars per tonne of cargo, especially in bulk trades. In the container business, costs are often expressed per teu, an abbreviation of Twenty foot Equivalent Unit, again because rates are expressed per container or box. It is clearly very important to be able to express prices and unit costs in the same way, so that profitability can be measured.

4.1.1 Short-run costs

In the short-run, the ability of any company to vary production or output is limited, because some of the inputs which are used in producing that output are fixed in quantity.

Economists define two categories of costs in a short-run period. These are:

Fixed costs, or indirect costs, and variable costs, or direct costs, sometimes called avoidable costs.

Fixed costs are defined as all those expenses which have to be met when producing the output of goods or services, but which do not vary with the level of production of that output. Basically, they are costs which are necessarily incurred, but their level is unaffected even if production fell to zero.

Variable Costs are defined as those items which do vary with the production of output. These may be quite a small proportion of the total cost of production, depending upon the business that one is examining.

It is important to note that this distinction is only valid in the short-run. Indeed, it defines the short-run, since its definition is not determined by a period of calendar time.

For example, the short-run time period for a ship operator may in effect be a matter of a few months. In most shipping situations, the largest cost item is the capital tied up in the ship. While the company is committed to owning that ship, it has to meet the implied capital cost of ownership, or opportunity cost. The company expects to receive a return on the capital invested in the vessel. The capital cost, in many cases the mortgage repayment, is a fixed cost for the simple reason that it does not vary with the output that the ship produces. It does not matter whether the ship sits at a lay-up berth for six months, producing no output, or is actively trading; the daily capital cost has to be recovered. This cost is clearly fixed, as long as the operator owns the ship or until the mortgage is fully paid off.

On the other hand, it is clear that fuel consumption, and hence bunkering expenses, are directly related to producing output. In other words, tonnes of cargo moved, or laden tonne/miles produced. Such items are, therefore, defined as variable costs.

4.1.2   The Behaviour of total costs and output in the short-run

Describing the link between total costs and output in the short-run is not at all straightforward.

Fixed Costs are unaffected by the change in the level of production. Hence it can be argued that they can be treated as a constant, independent of the level of output.

Figure 4.1 shows such an example, in the context of shipping. Assume for example, that the daily overhead costs attributed to a 50,000-dwt dry cargo vessel have been calculated by its owners as being $10,000 a day. The vessel is to be used to trade from the UK to Montreal and back, a round-voyage distance of some 6,000 nautical miles. The output produced by this journey can vary between zero and 150 million tonne/miles, assuming it is laden one way. Assuming the round trip takes 17 days, the total fixed cost attributed to the trip is $170,000.

Variable costs

The principal variable costs will be voyage related costs. Fuel consumption, both at sea, and in port, must be accounted for. In addition, there will be port and canal dues, where appropriate, and stores and provisions for the crew. In addition, there may be loading and discharge costs to consider. Fuel consumption will rise as the laden weight of the vessel rises, but port and cargo handling charges will increase with the volume of cargo being moved. If these increase at a constant rate per tonne, a line showing the relationship between total variable costs and cargo volume produced can be drawn, as in Figure 4.1 below.

Total costs and output

Adding the total fixed cost to the total variable cost generates total cost, for any given volume of cargo delivered, from zero to a full load, under our assumptions. This diagram assumes that the relationship between variable costs and output is a simple, constant proportional one.

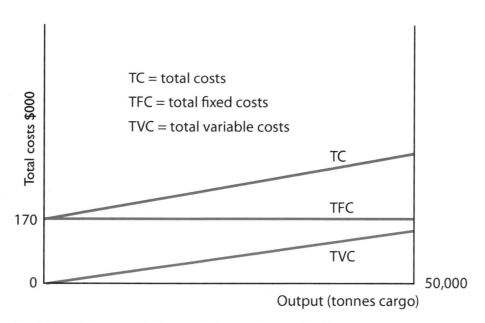

Fig 4.1 Total Costs and Output Relationships in the Short-run

Figure 4.1 will be used as the basis for a breakeven analysis, introduced in chapter 5.

Average costs

While examining total costs may be useful, market prices are not expressed this way. Market rates are expressed per tonne of cargo delivered. It is therefore useful to translate the total cost of producing output into its unit cost equivalent, or average cost. Average costs are easily defined. The total cost of producing output is simply divided by the output being produced. In the example above, the average total cost per tonne of cargo delivered can be found by dividing the total costs of delivering the cargo by the quantity of cargo delivered.

Similar calculations can be made for average fixed costs and average variable costs. But now, their behaviour will be quite different. In the example, average fixed costs will decline steadily, from $170,000 per tonne when only one tonne of cargo is delivered, to $3.4 per tonne when 50,000 tonnes are delivered. This implies that the average fixed cost value declines steadily, and is always minimised when the maximum output is produced.

The behaviour of average variable costs is quite different in this case. With a fixed journey length, and fixed vessel speed, plus the assumption of a fixed cargo handling charge per tonne of cargo delivered, average variable costs will be constant. They are the same whether one tonne or 50,000 tonnes is discharged. Note that total variable costs will increase. It is the unit cost, or average variable cost, that is constant.

Adding the constant average variable cost with the average fixed cost yields average total cost. In this case, it reaches its minimum at the maximum cargo volume which can be carried. This is inevitable, given the assumptions, but is not always the case in shipping, and it is definitely not the case in many other industries.

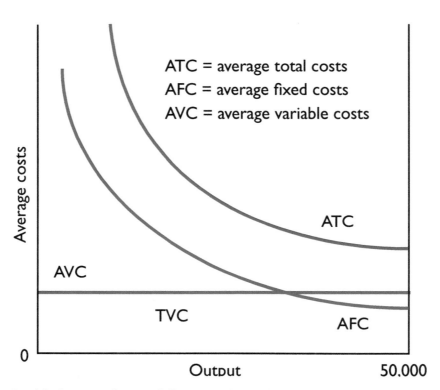

Fig 4.2 Average Cost and Output Relationships

4.1.3 The general relationship between short-run costs and output

In many circumstances, the linear relationship developed between output and costs is not an accurate one. Indeed, it is possible to find a more complex inter-relationship in shipping, which we will come to later in this chapter. In general terms, economists do not expect total variable costs to rise proportionately with output. This is because of the fact that variable inputs (such as the quantity of fuel in shipping), into the production process are combined with a fixed quantity of another input such as the ship.

The law of variable proportions states that there is an optimal combination of these inputs. This implies that if the mix of inputs is not optimal, efficiency is reduced and average variable costs are higher than can be achieved at a different level of output. There will be, for any given size of capital, a most efficient level of output. Efficiency here is being measured in terms of the lowest average total cost. In this situation, average variable cost falls at low levels of output and then begins to increase at higher levels of output. For example, a fully laden ship going faster will increase output but at a higher fuel cost.

Since average total cost is the sum of average fixed and average variable cost, this generates a U-shaped average total cost curve. The reason is simple; at low levels of output, fixed costs are a very large share of total costs. They fall sharply in share when output increases. When combined with a falling average variable cost curve, average total costs must fall. As output continues to increase, two things happen:

- the relative importance of the fixed cost element declines, and its rate of fall declines;

- average variable costs, which are now a larger and larger share of overall costs, start to rise rapidly. This makes the average total costs rise.

If average costs have this U-shape, there must be a range of output over which unit total costs are at their lowest. This range, or specific level of output, is the most efficient level of output associated with the quantities of capital, labour and the other inputs used in the production process.

Figure 4.3 Shows the typical cost relationships that are expected.

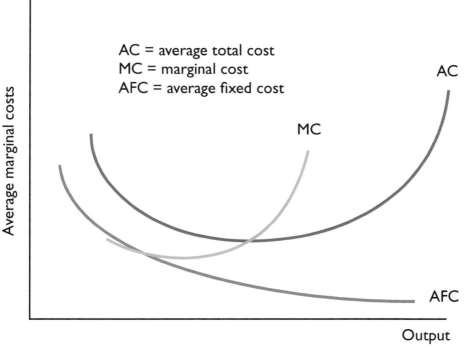

Fig 4.3 Traditional Cost Output Relationships

4.1.4 The concept of marginal, or incremental cost

The last cost concept to be introduced is very important for decision-making. This is the concept of marginal or incremental cost. Marginal cost is defined as the change in total costs generated by the production of an extra unit of output. In the short-run, marginal cost must be related to variable costs, since by definition of short-run, fixed costs cannot be altered. The only changes in total costs that can be generated are generated through the change in total variable costs associated with the change in output.

In the example used above, marginal cost is in fact the same value as average variable cost, because of the assumption that the cargo related costs are independent of the volume of output carried. But this is not always the case. When average variable costs rise, marginal costs will be rising even faster; when average variable costs fall, marginal costs will be lower than average variable costs.

The measurement of marginal cost itself can vary; it has to be defined very carefully. For example, what is the marginal cost of carrying an extra passenger on a bus or a train, or of taking an extra tonne of cargo on a vessel about to depart? If the carrying units are not already fully laden, the answer is usually an extremely small number. But this example is rather extreme. Now consider the same situation, this time assuming that the bus, train, or ship is fully loaded. The answer to the question is now quite different, since the costs incurred will constitute those associated with providing an extra train, an extra bus or an extra ship. In effect, assuming, on average, in the long-run, that capacity utilisation is close to 100%, the latter type of marginal cost is a measure of the long-run total cost of meeting that extra demand. On the other hand, if capacity is idle, the same marginal cost can be measured as a very small number, relative to the total costs involved.

It is often the case that the change in output which is being considered is not just one extra unit. It may be several thousand tonnes of cargo, which forms a consignment which a charterer wishes to move. In this case, the appropriate measure is the extra costs associated with accepting that consignment. This may be converted to a per tonne measure by dividing the estimated additional total costs related to the movement of the consignment by the tonnage of the consignment, to arrive at a per tonne figure for the incremental cost of accepting the business. This figure can then be compared with the extra revenue that the cargo brings. It should be clear that if the consignment generates additional revenues which exceed the extra costs incurred, the shipowner or operator will be better off by accepting the business.

4.1.5 Long-run costs in economic theory

The long-run is defined as the period of time in which it is possible to vary all the input quantities used in producing a given level of output. It is assumed that the unit prices of those inputs remain unchanged. Therefore, the amounts of capital, land, fuel and labour required to produce a given level of output can all be varied.

In the long-run, by definition, fixed costs do not exist. This is because every element used in the production process can be varied. In shipping, one of the key determinants of the output produced by a vessel trading on a particular route at a given speed is its size. Other things being equal, the larger the size, the larger the cargo volume, cargo tonne/miles or passenger numbers carried per time period. The long-run period for a shipping operator is therefore the period long enough for the size of vessels to be considered as a variable.

Given that there are no fixed costs, long-run costs can be described thus: the long-run average cost measures the total unit cost of producing a given level of output, given the prices of the inputs employed in the production process.

Long-run average costs can be related to output in three different ways:

- Long-run average costs may fall, as output levels rise. When this occurs, economies of scale are said to exist. Put bluntly, their existence implies that the larger the volume of output that can be achieved, the lower the unit or average cost of production.

- Long-run average costs may remain unchanged as output levels change. In this case, constant returns to scale are said to exist. Average costs are the same, irrespective of the level of production.

- Long-run average costs may rise as output levels rise. This situation is defined as one in which diseconomies of scale are present. Basically, this implies that it may be more efficient to produce lower levels of output, because unit costs will be less.

These categories are illustrated in the long-run cost curve shown in Figure 4.4 below.

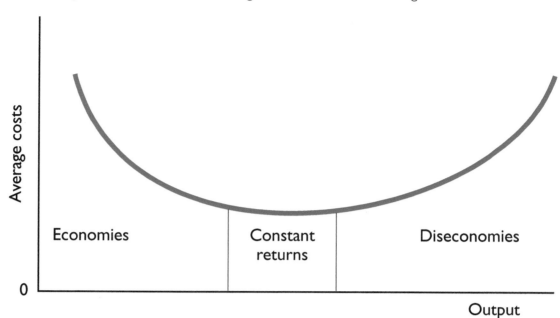

Fig 4.4 Long-run Average Costs and Returns to Scale

4.2 THE CONVENTIONAL ANALYSIS OF VESSEL OPERATING COSTS

Vessels' costs are often classified into three distinct categories, defined for a particular ship size. In a sense, the trade analysis is a short-run framework, but when several different sizes of vessel are considered, the information could be related to the long-run period discussed earlier.

The three distinct categories that are employed are:

4.2.1 Capital-related costs

These are the cost items incurred by the shipowner which can be attributed to the ownership of the ship itself. The principal items are:

a) Repayments of the loan principal, if a mortgage or other financial instrument has been used to purchase the vessel;

b) Payment of interest on the outstanding balance of any loan or mortgage.

Both of the above would be regular cash payments

c) The cost of capital for having the shipowner's capital tied up in the ship. These are not necessarily cash payments, but they are a legitimate cost item because they measure the value of the opportunities forgone, also called opportunity cost.

Many shipping consultants include a notional 8% on the capital value of the ship to represent the cost of capital, as they assume the shipowner would have such a return on its capital investment.

4.2.2 Direct operating costs

These are items which are necessarily incurred in the running of the vessel, but which do not vary with the vessel's use. They include such items as hull and machinery insurance, P&I cover, cargo insurance, crew costs, lubrication costs, repairs and maintenance expenditures, stores, etc. Table 4.1 lays out the major cost items.

4.2.3 Voyage-related costs

Voyage-related costs are those items which can be avoided if a voyage is not made. The major component is fuel costs, which are determined by the fuel consumption of the vessel on a particular journey, and of course, the price of bunkers. Fuel consumption is often computed at a particular vessel speed. Variations in a vessel's speed can have significant effects on the rate of fuel consumption, so assumptions about speed have to be made.

Other components of voyage-related costs include port and canal dues, pilotage and towage and cargo loading and discharging charges. The relative importance of these two cost components will be affected by the journey distance. Short haul trips will mean a large proportion of vessel time spent in port, with a greater weight for port dues and similar charges. Long haul trips will mean a longer time at sea, less port time and a greater weight for fuel consumption at sea.

Capital Cost	Direct Operating Costs	Voyage Related Costs
Interest on Loans Repayment of Loan Interest on Equity Taxation	Insurance Hull & Machinery Protection & Indemnity War risks Crew costs Repairs and Maintenance Stores Administration Expenses	Fuel costs Canal Dues Port Dues Cargo Handling costs Crew Provision

Table 4.1 Typical Cost Structure

Recalling the discussion of the economic theory of costs, it is clear that columns 1 and 2 of the above can be viewed as consisting of fixed costs; they are given no matter what the level of output produced by the vessel. The voyage related costs then become the variable costs, in the model developed earlier.

4.3 SPECIFIC FACTORS AFFECTING THE RELATIONSHIP BETWEEN COSTS AND SHIPPING OUTPUT

A number of assumptions have been made in Section 4.2. Firstly, vessel size has been taken as fixed. All costs are calculated with that assumption in mind. Secondly, the total and average cost of delivering the cargo to a specific port requires additional assumptions about:

a) the cargo load factor;

b) vessel speed at sea (affects time spent at sea relative to in port);

c) voyage distance (affects time spent at sea relative to in port);

d) cargo handling rates (affects time spent in port relative to time at sea);

e) the proportion of the journey spent in ballast;

f) the size of the vessel itself.

These items interact with each other; if speed is increased, fuel consumption rises. On the other hand, time spent at sea will fall, so the amount of overhead allocated to a specific cargo trip will fall. Whether the cost per tonne of cargo delivered falls or rises becomes an interesting question.

One way of analysing the effects of these changes is to allow only one factor to change, keeping all the other possible changes constant. This is what is done in the following analysis.

4.3.1 Changes in the vessel load factor

Variations in the vessel's average load factor will affect the average cost per tonne of cargo delivered. Increases in load factors will lower unit costs, decreases will raise them. Attempting to increase a load factor may be one of the key goals in certain sectors of the shipping business. As we have seen, industries with very high fixed costs and low variable costs will experience sharply falling average unit costs in the short-run, because the overhead can be spread over greater output volumes. The containerised liner trades are a good example. Shipping lines sail according to published timetables. The short-run average cost is minimised at a 100% utilisation rate. The lines are continuously striving to raise the load factor of their vessels, as this generates more revenue and lowers unit costs.

In the tramp trades, the load factor is not really an issue. Operators will be seeking cargoes that match their capacity, and usually they sail with full cargoes. In oil trades, the cargo flows are very unbalanced; usually one leg of the journey is carried out in ballast.

Until the mid 1970s, all tankers sailed fully laden. During the 1973 oil crisis and immediately after, part-cargoes became much more common, being a means of employing tanker tonnage that would otherwise be idle. As the tanker market recovered from this shock, part-cargoes became less common again.

Case Study: Distance and concept of cost per tonne mile

Distances at sea are measured in sea miles and the speed of a vessel is measured in knots. Since a knot is a certain amount of sea miles per hour, the journey time is easily obtained by dividing the distance by the amount of knots.

So a ship travelling at 16 knots will cover a distance of 2500 sea miles in 6.5 days.

To be able to compare cost/earnings of different journeys, shipowners need to take into account that the journeys cover different distances and, therefore, have different cost structures. To account for this, they calculate the cost/income per tonne mile. Following with our example, let's assume that the ship travelling 2500 sea miles carries 50,000 MT of coal with a daily running cost of $30,000.

Therefore, in the 6.5 days that it needs to cover the 2500 sea miles the ship will incur a cost of $195,000. Given that the journey generates 125 million tonne miles, the cost per tonne mile is then $0.00156/tonne/mile.

4.3.2 Changes in vessel speed

Shipping output can be altered by varying the speed of the vessel, as noted in chapter 3. Indeed, it has been argued by some authorities that speed variations are effectively the only way of varying short-run output in the tramp and bulk trades.

Ships are usually designed to run at a particular speed. This speed is determined by the vessel's size, technical characteristics and engine power. When designed, vessels are often optimised for a particular trade. So once built, the flexibility is reduced but there is still some room to vary speed and output.

Making a ship go faster does two things. Firstly, it alters fuel consumption. There is a well known approximate relationship between speed and fuel consumption; known as the cube rule. It says that a 1% increase in vessel speed will lead to a 3% increase in fuel consumption. This formula is calibrated for deviations from the vessel's design speed. Because the speed increase is less than proportional to the consumption increase, fuel consumption will rise, even when the journey time has been reduced.

But the reduction in journey time brings a second consideration into play, namely the daily overhead, covering capital and direct costs. A reduction in journey time means a reduction in the allocation of overheads to this trip, so that there are two opposing forces at work on costs.

Modelling these effects is best carried out with a simulation; taking particular vessel characteristics, a particular voyage and most importantly, assumptions about the price of bunker fuel and freight rates available for any extra cargo carried in the time saved by speeding up the vessel.

It can be shown that the average cost per tonne of cargo delivered falls, and then rises, around the vessel's design speed. The range of vessel speeds is often limited; at the top end, by the discomfort of the crew due to excessive vibration, and at the bottom end, by the loss of vessel manoeuvrability and steerability. A 14 knot vessel may have an effective speed range of 10 to 16 knots; this is still a range of -30% to +12% relative to the design speed.

It is important to note that this relationship is derived for a given price of bunkers. An increase in the bunker price will shift the entire relationship up and to the left, thus reducing the least cost speed. A decrease in bunker prices will do the reverse.

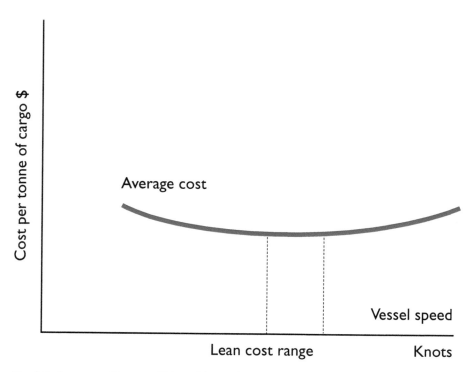

Fig 4.5 Average Cost and Vessel Speed

Note, too, that when freight rates are high, the profit rate increases, and it becomes worthwhile to increase vessel speed. This assumes that the short-run situation exists, since an even more profitable response may be possible in the long-run, such as buying and operating another vessel.

There is good evidence to back up the link between rates, bunker prices and speed in the bulk trades.

There are however, some trades in which speed variation is only used to maintain the published sailings timetable. The liner trades, in particular, have to meet deadlines in order to satisfy their contractual obligations to their customers. They have far less room to respond to variations in bunker prices. Indeed, they behave quite differently, inserting into their contracts a clause that permits them to pass on the effects of unexpected movements in bunker prices to the customer. This response is needed because of the different nature of the service offered in these trades. Recent developments in the world economy and increasing bunker prices in the year before the financial crisis showed that slow steaming in liner trades is possible as long as the savings outweigh the cost of adding an additional ship to the loop.

4.3.3 Changes in distance travelled

Altering the voyage length will automatically increase the total costs incurred by a vessel of a given size assuming all other factors are constant. There are two obvious reasons. With vessel speed held constant, longer voyage lengths mean larger fuel bills. But it also means a longer journey time and hence the direct operating and capital costs, which accrue to that journey, also increase.

Again, the relationship between costs and distance can be shown as a graph, as in Figure 4.6 below. The relationship is drawn for a given vessel size. The vertical distance 0X represents the fixed overhead that would be incurred if the vessel sailed no miles at all. After that, each extra mile requires fuel and additional time costs. These will rise proportionately with distance, assuming a fixed vessel speed.

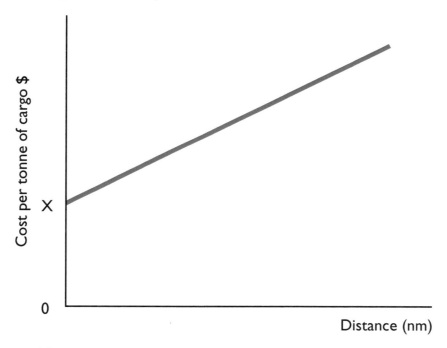

Fig 4.6 The Relationship Between Average Cost and Distance

This relationship can be developed by drawing a graph of the relationship between cost and voyage distance for successively larger sizes of vessels, measured in DWT. Let L_1, L_2 and L_3 represent three successively larger sizes of vessel. The fixed overhead element will tend to get larger as the vessel gets bigger, because larger vessels have larger daily direct and capital costs. On the other hand, the increase in fuel required to travel further will be lower, because fuel consumption at a given vessel speed rises less than proportionately with vessel size. This means that the slopes of the lines become flatter as vessel size increases.

Over the distance range 0A, it is clear that the smallest vessel size is the most economic. Over the range AB, it is vessel size L_2, whilst the largest vessel becomes more efficient as the voyage length increases. For voyage distances around 0A, vessels L_1 and L_2 will be in competition, whilst around 0B, it will be L_2 between vessels of differing sizes. and L_3.

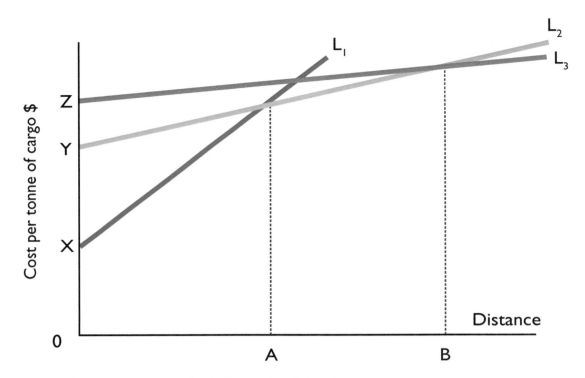

Fig 4.7 Costs and Distance for Different Sized Vessels

Figure 4.7 illustrates another interesting point. As the voyage distance increases, and the time spent at sea increases relative to the time spent in port, the preferred or optimal size of the vessel increases. This point will be considered in more detail below.

4.3.4 Changes in cargo handling rates

Changes in the rate of cargo loading and discharge will reduce the amount of time the vessel spends in port. Other factors being equal, this will reduce the constant terms, the vertical distances such as OX in Figure 4.6 shown in the earlier figures, but will not alter the slope or gradient of the line. The reduction in the constant terms will alter the critical distances at which one vessel size becomes more efficient than another. In general terms, higher cargo handling rates will reduce the distance at which the larger vessel becomes more economic than the smaller.

4.3.5 The proportion of journey spent in ballast

It should be clear that reducing the proportion of the journey that is spent in ballast will lower the average cost per tonne of cargo delivered. This is because the vessel is carrying more cargo, producing more output, with more or less no change in total voyage costs. Fuel consumption will increase slightly, but not significantly.

The effect is exactly the same as raising the vessel's load factor.

4.3.6 Changes in the vessel's size

There are two ways to alter vessel size:

Vessels can be 'jumboised' by the insertion of an extra section of the hull. The opposite operation can also be carried out to make the vessel's capacity smaller. This is clearly an expensive process.

The vessel's size can be altered on the drawing board. Prior to commissioning, the shipowner will have to consider the most appropriately sized vessel for the intended market.

Both of these are long-run decisions. For the sake of completeness, it should be noted that the cost-distance relationship for different sizes of ship can be calculated, which was shown in Figure 4.6. It should be clear that, for greater distances, the preferred size of the ship increases. But the full examination of the relationship between average costs and vessel size leads into an analysis of long-run costs, and this issue is discussed in the next section.

Addendum: Time spent in port relative to time spent at sea

Two of the factors discussed above have a direct effect on the relative proportions of time spent in port and at sea by a vessel. It should be fairly clear that port time costs will be affected by a vessel's size. There are two reasons for this. Firstly, larger vessels will incur greater port charges, as they are often based on either gt or nrt, so larger vessels will be charged more. A related factor to this is, of course, the opportunity cost of the vessel itself. The larger the vessel, the greater the value of capital tied up in the vessel and the greater the cost of capital and opportunity cost of idle port time.

But large vessels are often able to discharge their cargoes more rapidly than smaller ones. So that the time they need to spend in port does not need to be longer than that expected for a smaller vessel. The reason is simple; larger vessels lose more revenue than smaller ones when they do nothing. So it is often the case that they are equipped with higher capacity loading and discharging onboard facilities. Oil tankers are a very good example.

One implication of this is that, other things being equal, the larger the proportion of time a vessel spends in port per year, the smaller its preferred size. The reason is that less capital is tied up doing nothing. Multi-port operations also tend to reduce the optimum vessel size for similar reasons; hence the fact that feeder ships are often of a smaller size.

4.4 LONG-RUN VESSEL COSTS: ECONOMIES OF SCALE AND OPTIMAL SHIP SIZE

A vessel's capacity can be varied in two ways; by altering the dimensions of an existing vessel or by ordering a new, larger one. Information from shipbuilders about the costs of building different sizes of vessel, together with estimates of their running and voyage costs, can be used to estimate the average cost of delivering a tonne of cargo between two ports for different sizes of vessel.

It is important to note that the long-run relationship between average cost and vessel size, which is taken to measure output, is constructed with a number of underlying assumptions.

Input prices are assumed to be constant. In the long-run context, this means the price of capital or interest rates, the price of labour such as crew and the price of fuel are assumed to take the same values when comparing average costs at different sizes. Voyage characteristics, load factors etc. would also need to be kept constant.

In Section 4.1.5 above three different relationships between long-run average costs and output were identified. They were:

a) Economies of Scale;

b) Constant Returns to Scale;

c) Diseconomies of Scale.

Economies of scale exist in two principal areas of shipping, namely the ship and the port facilities, such as container terminals. This section discusses the reasons for the presence of scale economies in general, and then for their existence in shipping.

Economies of scale are essentially of two broad types:

Internal economies of scale as they are only enjoyed by a single company through that firm's individual policy;

External economies of scale, which result from the expansion in scale of the whole industry or a number of firms within the industry and cause a decline in costs to all the firms in the industry.

In the present discussion there will be a concentration on internal economies but readers should be able to see for themselves the effects these economies have on the wider external economies of the industry.

Internal economies of scale can be classified under five convenient headings:

- managerial;
- commercial;
- financial;
- risk bearing;
- technical.

While much of the remainder of this chapter will concentrate on the latter category, before proceeding it is important to look briefly at each of the former categories.

Managerial economies: These are concerned with the control of the organisation. This is part of the important process known as the division of labour where individuals increase their productivity by specialising in a specific task. Management becomes increasingly specialised in a particular aspect of the function of a large company. Senior management can concentrate on general policy, delegating subsidiary, often specialised, tasks to others, usually within a divisional structure.

A small shipping company with only one or two ships may find it cheaper and more efficient to have their ships managed by a specialist management company instead of employing its own staff. Thus the small shipowner will benefit from the economies of scale already achieved by a large management company.

This will apply to the point where the expansion of the fleet makes management expenses greater than for the company employing its own management staff. As with any business, larger shipping firms will be able to have their own specialist legal and insurance departments for example, hopefully saving fees and making more informed management decisions.

Such economies are also applicable to the major liner companies, which have offices all over the world. As part of their company policy, they transfer staff to other places in the world in order to create an all-round management structure.

Commercial economies: Sometimes referred to as marketing economies, large production allows bulk buying at a discount. In selling the marketing cost per unit of output and advertising is cheaper in larger volumes, the shipowner or operator can achieve economies of scale by placing regular orders in respect of such things as maintenance or bunkering.

Financial Economies: Large companies have advantages in raising finance for expansion either through banks or by going to the public through the sale of shares. It is much more difficult for the small company to convince potential lenders of their financial stability.

Risk bearing economies: There are three types of risk.

Insurable risk: often large companies can insure at low premiums simply because of the size and the limitation of risk. For the same reasons some large companies will insure themselves internally, rather than give their business to insurance business.

Risk bearing: large businesses can usually bear their own risks by introducing a new commodity because they will have secured the confidence of their customers.

Uncertainties: uncertainties are those risks which cannot easily be insured against. Such uncertainties can, and often do, cause the bankruptcy of small companies. Larger concerns can diversify their product industrial section or market and thereby compensate for the difficulties in one area by the buoyancy in another. This is one of the basic strengths of the large multi-national company. Increasingly shipping companies are diversifying their interests and investing in related services, such as through-transport and leisure services. Larger shipping companies can more easily switch vessels from one trade to another trade should the need arise. If, for example, a certain vessel has to undergo major repairs, then the services of that vessel can be taken over by another vessel of their fleet and so save the cost of having to charter a vessel. Pooling arrangements also offer the opportunity to spread risk.

As can be seen in Table 4.2, there is a decrease in average construction costs as measured by deadweight or teu, with increases in vessel size for all three vessel types. But it should be stressed that these are newbuild prices, not costs. Newbuild prices are market driven as well as cost related, so they may reflect demand conditions as well as the costs of production.

The final column expresses the unit cost reduction as a percentage of the cost per dwt of the smallest size vessel of a given type. It is clear that container vessels, because of their greater complexity, experience much smaller economies than are found in the tanker or dry cargo sectors.

Dry Cargo DWT	2000		2006	
	Price $mn	$/DWT	Price $mn	$/DWT
30,000 Bulk Carrier	20	667	34	1133
70,000 Panamax	23	329	37	529
150,000 Capesize	40	267	68	453

Tankers (double hulled) DWT	2000		2006	
	Price $mn	$/DWT	Price $mn	$/DWT
32,000 Products	25	781	46	1438
80,000 Aframax	35	438	64	800
110,000 Suezmax	44	400	75	682
250,000 VLCC	78	312	126	504

Containerships TEU	2007	$/TEU
1,700	33	19412
4,000	66	16500
5,750	123	21391
11,600	161	13879

Table 4.2 Newbuilding Prices, 2000 and 2006/7 (source: SSY Monthly Shipping Review, various issues. Worldyards Newsletter, May 2007 (for containership prices)).

Using the above data to approximate the elasticity of ship price with respect to size, it turns out that the relevant estimates for 2010 are:

0.78 for crude oil tankers,

0.69 for dry bulk vessel,

0.65 for containerships

These figures all imply the presence of significant economies to the owner derived from purchasing larger ships. The smaller the elasticity value, indicating inelasticity, the greater the unit cost reduction. In 2010, the largest benefit to owners appeared to be available in the container sector.

Determining the appropriate size vessel for a given route length

Even though the cost per tonne of the ship itself declines with vessel size, other cost elements involved in the operation of a ship may not do so. Indeed, there is a trade-off in existence, between the lower unit costs brought about by operating a larger size vessel, and the extra time it requires to load and discharge them, assuming that cargo loading and handling rates are constant. In essence, this boils down to the gains from larger ship sizes when the ship is at sea being offset by the extra port time implicitly required to load and discharge. Where the voyage length is short, the ship will spend more of its time in port in a year, compared to if it traded on a long distance route. This means that there may be a point at which the potential cost savings from using a larger vessel when at sea are more than offset by the higher costs involved with the same ship sitting idle in port.

This idea can be more formally expressed in a model of ship costs. Basically the model can be reduced to three elements:

1. The daily capital cost of running a vessel;

2. The daily operating cost of running a vessel;

3. The voyage related cost (primarily fuel).

This model ignores cargo loading and discharge costs. When the ship is in port, the first two elements must be covered, as these costs have to be financed in the long-run at all times. When the ship is at sea, the vessel also incurs the third set of costs. The relative importance of the components clearly depends on the number of days spent at sea and the number of days spent in port. A Calais–Dover ferry will spend a large proportion of its working year in port, compared to a 310,000-dwt VLCC trading from the Middle East to Japan and China. Thus short route lengths will raise the number of port days relative to sea days, and will affect cost structures.

Second, increases in ship size lowers average costs, but the relationship between ship size and capital cost is not the same as the relationship between ship size and daily operating cost. The relationship between ship size, vessel speed and fuel consumption is complex, and this affects the third component of the cost model.

In the past, the elasticity of capital cost with respect to ship size has been estimated at around 0.7. In other words, a 10 per cent increase in ship size would raise the newbuild price of a vessel by seven percent, thus leading to a fall in the average cost per deadweight.

Let us assume that, for direct operating costs, the elasticity was much lower at 0.5. This means that direct operating costs only rose by five percent for a 10 per cent increase in ship size, implying larger savings than from capital. This assumption is not unrealistic as direct operating costs do not increase relative to size. A good example of this is crew. A ship five times larger does not require a five times larger crew.

For voyage costs at sea, the primary determinants are assumed vessel operating speeds, both laden and in ballast, and fuel consumption of main engines, which is affected by assumed vessel speed. It is simplest to assume a constant voyage speed which is the same on both legs of the voyage. In the model, the assumed elasticity of fuel consumption with vessel size is set at 0.75, implying that a 10 per cent increase in size will increase daily fuel consumption by 7.5 percent.

To construct an estimate of costs per tonne of cargo delivered, we make the following assumption for the calculation:

The ship is a dry bulk vessel of 170,000-dwt

The new building cost was $97,000,000

The economical life is 18 years

Interest rate is 5%

Capital cost elasticity is 0.7

Trading life of 350 days per year, ignoring time and cost for its five year surveys

Daily operating costs elasticity is 0.5

Assumed operating costs for the base vessel is $2,700,000 per year

The constant speed is 15 knots and the base vessel consumes 100 tonnes a day at a price of $720 per tonne

The time in port is based on a load and discharge rate of 5,000 tonnes per day

Fuel consumed during the time in port is ignored.

The model calculates the average cost per cargo tonne, which is a long-run concept, because capital and direct operating costs have been included, and reveals some interesting trends:

1. For a very short route length, smaller size ships have lower unit cargo costs per tonne than larger ships

2. As the route length increases, larger ships will have lower unit cargo costs than the smallest ship size, but the very largest ships may have marginally higher unit cargo costs per tonne. In other words, there is a range of ship sizes that generate lower unit costs; both smaller and larger ship sizes will have higher unit costs. This means there is an optimum range ship size for these route lengths.

3. As the route length gets longer, the optimum ship size gets larger and the range of sizes shifts to the right.

These results show that there is a range of optimum sizes. Manipulation of the basic elements of the model, such as ship prices, fuel prices, and the assumed values of the elasticities, will all affect the precise ship sizes that are optimal. The key insight, however, relates to the behaviour of costs at sea and costs in port.

The reason why the optimal ship size range gets larger with longer route length lies in the fact that as the proportion of sea time rises, fuller exploitation of the economies of scale are to be gained from using larger ships, as the cost penalties from so doing, including longer time in port with longer loading and longer discharging times, are offset by the longer distance voyages.

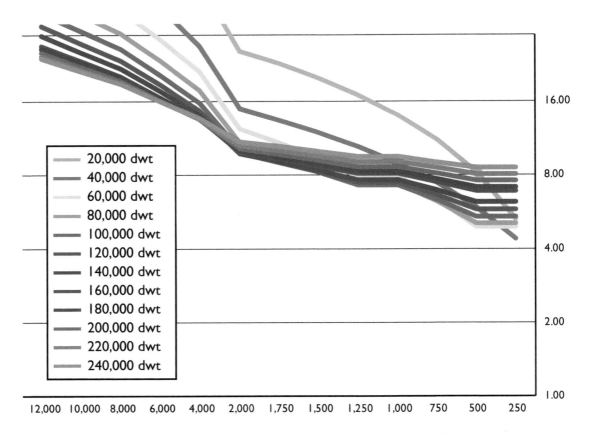

Fig 4.8 Long-run Average Costs per Tonne of Cargo by Voyage Length (Source: Derived by Author from Evans and Marlow model)

Note: Port load and discharge costs excluded. Bunker prices assumed to be $180 per tonne.

Even though the model has been developed for dry bulk vessels, there is no reason to assume it is just limited to that ship type.

This helps to explain the use of Hub and Spoke networks on the liner trade. In a hub and spoke network, the liner company will have a main terminal or port in a geographical area called the hub to and from which the cargo is brought and distributed to the other ports in the area, the spokes.

Large container ships are very expensive. The rapid growth in world trade in the past 15 years has led to a big increase in the demand for container movements from the Far East to North America and Europe. The *Emma Maersk*, in 2007 the world's largest container ship, carried around 11,000-teu although industry sources claimed its true capacity was 14,770. Engineering studies have argued that there is no engineering obstacle to building an 18,000-teu vessel, the maximum size capable of transiting the Straits of Malacca. After that two main engines would be required to maintain a service speed of 24 knots, with implications for fuel consumption and voyage costs. Such large vessels will have very high daily capital charges, and their time in port must be kept to a minimum. The *Emma Maersk's* main voyage is from North West Europe, calling, for example at Bremerhaven and Felixstowe, and then next calling at Singapore, before sailing on to China and Japan. Its port time is kept as short as possible and its sea time maximised. Some modern large container ships will be calling at Southampton container terminal, their only UK port call, for 12 hours before sailing again. These observations are consistent with the model above.

One other observation should be made. The assumption is made that the ship is sailing fully laden. With tankers, the standard assumption is of laden one way, ballast back. Dry cargo ships have more possibility of back haul cargoes, but the model assumed one cargo in one direction, fully laden. It is clear that if demand levels do not generate cargo lot sizes that are the same as the ship, then the average cost per cargo unit will rise, as the greater capital costs of a larger ship will be spread over the same cargo volume as those incurred if a smaller ship had been used. The model thus assumed ships size and average lot size are the same.

4.5   THE EFFECT OF DIFFERENT FISCAL REGIMES ON COSTS

The discussion has ignored the tax treatment of investment in shipping. But the way that national governments set the tax regime on ship investment plays a critical role in influencing the long-run average cost of operating vessels under the national flag. Because ships are large, expensive and long-lived assets, the way that their purchase can be written off, and the way that ship purchases can be offset against a shipping company's liability for tax on its overall operations, can have a highly significant effect on the overall profitability of a company's shipping operations.

The most thorough research into this issue has been conducted by Gardner, Goss and Marlow. They developed a model which allowed them to compare the effect of different tax regimes on £1m worth of shipping investment. Their ground-breaking work has been updated by the UK Chamber of Shipping, whose data is reproduced below.

Registry	Ranking	Net present value of £1m invested in 1995 (£)
Germany	1	125,860
Norway (Norwegian International Shipping)	2	120,430
Liberia	3	120,000
Greece	4	104,710
Netherlands	5	94,990
Norway (National Register)	6	59,580
United Kingdom	7	59,670
Italy	8	5,780

Table 4.3 The Effect of Different Fiscal Regimes on Ship Investment
(Source: Farrington (1996))

Table 4.3 above illustrates that wide differences exist for the profitability of investment across different countries. They are based on a standard vessel, a £15m dry bulk cargo vessel of 68,000-dwt, 36,000 gt, 23,000 nrt. A 10% rate of return on capital is assumed, together with assumptions about the vessel's economic life, rates of inflation, and discount rates. The table implies that even if every other factor that affects costs is held constant, the choice of country of registration affects overall profitability, because of its effect on the cost of investing in shipping. One issue for the European Union, with its commitment to equality of opportunity within its boundaries, is the question: should all European shipowners face the same fiscal regime? The EU's drive for a single market would appear to imply this; it is clear that there is a long way to go.

In the past decade, a number of countries have introduced what is known as a 'tonnage tax' regime in an effort to encourage shipowners to register their ships. The United Kingdom introduced its regime in 2000, and it has been quite successful in attracting some tonnage back to the UK register, which had become much reduced. Essentially, under the scheme, owners pay a fixed amount per tonnage registered, irrespective of profits made. Provided that the company is profitable, the actual tax paid under this scheme is lower than the standard rate of Corporation Tax which would otherwise have been levied. The UK scheme has a twist, in that owners electing for this optional tonnage tax have to commit themselves to training one cadet officer for every 15 qualified personnel they employ. This is designed to encourage the training of officers in the UK, which fell to very low levels in the 1990s. Tonnage tax schemes have been introduced in other countries, such as the Netherlands. From a European perspective, it is clear that industry directed tax schemes may lead only to the owners benefiting at the expense of European taxpayers, as national administrations compete against each other through these schemes. Japan has also made efforts to introduce a similar scheme.

What difference has the change in tax regimes made to the relative tax burdens of the different registries? In 2008, Marlow and Mitroussi in their 'EU Shipping Taxation: The Comparative Position of Greek Shipping' have calculated the present values of tax payments required under five different tax regimes for five different specific vessels, assuming the ships are new, operated for 15 years. They compare Panama, Liberia, Greece, Netherlands and the UK flags. They find that for four of the five cases, Panama and Liberia rank first and second, with the UK last. Greece is worst for the 75,000 DWT bulk carrier but second or third for the two container ships and tankers (of different sizes) that make up the five examples. All the calculations assume a discount rate of 10% per annum. It should be noted that the difference between the UK and Dutch figures are very small, so the ranking is perhaps a little misleading. For example, at the 10% discount rate, the present value of tax payments for a new 299,700-dwt tanker was £368,182 for the UK, £363,253 for the Netherlands and £155,544 for Greece. The tax payments to Panama and Liberia were found to be £44,911 and £164,375 respectively. Whilst tax payments are one factor, the magnitude of these figures is relatively small when considering the overall capital and operating costs of such a vessel. A flag is not always selected for tax reasons.

4.6 THE EFFECT OF FLAG OF REGISTRY ON COSTS

Ship operators face very competitive conditions. One of the post war developments in shipping has been the rise of what are known as Open Registers or Flags of Convenience. These were terms denoting national shipping registers that have two principal characteristics:

1. The ability to repatriate profits to the beneficial owner's home country, with light or non-existent taxation.

2. Light or non-existent machinery for the enforcement of internationally-agreed regulations.

The former allowed the owner to repatriate profits; the latter allowed them to avoid domestic wage agreements, permitting the use of low-cost crew from non-domestic sources, and often avoiding the enforcement of social and safety regulations.

Basically, the Open Register permitted owners to exploit lower labour costs and lower tax rates. Thus similar sizes and types of ships may well be operated at significantly lower costs than under national flags. Some have estimated the cost differential at about 10%, allowing for vessel size, age, and other factors determining costs. There is a range of costs for a given size, depending on the nature of the vessel's flag; this cost range is shown in Figure 4.9.

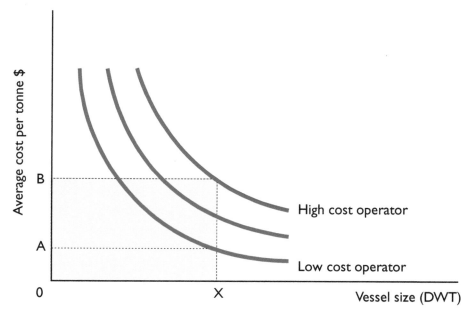

Fig 4.9 The Cost Margin Zone: Long-run Average Costs for Operators Facing Different Cost Conditions

At vessel size OX, unit costs for the low cost operator are OA per tonne, whereas those for an equivalent sized high cost operator are OB per tonne. The figure has been drawn to exaggerate the difference, relative to the overall unit cost value. If it is the case that Open Registers permit a higher proportion of profits to be retained and also permit the lowering of daily operating costs by the use of crew paid at lower wage rates, then there is a strong incentive for the shipowner or shipping company to switch registries to exploit these advantages.

The pull of these registries is quite large. Table 4.4 shows that traditional maritime countries' shares of world tonnage steadily declined over the past 30 years, with the share of Open Registries rising to nearly 50% of the world merchant fleet.

	2004	2005	2006	2007	2008	2009	2010	2011
Developing Economies	21.20	22.60	22.70	17.15	25.51	25.21	25.23	25.50
Developed Economies	26.90	27.00	26.90	28.43	18.54	18.23	17.89	16.96
Economies in Transition	1.80	1.60	1.50	0.13	1.15	1.06	1.00	0.93
Open & International Registries	46.60	45.10	45.00	54.26	54.35	55.11	55.44	56.10

Table 4.4 Market Shares of World Registered Tonnage (Source: UNCTAD Maritime Review, 2006 , Table 14, p.29)

Note: Figures in percentages except for Total, which is in millions of tonnes deadweight.

Some traditional maritime nations have responded to this trend by introducing their own version of an Open Register. The best known of these is the Norwegian International Shipping Register, which among other things, permits Norwegian owners to avoid national crewing regulations. It has attracted a large volume of tonnage owned by Norwegian shipowners back from other Open Registries, since its creation in 1990.

The increasing trend in the use of Open Registers is very clear from Table 4.4. It should be noted that the fall in the share of traditional registers' maritime tonnage does not necessarily imply a fall in the share of ownership, since many beneficial owners of Open Registry vessels are resident in those countries. For example, many owners of Liberian tonnage live in the USA or West Europe; few live in Monrovia.

There are a number of other points to note from the table. Whilst the Open Registers share stood at 45 per cent in 2006, this is in fact a slight decline from 2000. The developing countries' share now stands at 22 per cent, up from 10 per cent in 1980, but stable over the past 15 years. The central and East European economies' share fell over the period 1990-2005, largely driven by the break-up of the Soviet Union and the decline of the Russian economy over the period 1990-1995. Whilst the Russian economy has recovered, helped by rising commodity prices, the fleet share has not.

4.7 COSTS AND QUALITY: THE PROBLEM OF SUB-STANDARD SHIPS

Economists assume that markets trade fairly. The product being offered is of merchantable quality, and is fit for the purpose. Many observers of the shipping industry, and indeed participants, have become increasingly concerned over the continued existence of poor quality tonnage in the market. Some national governments have become so concerned that they have enacted their own laws regarding the age and quality of vessels that may enter their ports.

20 yr old bulk carrier: 30 000 DWT US$/Day		1990 products tanker: 40 000 DWT US$/Day
7 500	Ceiling (1)	9 500
4 500	Good Practice (2)	4 850
3 750	Common Practice (3)	4 250
3 250	Standard (4) (6)	3 750
2 750	Floor (5)	3 100

Table 4.5 Vessel Operating Cost 'levels' and Financial Advantages (Source: Non-Observance of International Rules and Standards: Competitive Advantages Annex, page 5, Directorate for Science, Technology and Industry, Maritime Committee, OECD, Paris, January 1996.)

Key:

(1) Ceiling = level of maximum expenditure
(2) Good Practice = high level of expenditure adopted by minority of shipowners.
(3) Common Practice = average level of expenditure adopted by majority of shipowners
(4) Standard Practice = minimum level of expenditure to ensure owner's compliance with basic standards of safety.
(5) Floor = level of minimum expenditure, still keeping vessel operational.
(6) Shaded area = margin of sub-standard operation within which the shipowner is able to operate a vessel subject to non-detection by regulatory authorities such as flag States and classification societies acting on their behalf, port States and so on.

The incentive for unscrupulous shipowners to cheat is quite large. As long as charterers are solely concerned with price, there are pressures placed which may lead owners to reduce repair and maintenance expenditures to below that necessary for the long term quality of the vessel. A 1996 study by the OECD provides some estimates of the margins available.

The estimates translate into a 13% saving on the annual running cost for the dry cargo vessel, and 15% for product carriers. These illustrative figures indicate the very strong incentives to cheat, if charterers pay the same rate to good and bad shipowners alike.

One means of reducing the incentives to cheat is to raise the overall standard of management in the shipping industry. The successful introduction of the International Safety Management Code by the IMO in 1998 appears to have improved the industry's performance overall. The appointment of an onboard officer who is responsible for the day-to-day implementation of the regulations appears to have led to significant reduction in accidents and an increase in ship quality.

Enforcement of ship quality by more frequent ship inspections, carried out by Port State Authorities, has also helped. In the European Union the EQUASIS data base permits national administrations to swap information on ship detentions and thus improve the targeting of ships calling at European ports. Following the Erika and Prestige disasters, the IMO accelerated the phase out of single hull tankers, from 2015 to 2010. This has reduced the average age of the tanker fleet and the probability of oil spillage in the event of a tanker accident with the ship's shell plating being breached.

The past strong growth of shipping markets has encouraged shipowners to increase investment and lower the average age of the world's fleet. In the current economic climate owners are again seeking to limit their costs. One way is scrapping the older, uneconomical tonnage. Another possibility is cutting costs and making savings on maintenance and safety.

The figures also highlight the important role of the regulatory bodies in ensuring that competition between shipowners is equitable. It is clear that the maritime sector must always be vigilant in this regard if it is to improve its public image in terms of pollution and the treatment of its workers.

4.8 THE EFFECT OF DEMAND AND INVENTORY ON OPTIMAL SHIP SIZE

It is, in fact, the volume and characteristics of demand and the level of inventory costs that help determine the preferred size of the vessel.

As noted in Section 4, the ability to exploit the fact that in general, larger ships deliver the cargo at a lower cost per tonne than smaller ships, is clearly limited by the volume of cargo to be moved. This can be measured in two ways. First, the average lot size, or parcel size, of cargo, and second, the frequency with which cargo needs to be moved in a given period of time.

Other things being equal, the larger the average lot size, the larger the optimal size of vessel. The more frequent the required delivery, the smaller the optimal size of vessel. If demand volumes, and average parcel sizes rise, then there is scope for using a larger vessel, provided that unit costs continue to fall.

If demand levels are not sufficient to allow very large vessels to be used at the appropriate service frequency, demand acts as a constraint on the ability to exploit larger ship size.

Two examples illustrate this point. The rapid growth in world trade in the past 15 years has led to a boom in demand for liner shipping services. The most notable has been the trade with China, prior to and after it joined the WTO (World Trade Organisation) in 2001. Two of its principal trading partners have been the European and North American economies. These are long haul routes. As cargo volumes grew, larger container ships are introduced on these routes. As even larger vessels were introduced, the previous larger vessels are cascaded down to trade on the less busy long haul routes, and then as economic trade volumes grow over time and the new ships become older, they are progressed onto shorter haul routes, where demand volumes grow.

This process is observed in many industries. In aviation, the same thing happens to new, larger aircraft. In the dry cargo market, China has again been instrumental in raising the demand for coal, iron ore and steel to record levels. Ships as large as 400,000-dwt have been ordered to serve this trade. Brazilian mining company Vale ordered or underwrote the building of 35 such vessels, the first of which was delivered in 2011. This contrasts with the sharp difference in sizes observed between the sectors in the 1980s, when oil demand had peaked in 1981 after rapid growth. This illustrates the fact that demand volumes also help dictate both the largest economic ship size, and by implication, average ship size, in the different trades.

The discussion of operating costs in Sections 3 and 4 above focussed entirely on the costs of operating the ship. But in some cases, ship operators also own the cargo. This then leads to the following question:

What effect will incorporating inventory value have on the determination of the optimal vessel size for a given trade?

Inventory costs are also important as the cost of holding the cargo in store on the vessel increases directly with the size of that vessel, assuming a fixed interest rate and a fixed average value for the cargo. When inventory costs are included in estimating the overall cost of cargo per tonne to be delivered, it is possible to generate a u-shaped average cost curve, as shown in Figure 4.10.

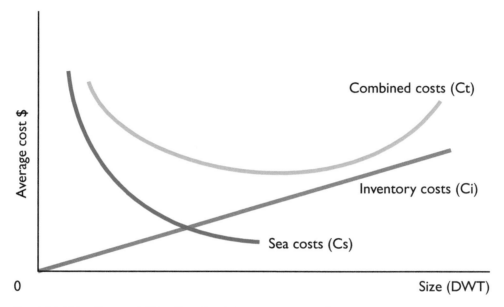

Fig 4.10 The Optimal Ship Size (with inventory costs)

It is clear that the higher the inventory cost, the smaller the optimum vessel size, as the slope of the inventory cost line will increase. Therefore, high cargo unit prices will tend to reduce the optimal size, and vice versa.

Any shipowner which also operates a terminal or port, or which has an interest in the cargo, which it also owns, would be interested in the combined costs. For example, a major oil company moving its own oil in its own vessel might consider both the inventory costs of the cargo as well as the operating costs of the ship when modelling overall costs. The classic case of this would be the traditional large multi-national oil companies, at their peaks in the 1970s, with large tanker fleets and direct control of oil from field to consumer.

It should also be pointed out that increased ship size means increased draught, beam and length. Many parts of the world have draught restrictions because of shallow waters. The Suez and Panama canals also impose an upper limit on vessels designed to transit them. Many ports do not have the facilities necessary to handle the largest vessels. Thus the trading flexibility of very large vessels is more limited than the smaller ones. Provided that demand conditions are satisfactory, the vessel may survive on these restricted opportunities, but that may not always be the case.

4.9 TRENDS IN SHIP SIZE AND THE CONCEPT OF THE OPTIMUM SIZE OF VESSEL

Table 4.6 indicates the trend changes in the average size of vessels of different ship types over the past 40 years. A number of points are worthy of note. Firstly, there has been a general increase in the average size of all ship types over the period. There has also been a marked increase in trade volumes, so this is hardly surprising.

What is much more interesting is the differences that have emerged between the ship types themselves. The average size of oil tankers peaked in 1980 at around 100,000-dwt. From there it declined to the current 85,000-dwt mark. It must be stressed here that the figure is the average size.

Dry Cargo vessels have steadily increased in size, and have closed the gap with oil tankers on average. In 1995, they were, on average, half the size. By 2005, they were two thirds of the average tanker size. Container vessels have also increased their average size, growing rapidly over the period 1995-2007. In teu terms, the average size of a 1995 containership was 1,431. By 2006, it had risen to 2,316, an increase of 56% over the original value.

4.9.1 Why the differences?

It is clear that some ship types have been able to exploit the potential of scale economies to a greater extent than others. In a similar fashion, the ability to exploit the fact that in general, larger ships deliver the cargo at a lower cost per tonne than smaller ships, is clearly limited by the volume of cargo to be moved, in other words, by the size of the market. Figure 4.11 and Table 4.6 provide some information on the trends in average ship size for a number of major ship types.

The increase in tanker sizes in the 1970s can be seen as exploiting the growth in volume demand, the growth in average parcel sizes, and the shift toward longer hauls. In earlier sections, it was noted that increases in journey distances tend to increase the optimum vessel size. In addition, average journey lengths increased rapidly with the closure of the Suez Canal in 1967. Larger and larger vessels were built, culminating in a number of ULCCs of 500,000-dwt.

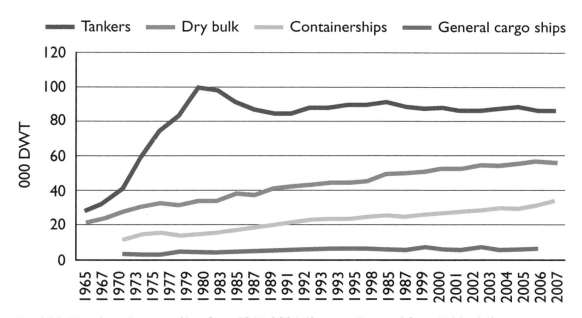

Fig 4.11 Trends in Average Ship Size, 1965-2006 (Source: Derived from Table 4.6)

The increase in average size was reversed in the early1980s. Crude oil prices had risen to their highest ever value, thus raising inventory costs significantly. Average tanker voyage lengths have declined since the early 1980s; cargo volumes also stagnated. The ideal parcel size, even on the long haul major routes, fell. These pressures led to a decline in the average size of tankers in the years 1981 to 1987, although the trend has again reversed.

In the 1990s, the price of crude oil had fallen to its lowest level in real terms since 1973. Since 2002, demand for crude oil has grown and is close to projected maximum refinery capacity, creating a volatile market price which is now much higher, trading well above $100 a barrel. This raises inventory values again and tanker average sizes have fallen slightly in the past few years. Tanker average size has now stabilised at around 86,000-dwt.

Dry bulk cargo lot sizes have increased as coal and iron ore trades have grown rapidly, as seen in Chapter 2. As a result, dry cargo bulk vessels have also grown in size, with Capesize vessels going above 200,000-dwt and the largest measuring 400,000-dwt. The expansion in size again reflects the longer route structures and greater volumes traded in the Chinese and Asian markets. These trends are consistent with the model outlined above. Again, larger sized vessels need improved cargo handling rates in order to prevent port time increases offsetting any potential cost gains when the larger vessels are at sea. Higher rates of cargo handling mean less time in port, and raise the optimal size. Larger average lot sizes also raise the optimal size of a vessel.

Year	Tankers '000s dwt	Dry Bulk '000s dwt	Containerships 100+gt	General Cargo 100+gt
1965	28.123	21.046		
1967	32.902	23.996		
1970	42.982	27.596	11.425	3.268
1973	58.252	30.465	14.972	3.249
1975	73.487	32.185	14.902	3.296
1977	83.973	32.599	14.878	3.494
1979	99.900	33.700		
1980	97.300	34.468	17.030	3.593
1983	91.000	38.500		
1985	86.900	38.500		
1987	84.100	40.959		
1989	85.300	42.367		
1991	86.600	44.023	22.701	
1992	87.200	44.465	23.248	5.927
1993	88.500	44.746	23.583	
1995	89.062	45.922	24.435	5.822
1998	90.715	49.218	25.377	5.802
1999	87.414	49.981	25.691	5.639
2000	87.672	51.113	25.973	5.795
2001	87.661	52.714	26.800	5.796
2002	87.286	52.695	27.928	5.732
2003	87.068	54.241	28.828	5.805
2004	87.060	54.944	29.715	5.773
2005	87.494	56.492	30.804	5.863
2006	86.472	57.670	31.777	5.888
2007	86.475	57.911	33.148	

Table 4.6 Trends in Average Ship Size, Selected Years (Sources: 1965-1995 1995 on SSY Monthly Shipping Review; Shipping Statistics and Market Review, ISL, Bremen. DWT from 1995 on)

Notes:
1. As at 1st January of each year
2. Series from 1995 on all in dwt
3. General Cargo and Container Ships greater than 300gt after 1995

Vessels in container trades spend a considerable amount of time in port, despite the container revolution. They also need to sail at regular intervals and journey lengths may be short. They carry a mix of cargoes, a lot of it with high unit value and high inventory cost. All these factors tend to make the optimal vessel size smaller than in the bulk trades. But it is interesting to note that cargo volumes have boomed in the past years, especially between 2003–2008 and there are now 12,000-teu vessels. The size of container ships has grown rapidly since 1995, as globalisation and greater trade volumes have led to increased viability of very large containerships. This process echoes the rapid development of tanker sizes that occurred in the 1970s.

General cargo ships show the least increase in size. Given the amount of time they have to spend in port, and the low growth in demand for their services, this is hardly surprising.

The above analysis and argument can be shown up clearly with the aid of Figure 4.12 below. It is assumed in the diagram, that the long-run average cost relationship for a particular ship type is known. This is represented by the LRAC curve in the diagram. To simplify matters, it is assumed that the shipowner is not the cargo owner, so inventory costs can be ignored.

Two trades are represented on the diagram. D1 and D2 represent the long-run level of demand per time period expected on that route. The lower demand volume represents a smaller trade in total tonnage, assuming voyage distance, load factors and other relevant factors are similar. This demand volume can be viewed as representing the average cargo lot size for a particular trip; low total volumes, for a given frequency of service, will imply low cargo lot sizes.

If we question what size of vessel would provide the least average cost for moving the cargo volume, the answer is clear. Figure 4.12 implies that the lowest unit cost for D1 can be achieved by using a vessel of OX dwt capacity; for D2, it would be OY. Note the emphasis on average cost; it should be clear that even though the average cost per tonne of cargo is lower in the case of D2, the total cost will be larger, as, indeed, is the total cost of the vessel, as Table 4.2 above makes clear.

It would not be efficient to use the larger vessel, which is appropriate for average lot size D2, on the trade D1, because it would be trading at much less than full capacity, so that its average cost per tonne would not be that read off from the LRAC at OX. This curve was drawn assuming that all vessels traded at the same full load factor. It is highly likely that the unit cost per tonne actually carried by the much larger vessel, when trading at 25% load factor, say, will be higher than the average cost achieved by the smaller vessel when trading at 100% load factor.

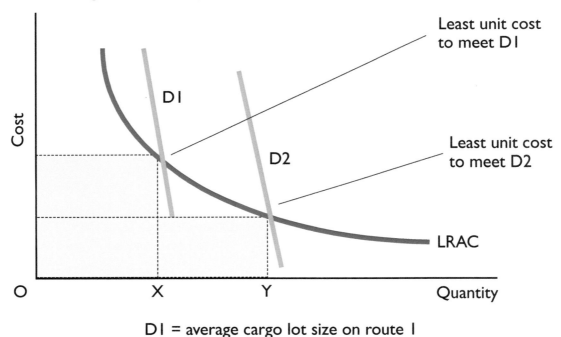

D1 = average cargo lot size on route 1
D2 = average cargo lot size on route 2

Fig 4.12 Choice of Least Cost Vessel Size

4.10 CONCLUSION

This chapter has developed some basic ideas about the determinants of shipping costs. After a short review of basic economic cost concepts, both short and long-run cost relationships were explored in the shipping context. The principal conclusions were that:

1. Short-run variations in output and cost were primarily driven by variations in vessel speed, assuming that other important factors are held constant.

2. There is a complex relationship between long-run unit costs and vessel size; as route lengths increase, larger vessel sizes will have falling unit costs, but, if the size becomes too large on a given route length, unit costs may rise. This leads to the concept of an optimal size range of ships for a given route and for trade volumes.

3. The choice of optimal vessel size is affected by the long-run cost curve, demand conditions and the cost of inventory.

4. Cost levels are affected by:

   a) The choice of flag;
   b) the fiscal regime;
   c) the degree to which regulations are actually enforced.

Chapter 5
. . . .
COMPETITIVE SHIPPING
MARKETS: DRY BULK CARGO

Coins have a grooved edge because in the past dishonest traders filed down the edges to remove some of the precious metal. Many countries print images or writing at the very edge of the coin to prevent this same dishonest practice.

5   INTRODUCTION

The dry bulk trades have been transformed over the past 25 years. The average size of the vessel engaged in these trades has doubled in size, as was shown in chapter 4. There is now a large range of vessel sizes, with ships of 10,000-dwt now being regarded as relatively small.

Dry bulk trades have in fact evolved from the tramp market. Traditional tramp markets were served by small, general purpose vessels, essentially scouring the world's ports in search of business. That business was primarily undertaken on the spot market, with owners using the global network of shipbrokers to seek business for their vessels. At the same time, charterers would contact the same set of brokers to inform the market of their chartering requirements. Brokers perform a fundamental function in providing information to both sides of the market place, to enable contracts to be agreed.

Nowadays, as vessel sizes have increased so much, there is a tendency for really significant charterers to use long timecharters, consecutive voyage charters and contracts of affreightment. Owners have to be able to offer several vessels to fulfil these types of contracts, but if the company operates large vessels, such contracts provide greater continuity of employment.

Despite the growth in these types of contracts, there is still a huge volume of spot charters. This market is widely regarded, by both practitioners and observers alike, as being very competitive. In this chapter, the focus is on the development of a simple model of the competitive process that will then be used to analyse market behaviour in these trades. The centre of attention, throughout this chapter, will be the tramp.

5.1   DEFINITION OF THE DRY CARGO SECTOR

The dry cargo sector can be defined using two basic methods. Firstly, it could be defined as the basic unit that provides the service, the tramp ship. Alternatively, a broader based approach could be adopted, defining the sector in terms of its major market characteristics. These two approaches will overlap to a considerable extent.

The tramp ship

The first approach, used by several authors, is to define the sector in terms of the vessel itself. Gripaios defines the tramp ship as follows:

'A deepsea tramp ship is prepared to carry any cargo between any port at any time, always providing that the venture is both legal and safe'.

This definition focuses upon the nature of the market that the vessel serves. During the 1960s, vessel size increased, prompting a different definition, suggested by the late Professor B.N. Metaxas:

'Any vessel with a tonnage of 4,000-dwt or above, which in the long-run does not have a fixed itinerary, and which carries mainly dry cargo in bulk over relatively long distances and from one or more ports to one or more ports is an ocean or deepsea tramp'.

Notice that both definitions emphasise the fact that the vessel has no fixed pattern of employment. It is this feature that has been labelled tramping. But Metaxas' definition differs in several respects from the earlier one. Firstly, a minimum vessel size is introduced, in order to exclude small vessels from the market. Secondly, attention is drawn to the term relatively long distances, which is a way of focussing on the deepsea nature of the tramping operation. Finally, Metaxas also states that the vessel trades mainly in the dry cargo sector.

Market characteristics

The problem with defining a market in terms of a set of specific vessel characteristics should be obvious to most people. By including a specific vessel size, Metaxas has dated his definition. The growing average size of most vessel types over the past 25 years, as we saw in chapter 4, means that 4,000-dwt appears to be a very small vessel nowadays.

In the past two decades, dry bulk vessels have increased their size range, varying from 10,000-dwt, through 50-80,000 DWT-dwt or (Panamax size), up to 400,000-dwt or capesize. These vessels are more specialised than the old tramps, as some are clearly too large to trade from any port to any port; indeed the very largest cannot transit the major canals of Panama and Suez, hence the terms Panamax and Capesize.

In addition such vessels are often employed on contracts of affreightment, which permits the shipowner to meet the charterer's requirements by using more than one vessel, or by consecutive voyage charters, which oblige the shipowner to commit the vessel to several voyages in a row for a particular charterer. These longer term commitments from both sides of the market do not fit neatly with either definition.

A modern definition would need to include the development of these longer term commitments, which have been brought about by two major trends.

Firstly, cargo volumes and average lot sizes have increased, therefore creating the bulk dry trades sector. Secondly, the most efficient way of meeting these trends is to use larger vessels. But, as we have seen, larger vessels require larger capital requirements from the owners; they are only prepared to risk the commitment to such large vessels if they have a better guarantee of employment; and this is what the above contracts provide them with.

It should be clear that freight rates arrived at for these contracts are still influenced by the spot market. The analysis that follows focuses on this sector of the market, noting that there are other contract types available.

A definition that was based upon market structure might be more generally applicable, as it would be less affected by changes in the size of vessels which were used to serve it.

One of the key features of dry cargo markets is the fixing of many contracts in an open market situation. What is meant by this is the fact that most contracts between charterers and shipowners and ship managers become well known to all the market participants, through the activities of the essential market intermediaries, the shipbroking companies. This openness means that all agents in the market know the prevailing levels of freight rates, and can make their own decisions accordingly.

The markets publish details of all types of charter. It is important to note a major difference between time charter contracts and voyage charters. Rates for the former are expressed in terms of dollars per day, and are effectively the hire rate for a vessel, independent of its place of operation. Spot voyage contracts include port and voyage expenses for the owner's account. In timecharter instances, these are paid for by the charterer in addition to the time charter hire.

The market includes many types of contract from spot fixtures, to be started in a matter of days or weeks, through consecutive voyage and contracts of affreightment, to time charters of varying durations.

Open market fixtures are contracts made in the spot market. The basic elements of the spot market are:

1. The provision of a vessel to load cargo for a specific destination at short notice;

2. To offer a vessel for hire for a single voyage or period usually four to six months or five to seven months. There is usually an upper limit of up to one year. The market for long term and short term fixtures is intimately related for open market fixtures and will have an important influence on other fixtures. UNCTAD defined an open market as follows:

The open market embraces the aggregates at any given time of tramp shipowners seeking employment for their vessels and shippers requiring the services of tramp ships for a limited period.

The keynote of the open freight market is the quick and easy communication of information. The basis is an international network of shipowners, shipbrokers and charterers, closely and continuously linked by telecommunications. Thus, any charterer needing a ship of a certain size and type available at a specific port on or about a specific date can be assured that his needs will be made known to shipowners in all countries which possess merchant fleets.'

Hence for the purposes of this ICS course, the clearest definition may be found in the market characteristics rather than in the particular specification of the vessel.

5.2   MARKET CHARACTERISTICS

The economic characteristics of the dry cargo bulk freight market has led some authors to argue that it is a very competitive one, close to the perfectly competitive model used by economists. There are a number of important features of this model which have to be satisfied in real life if it is to be usefully applied to the analysis of the dry cargo market. The assumptions are listed below:

1. Every supplier in the industry seeks to maximise its profits, which are defined as the difference between their total revenues and total costs. Put differently, profit maximisation requires that shipping companies sell only that output level which maximises the total profit they make;

2. There are numerous buyers and sellers in the market;

3. The service offered by each shipping company is exactly the same as every other company on the market. In the dry cargo market, what is being provided is cargo space, which can be argued to be exactly the same, no matter what ship or what company. After all, grain or iron ore are indifferent to their surroundings, unlike human cargoes;

4. There is easy exit from and entry to the market;

5. There is full information, in the sense that all participants in the market place know the same as everyone else; market rates are known to all, and cost information is also widely available.

Under these circumstances, a perfectly competitive market is said to exist. The dry cargo market fulfils all of the above conditions. Allegedly, charterers and shipowners are both driven by the profit motive.

Assumption two is clearly satisfied. There is a large number of charterers and shipowners in the market, and even the very largest shipowning company owns a tiny percentage of the total dry cargo tonnage business; the largest charterer is responsible for a small percentage of turnover. This means that no single supplier or single user of the market can influence the behaviour of freight rates in the market. Rates cannot be fixed, but are driven by overall demand and supply conditions.

Assumption three is also easily satisfied. The basic service being provided is the safe transportation of cargo in a timely manner. Provided that all ships trade with the relevant classification certificates, their crews are properly trained, and the vessels are well maintained, and loading and discharging procedures are carried out correctly, it makes no difference as to the ship used. The one area of concern might lie in the presence of sub-standard ships. If these have a greater risk of foundering, of cargo damage or loss or of unreliability, then the cargo space in these vessels is not quite the same quality as in those vessels that do meet the requirements listed above. With that proviso, it will be assumed that the analysis is based on ships of an acceptable standard.

Assumption four is also easily satisfied. If a shipowner earns unsatisfactory profits from the ship, and sees no long term prospects for recovery, then they can put the vessel up for sale. This may take a few months, providing there are willing buyers. If it is loss making, the capital value will be low, but at least the owner has exited. Although, if the shipowner would incur a loss when existing the market this could be a barrier to exiting. The new owner may be able to make a profit because of the fact that its capital investment is lower than the previous owners. If many owners cannot make profits, and buyers are few, they can either lay-up or scrap the vessel. Exit occurs if the vessel is scrapped, since less tonnage is now available for supply.

Entrance is the opposite. One can enter the market by buying a second-hand vessel, or by ordering a newbuild. It is the newbuild component that alters the supply of tonnage in the long term.

Entry and exit is easy in this market, because existing shipowners have no way of preventing such a process. This is in contrast to other types of markets, where existing companies may have several different ways of preventing new firms from entering and competing. Note that easy does not mean costless; it is an expensive process to set up a shipping company. What is meant, however, is that economists do not expect the operating costs of a new entrant to be any higher than those of companies already in the business; they would not suffer a cost disadvantage from entering.

Assumption five is best justified by two words; Baltic Exchange. Although little direct trading is now done on the floor of the Baltic, it symbolises the fact that there is a meeting point at which charterers can find ships and shipowners can find charterers and at the same time learn what current market rates are. Nowadays, most transactions take place on computer screens in shipbroking houses; the effect is the same. The brokers act as information transmitters, ensuring that all players are kept fully informed of any event that might affect the market.

An important characteristic of a competitive market is that shipowners have no individual influence over market rates. But since profit is made in the margin between revenues and costs, the only element that they have control over is costs. Competitive markets tend to be driven by cost trends, rather than by demand features. In other words, continuous attention to all aspects of costs, keeping them as small as possible, is a hallmark of a competitive industry.

The assumption of a competitive industry permits the use of a simple model of industry behaviour. Before that, the structure of the dry cargo fleet, and the use of breakeven analysis in tramp operating decisions, will be explored.

5.3 DRY BULK MARKET DEMAND STRUCTURE AND TRENDS OVER THE PAST 25 YEARS

Table 5.1 provides annual data on the growth of dry cargo demand over the past 20 years. Column one reveals that the total volume of cargo, measured in cargo tonnes, has nearly trebled in that period. This works out at an annual average compound growth rate of 3.2% per year. This rate of growth is quite a respectable one; the UK's growth rate has been around 2.5% per year for the same period, although of course, other developed countries have grown faster.

The average growth rate hides two points worthy of note. Firstly, demand growth is much more uneven on a year to year basis. Column two shows the annual growth rate over the previous year's level of demand. This column reveals many interesting features. It is clear that the highest rate of growth to be observed occurred in 2004, at 11.4%, more than three times the long term average. Since 2001 the tonnage growth rate has fluctuated between -0.1 and +11.4%, which is a large variation. Secondly, it should be noted that growth rates seem to go in spurts; the rate peaks, declines, and in some years becomes negative, before recovering again. In other words, demand growth tends to move in cycles; of good years, medium years, poor years, and back again. These cycles exist around a rising trend in the total volume of cargo moved.

Year	Dry Cargo million tonnes	Annual % growth	Dry Cargo Tonne/ miles billion.	Annual % growth	Average haul nautical miles	Ore and Bulk Fleet million grt.	Ore and Bulk Fleet million dwt	Annual % growth	lay ups % of dwt.
1985	2,217	7.1	7,908	1.7	3,767	134	222.7	3.6	22.5
1986	2,122	-4.4	7,657	-3.2	3,608	132.9	215.4	-3.3	14.3
1987	2,178	2.6	8,284	7.9	3,803	131	213.8	-0.7	13.1
1988	2,308	5.8	8,789	5.9	3,808	129.6	220.6	3.2	10.6
1989	2,400	3.9	9,109	3.6	3,795	133.2	225.4	2.2	7.5
1990	2,451	2.1	9,300	2.1	3,794	135.9	228.7	1.5	8.5
1991	2,537	3.4	9,586	3.0	3,778	136.8	235	2.8	8.8
1992	2,573	1.4	9,638	0.5	3,746	140.9	237.3	1.0	10.6
1993	2,625	2.0	9,828	2.0	3,744	143.3	238.6	0.5	9.9
1994	2,735	4.1	10,271	4.4	3,755	149.3	242.6	1.7	8.4
1995	2,875	5.0	10,517	2.4	3,658	0	277	14.2	7.1
1996	2,923	1.7	11,143	5.8	3,812	0	285.1	2.9	6.7
1997	2,781	-5.0	11,945	7.0	4,295	0	290.6	1.9	3.9
1998	2,884	3.6	11,729	-1.8	4,067	0	291	0.1	3.3
1999	3,196	10.3	11,958	1.9	3,742	0	281.8	-3.2	3.2
2000	3,703	-	13,428	-	3,626	0	279.4	-0.9	1.5
2001	3,717	0.4	13,706	2.0	3,687	0	280.2	0.3	1.1
2002	3,819	2.7	14,257	3.9	3,733	0	267.7	-4.5	0.9
2003	3,965	3.8	15,282	6.9	3,854	0	286	6.8	1.2
2004	4,442	11.4	16,400	7.1	3,692	0	298.3	4.3	0.6
2005	4,687	5.4	17,340	5.6	3,700	0	312.9	4.9	0.6
2006	4,684	-0.1	18,536	6.7	3,957				
Average2001-2006	3.9		5.4					2.4	0.9
Average1985-1999	2.9		2.9					1.9	9.2
Average1985-2006	3.2		3.6					1.9	6.9

Table 5.1 Dry Cargo: Seaborne Trade, Fleet and % Surplus 1985 - 2005 (Sources: Trade Data: Fearnleys Reviews, UNCTAD Maritime Reviews, various issues. Fleet and Lay Up data: UNCTAD Maritime Reviews, various issues)

Notes:
1. Break in data in 1999 due to change in sources. Data from UNCTAD differs from Fearnleys
2. Percentage growth of fleet based on GRT up until 1995, dwt thereafter
3. Fleet total in dwt may not match other tables because they are annual averages.

The above analysis examined demand measured in tonnes of cargo moved. This may well give an incomplete picture if the voyage distance alters, since the basic unit of output is the cargo tonne/mile. Column three provides information on the volume of tonne/mile movements over the past 10 years. In this period, tonne/mile demand increased by 3.6% per year compound, whereas cargo tonnes moved grew by 3.2% per year. The growth rate of tonne/mile demand has varied between 2.0 and 7.1 per cent in the period 2001-2006. Differences in the growth of tonnage demand and tonne/mile demand imply that journey distances have fluctuated, as column four reveals. The average haul has not increased by much though; it has moved from 3,567 nautical miles in 1985 to 3,658 nautical miles in 1995 and 3,957 in 2006, with a peak of around 4,300 in 1997.

Column five provides information about the growth of the dry bulk fleet, which has averaged 1.9% per year over the period 1985-2006 in dwt terms. Note that this growth differs from that of tonnage demand; it would not be fair to conclude that supply capacity has not kept pace with demand just on the basis of these figures, as supply capacity should properly be measured in terms of tonne/mile potential. After a short period of decline in the 1980s, the dry bulk fleet has expanded more or less continuously since 1999 and rose very strongly after 2003.

The decline in the lay-up rate coincides with a small increase in the fleet size and a recovery in demand growth.

Case Study: Elasticity of derived demand

The elasticity of derived demand is the measure that expresses the strength of the change in a derived demand when there is a variation in prices. To continue the example of the car industry, it is known that shipping is rather price inelastic as the price of transport, for most goods, is a very small part of the total cost.

Let us assume that the derived demand elasticity is -0.15.

From the example of demand elasticity we know that at a price of £10,000, the demand for cars is 100,000. If we assume that 8,000 cars are transported in one Car carrier, a minimum of 13 carriers are needed.

Now as the price increased to £11,000 the demand fell to 88,000 cars. A simple calculation would reveal that only 11 ships would be needed. However, following the derived demand elasticity calculation, the demand for shipping would only drop by 1.5% (-0.15*10) meaning that still 13 ships would be needed, but that overall they will carry less cargo.

5.4 AN ANALYSIS OF THE COST STRUCTURE OF TRAMP SHIP OPERATORS

Chapter 4 introduced the basic concepts of cost analysis employed by economists. In the short-run, tramp operators will have to identify their costs in terms of those items which are affected by the amount of output that the company produces, and those that are independent of any variation in that output, i.e. splitting their costs between fixed and variable. In the cost model presented in chapter 4 it was argued that in the shipping context, most variable costs related to those items specifically related to producing output, which of course implies those cost items related to undertaking a voyage, and the speed at which that voyage is undertaken.

The other way of viewing short-run costs is to ask a simple question. What costs are avoided, if I do not carry out a particular activity? The distinction between avoidable and unavoidable costs is also useful when making operational decisions.

Chapter 5

5.4.1 The lay-up decision

Here is an example. What costs should be considered relevant in the decision of a tramp ship operator to lay-up their vessel, or to continue to trade?

A common sense answer might be to estimate the total costs incurred if the ship were to continue to trade, undertaking another voyage that takes six weeks, say, and compare that to the freight revenue obtained from the trip. If the trip loses money, in the sense that freight revenues are less than the total costs, then the vessel could be laid-up.

There are in fact two things wrong with this analysis. Firstly, it assumes that lay-up is a costless activity. Lay-up costs money; the vessel has to be maintained, it has to be provided with some power, and it may have to be moved to a safe lay-up position. On the other hand, the vessel will no longer have a full crew. Provisions and maintenance will be less, so that the costs associated with owning the vessel will be reduced.

The second error is that the analysis includes costs that will be incurred by the owner whether the vessel trades or not, but if these costs are common in both situations, they cannot affect the outcome of the decision; they can in effect be cancelled out.

Suppose that the owner estimates that daily operating costs are $10,000 for a vessel in a trading condition, and $4,000 in lay-up. $3,000 of this cost is assumed to be the capital cost of owning the vessel; it is not avoidable, whatever one does with the vessel. It therefore can be cancelled out. The relevant costs become $7,000 per day when trading, and $1,000 per day when laid-up.

Suppose the owner is now offered a charter which takes 42 days, and will incur voyage-related costs of $380,000 in the period. On a total cost basis, the owner will require $800,000 revenues; if the vessel has a 50,000-dwt carrying capacity, this implies a rate of $16 per tonne of cargo delivered. But suppose the market rate is only $14. Should the owner lay-up the vessel?

If the owner lays-up the vessel, it faces extra costs of $42,000, say 42 days at $1,000.

If the owners takes the charter, they gain $700,000 in extra revenues. This comprises freight of $14 x 50,000 tonnes of cargo. But they spend operating costs of $7,000 x 42 + $380,000 = $674,000. The owner therefore gains $26,000, compared to the loss of $42,000 resulting from lay-up. They should take the charter, even though the rate is less than the full cost of the trip.

The same conclusion would of course be reached if the capital costs of $3,000 per day had been included. The total costs of lay-up would be $42,000 + (42 x $3000) = $168,000, whilst the total loss from trading would be $700,000 - $420,000 -$380,000 = -$100,000 . This is of course, a loss-making situation, but it is in fact the best that the owner can do in the circumstances. The $100,000 loss is in fact smaller than the loss made by the owner if the lay-up option were chosen. Note that the difference between the loss ($68,000), is exactly the sum of the cost saving from not laying-up, $42,000, and the net revenue, extra revenue minus extra costs resulting from continuing to trade; $26,000.

The hypothetical example ignored any additional costs incurred with the lay-up itself; including these would of course only serve to emphasise the fact that trading will often take place at market rates which are less than the long-run costs of providing the service.

At what point will it become worthwhile to lay-up? One way of answering this is to develop a model of the breakeven level of freight rates needed to maintain trading. This will be explored in section 5.5 below.

The analysis carried out so far has implicitly assumed that the basic unit of analysis is the vessel itself; that the shipping company is a one-ship operation. While this assumption may be reasonable for many small dry cargo companies, it is not true for a large number of dry cargo firms who operate several vessels, maybe dozens. As the number of ships operated by a company increases, the role of ship management, of planning and communications, all become more significant. It might be expected that these costs are generally unrelated to the level of output produced by the company's vessels. But they may be related to the number of vessels operated and controlled and will increase as a share of total costs, as the company size expands. On the other hand, the discussion in chapter 4 also indicated that larger firms may experience lower unit costs for a number of reasons; there are two forces at play here which can work in opposite directions.

It is widely argued that tramp operators tend to have a higher proportion of their costs as variable costs when compared to other market segments. S. A. Lawrence pointed out that:

'tramp companies operate with smaller overheads than liners and have no commitment to maintaining a regular service, enjoying greater flexibility in the use of their ships.'

As a final point in this section, it is worth emphasising that the distinction between short-run fixed and variable costs is not clear cut. It depends on the nature of the problem being considered, and on the type of vessel under analysis, as well as the time period involved. In our discussion of the lay-up problem, some items of daily operating costs could be avoided, so were treated as variable. But if the owner was considering between two trading options, the entire daily running cost would become fixed, because all those elements could not be avoided. Time is also an important factor; the shorter the time period under consideration, the greater the proportion of costs that will be fixed. Once a vessel is at its loading berth or a voyage is commenced practically all costs become unavoidable.

5.5 THE USE OF BREAK-EVEN ANALYSIS IN DETERMINING MINIMUM FREIGHT RATES

A well-known method in both economics and management is to present information on revenue and costs in the form of a break-even analysis. The normal procedure is to calculate the load factor or level of utilisation required to break-even. If actual load factors or utilisation levels exceed the calculated number, it is clear that profits are being made. If, on the other hand, the target load factor figure does not materialise, losses will be made.

Defining the load factor may well be significant in the liner trades, where vessels operate to a timetable, whether or not they are fully loaded. This is not normally the case for dry cargo shipping, where full cargo loads are usually the rule, rather than the exception.

Instead of applying the model to working out the break-even load factor, it can instead be employed to work out the break-even rate. That is the freight rate which will ensure that a full cargo load will generate sufficient revenue to cover costs. This is a very plausible use to put this model to, because freight rates in dry cargo trades are quite volatile; it is therefore useful to work out the minimum rate required to break-even.

The model is based on the following assumptions:

1. The vessel is taken as the basic unit of analysis;

2. Costs and revenues are assumed to be linear, i.e. total variable costs rise in constant proportion to output, and total revenues also rise in constant proportion to output. This implies that the average revenue, or unit price, of freight rate per tonne of cargo, is constant over the volume of output being examined, and the average variable cost is also constant as output changes;

3. The market contains many shipowners and many charterers who cannot influence the market rate on their own;

4. This means that the actual freight rate is taken as fixed, since no individual has any ability to alter it. Each individual is said to be a price taker.

Figure 5.1 below shows the standard break-even model, drawn for the current market rate. The slope of the line OF represents the market price; since total revenues rise in line with volume carried, the price is constant all the way along OF.

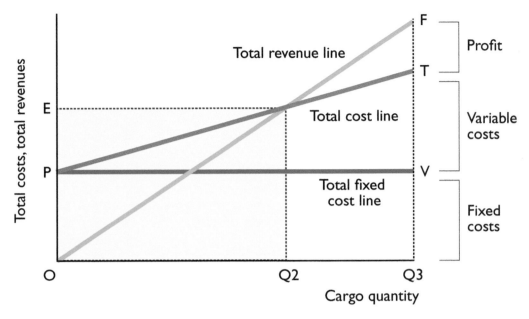

Fig 5.1 Break-even Model

At cargo quantity Q3, which represents a full cargo load, total revenue is given by the vertical distance Q3F. On the other hand, if no cargo is carried at all, total revenue is zero. Total fixed costs are P, which is the same value as Q3V. Total fixed costs are the same, no matter what cargo quantity is loaded. Total variable costs are the difference between total costs and total fixed costs; at zero cargo quantity, they are zero, so total costs equal P. When the maximum cargo quantity is loaded, total costs rise to Q3T, and the distance VT represents total variable costs at that level of output.

It is clear from Figure 5.1 that total revenue equals total cost at cargo quantity level Q2, with associated total cost = total revenue = E. This cargo quantity is called the break-even quantity, because it is at this point that total revenues cover both variable and fixed costs. The figure is often expressed as a percentage of the maximum quantity that can be carried or produced, a number which is found by measuring the ratio of Q2/Q3, then multiplying by 100.

5.5.1 Finding the break-even rate

The above analysis was outlined in Chapter 4. In a tramp shipping context it is perhaps more useful to use this model in a slightly different way. Instead of discovering what cargo quantity is required in order to break-even, the calculation might be used to discover what freight rate is needed to break-even.

The assumption that is needed for this analysis is that the vessel will always trade at or very near its full cargo carrying capacity for the voyage being considered. Figure 5.2 shows the new situation.

Two additional total revenue lines have been added to Figure 5.2. Each represents the behaviour of total revenue at different freight rates. The slope of TR2 represents a lower level of freight rate than TR1, and TR3's slope corresponds to a lower rate than TR2. In other words, the flatter the slope of the total revenue line, the lower the freight rate per tonne of cargo.

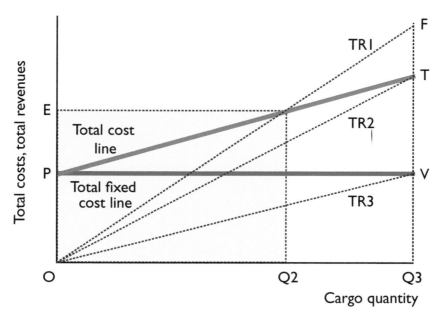

Fig 5.2 The Break-even Freight Rate Model

Given the assumption that the vessel is always fully laden, it is clear that the break-even rate must be given by the line TR2. If Q3 tonnes of cargo are carried, a total revenue of Q3T is obtained, and total costs of OQ3T are incurred.

It follows that, if the freight rate is above that implied by the line TR2, then the tramp operator will make a profit. On the other hand a rate of TR3 will incur a loss.

Again, the quest might be to discover the lowest rate which the owner should accept. Or put another way, will the owner ever accept a rate lower than TR2?

The answer to the latter question is yes. The minimum short-run rate that is acceptable depends on whether the losses incurred in accepting the business are smaller than the losses incurred from being idle. As long as total variable costs are covered, it is worthwhile accepting the business; if the loss so incurred is smaller than the loss arising from the vessel doing nothing.

In fact TR3, which represents that rate, must also reflect the slope of the total variable cost curve. Under the special assumptions of this model, it is the same as the marginal cost of moving one more tonne of cargo. Put another way, the price must never be below the marginal cost of producing the output, and must never be less than the average variable cost of production. This is in fact a general rule that always applies, no matter what the relationship is between costs and output.

It is worth recalling the discussion of lay-up. It is clear that the lower the proportion of variable costs to fixed costs in a shipowner's company, the greater the scope for the freight rate to fall below the long-run total cost of producing that output, or of maintaining the ship. This is an important point to note, because it is one of the factors that helps to explain the sharp fluctuations that are observed in freight rates in the dry cargo trades, especially when contrasted with those set in the liner trades. Owners, in depressed markets, may well accept short-run trip charters at rates well below those required to cover their long-run costs, if the proportion of variable costs are low.

5.6   MODELLING THE DRY CARGO MARKET

A very simple cost model of a tramp shipowner has been discussed, in which freight rates were taken as given. In what follows, it is assumed that the market can be separated into specific segments, one of which is being modelled. The bulk dry trade is taken as an example, leaving the segment of smaller vessels and the markets that they serve to one side for the moment.

The analytical framework developed here can still be applied to these other segments as well, provided that they satisfy the following assumptions:

1. Each shipowner and ship management company is seeking to maximise their profits, or to minimise their losses;

2. Each charterer is seeking the cheapest rate consistent with an acceptable quality of service offered by the shipowner;

3. There is a large number of fixtures, the details of most of which are readily available to all market participants;

4. The model of perfect competition is assumed to be an appropriate framework for analysing market behaviour (the assumptions underlying this model have been discussed in section 5.2).

5.6.1 Modelling demand

Readers may like to review their knowledge of demand from their studies in chapter 2. The individual shipper's firm requiring transport and shipping services regards the freight rate as a given value which they cannot alter through their own individual action. It is assumed that there is a downward sloping relationship between the cargo volumes required to be moved and the level of freight rates, other things being equal. The higher the rate, the smaller the demand for cargo movements and vice versa.

Will market demand be responsive, or unresponsive, to a change in the freight rate? Both are possible and consistent with a downward sloping relationship between rates and cargo quantities. The discussion in chapter 2 helps us to answer this question.

The demand for dry cargo tonne/miles is a derived demand. Chapter 2 reviewed the basic principles underlying the estimation of price elasticities for derived demands.

The principal factors were:

1. The value of the own price elasticity of demand for the final goods;

2. The existence of close substitutes;

3. The proportion of the total final price which transport constitutes.

Take grain as an example. Grain movements are driven by production and consumption trends in different regions, by local weather conditions and crop yields and by changing patterns of food consumption. Grain is itself an input; it is used to make bread or pasta, or is fed to animals to produce meat. But bread, meat and pasta all have low price elasticities of demand. Most empirical evidence suggests that they are price inelastic.

Grain movements from major exporting regions such as South America or Australia have to go by sea. Air transport, while perhaps feasible for very small volumes, is a very expensive alternative.

Freight rates are now about 6% of the final price of most traded commodities in Western Europe; these details have been covered in chapter 2.

The conclusion is that, taken as a whole, market demand is likely to be extremely inelastic with respect to changes in freight rates. The demand curve can be represented as an almost vertical line, as in Figure 5.3 below.

Note that this conclusion is for the market as a whole. It does not follow that demand conditions on any one trade route are also necessarily inelastic. It could be the case that the possible sourcing of demand from other countries and other routes makes the demand on each route much more sensitive to changes in the specific route's freight rate. Indeed, owners will always be seeking out trades which are more profitable than others. But the ability to switch vessels from one route to another at relatively short notice implies that rates should not get too out of line with each other, although there are specific additional costs attached to certain trades.

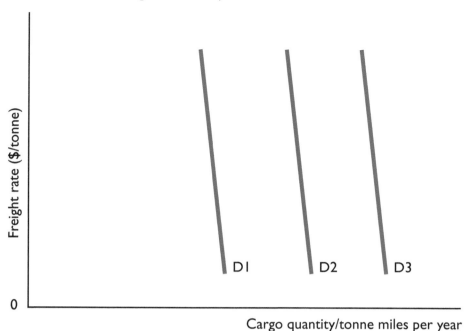

Fig 5.3 Inelastic Freight Demand Schedules

Freight rates are measured on the vertical axis and quantity of the commodity or cargo tonne/ miles are measured on the horizontal axis. D1, D2, and D3 show three different demand schedules, each further out to the right. These represent different volumes of demand, generated by higher and higher levels of economic activity, industrial production or world trade volumes. A fall from D2 to D1 would represent a decline in tonne/miles demanded, or cargo tonnes moved. A rise, or shift, of the demand schedule from D2 to D3 would represent long term expansion.

Recall that there are cycles of demand growth. In some periods the demand schedule will be shifting rapidly out to the right, reflecting boom conditions. In other years, it will be hardly shifting at all, and perhaps even declining. Over a long time period, it is generally anticipated that the trend will be a slow shift out to the right.

Case Study: Derived demand for shipping

The demand for shipping is a derived demand as the product being consumed is not the transport itself (except in passenger transport), but the goods that are being transported.

The shipping demand of the car industry is a very good example. Cars are produced all over the world in a wide variety of makes and models. Not every country produces each make or model and so cars need to be transported to satisfy customer demands. Therefore, when demand for cars increases, demand for transport increases. For example if more American families decide to order cars produced in Japan, Japanese cars will need to be transported from Japan to the United States. To transport these cars more ships will have to be chartered. Therefore, the transport by ship is a derived demand from the purchase of the car.

5.6.2 Supply

Given the discussion of short-run costs in chapter 4, and the discussion of short-run supply in chapter 2, it is time to try to integrate these two. Under competitive conditions, it was pointed out that the shipowner should never accept a freight rate that is less than the average variable cost of the ship's output. It has also been pointed out that different ships have different costs, because either they are of different ages, or they operate under different flags, or they face different wage costs.

Imagine that all these costs were known, and that a ranking could be organised, starting with the dry cargo bulk vessel with the lowest average variable cost, moving up to the next, and so on until the last, most expensive vessel is brought in. If freight rates were high enough and cargo volumes large enough, all these vessels would be employed. Now if one imagines that the rate is steadily reduced, one can see which vessels will cease trading first; those with the highest variable, or avoidable costs.

As the rate is remorselessly lowered, more vessels are forced into idleness, until none is trading. Furthermore, it was earlier demonstrated that capital costs should play no role in the lay-up decision in the short-run, since these costs have to be met whether or not the vessel is being traded. Older vessels will tend to have higher operating costs than newer vessels, partly because they will be designed with older, less efficient equipment in place, partly because they will require greater crew numbers than modern ships, and partly because they may have older, more fuel inefficient, engines. It is not surprising then, to observe that the majority of laid up vessels are the older ones of the fleets.

The discussion to date has ignored the fact that, in the short-run, vessels' variable costs can themselves be altered by varying the operating speed of the ship. Lower speed means lower output and lower costs. If freight rates are low because demand is low, the loss of output is more than offset by the benefits of slower steaming. Thus it is possible to expect the supply of tonne/miles, the supply curve mentioned in chapter 3 to be directly related to the cost considerations covered in chapter 4.

The shape of the supply schedule is repeated below from chapter 3, section 3.8. It is drawn so that it becomes steeper in slope as maximum tonne/mile production is attained. There are two reasons for this. Firstly, the additional tonne/miles being created near full capacity are being created by the more inefficient vessels in the fleet, the ones with higher variable costs. These vessels add a lot to costs without adding that much extra to output. Secondly, speed increases are a limited way of raising output. The extra costs of fuel consumption increase more rapidly than the extra output, so the required supply price increases.

The curve eventually becomes vertical, representing the notion of full capacity utilisation. No more output can be obtained from the existing fleet, in the short term.

In the language of economics, the supply curve represents additional or marginal costs of meeting the extra output required. This proposition is only valid if the market is itself competitive.

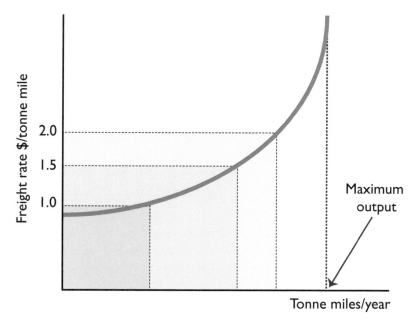

Fig 5.4 Short-run Shipping Supply Curve

5.7 DETERMINING THE EQUILIBRIUM FREIGHT RATE

The market is defined as the interaction of supply and demand, which both together determine the equilibrium freight rate and quantities sold at that rate. Figure 5.5 below shows several different possible short-run market equilibria, each determined by different demand conditions. The key factors that make demand conditions alter relate to the volume of world trade, which is driven by overall economic activity, and changing degrees of openness towards trade by individual nations. Demand curves further to the right represent larger trade volumes.

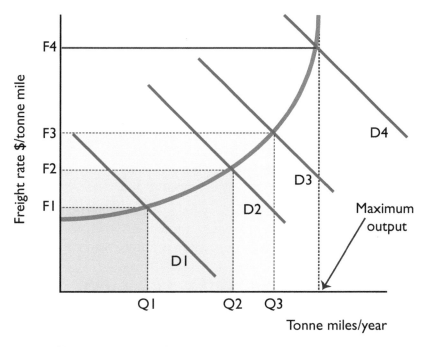

Fig 5.5 Short-run Market Interaction

Demand volumes increase from D1 to D4. Between D1 to D3 there is a relatively small rise in the market freight rate and a large rise in tonne/miles produced. But between D3 and D4, the increase in demand is translated into large increases in rates, because supply becomes very inelastic and the scope for increases in supply becomes increasingly limited.

The above model can be used to examine short-run fluctuations in market conditions, but not long-run ones. This is because the supply schedule represented in Figure 5.5 is drawn for a given stock of ships. However, it is a useful framework to explore fluctuations in freight rates in the short term.

Consider the shift in demand from D3 to D4. Rates move up very sharply, and supply does not increase much. This creates large profits for existing shipowners, who will be encouraged to order new vessels. The value of existing vessels will also rise, reflecting the market's expectation that profits are going to be healthy in the future. The increased number of orders will translate into a rightward shift in the supply curve in the long term and this will lead to a fall in rates if demand remains at D4.

On the other hand, a fall in demand from D2 to D1 will bring about a reduction in supply and a rise in vessel lay-ups. Remember that in the short-run, some vessels will be trading at rates which do not cover their full costs. While this is acceptable in the short term, it is not the case in the longer term. Some vessels will be laid up or scrapped. The scrapping of vessels leads to a leftwards shift of the supply curve. This process will help raise rates if the supply shifts far enough.

Extending the model

More detail can be incorporated into the basic model by considering, first, how the increase or decrease in short-run supply can be implemented. A rise or fall in demand generates the rise or fall in rates. The higher or lower rates create incentives to increase or to decrease tonne/miles supplied through the following mechanisms:

a) Higher or lower rates encourage a higher or slower speed;

b) Higher or lower rates will encourage owners with high variable cost vessels to bring them out of or drive them into lay-up;

In the long term, fluctuations in freight rates and lay-up numbers will encourage owners to embrace or reject newbuilds or progress or delay scrapping. These processes will shift the supply curve out to the right in the case of an increase in demand, or to the left in the opposite case.

A key factor influencing this decision is the expectation of shipowners. Expectations of future levels of freight demand and freight rates will be critical in determining how the market reacts to short term changes in demand and rate levels.

If owners are fundamentally optimistic about the future, falling rates in the short term may not lead to a longer term reduction in shipping capacity. If that expectation is false, however, it will be revised, and those changes will take place.

On the other hand, pessimistic expectations about the future will reinforce any short term downturns, and may lead to a shortage of capacity if demand grows at an unexpected pace.

Expectations can be very volatile, and their volatility helps explain the sudden increases and equally sudden falls that have been observed in rate movements, particularly when political events, wars or other events can have strategic impacts on dry cargo markets.

5.8   CONFRONTING THE MODEL WITH THE EVIDENCE

The above model implies:

1. That freight rates should be sensitive to short-run market conditions, reflecting both present and expected future situations;

2. There will be a strong positive correlation between demand growth and new orders, provided that the present stock of vessels is highly utilised with low levels of lay-up;

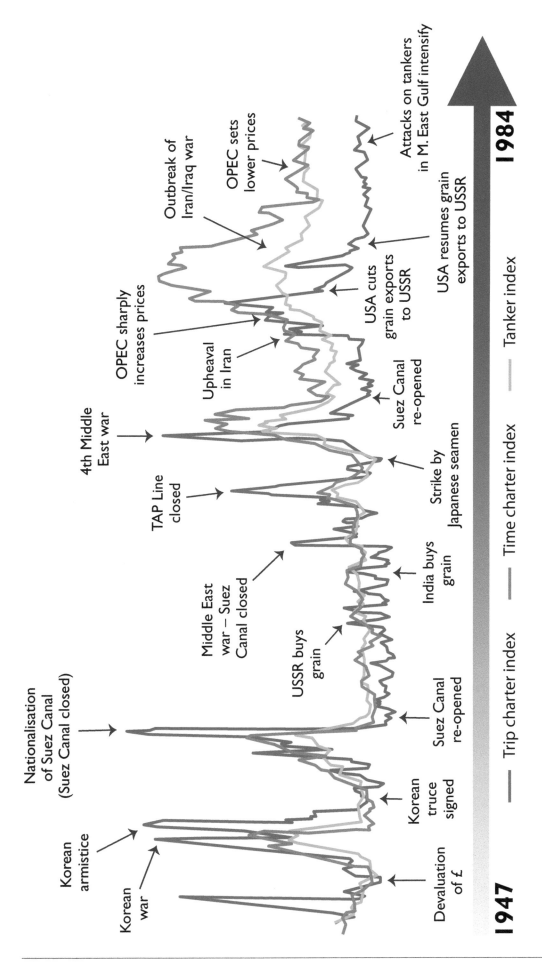

Fig 5.6 Development of Shipping Freight Rates, 1947- 1984

— Trip charter index   — Time charter index   — Tanker index

3. There will be a strong positive correlation between freight rates and new orders, with periods of high rates associated with higher than average orders, lower than average lay-ups and scrapping;.

4. Exceptional events will generate significant increases in rates, if they occur when existing shipping capacity is being fully stretched. These are usually anticipations or outbreaks of war, or strategically important changes, such as the closure of the Suez Canal or an international embargo on certain resource-rich countries.

Figure 5.6 shows the movements in tramp voyage rates for 28 trade routes and includes tankers engaged in the grain trade, for the period 1947-84. It also shows the movements of the tramp charter index, and a tanker index. An important point to note is that these indices are based on a notional value of 100 for 1965-66. It therefore takes no account of rates of inflation. If price level changes were allowed for, the later booms would look larger, and the earlier booms look smaller.

Note that there are substantial periods of demand growth in which freight rates do not fluctuate all that dramatically. In these periods, either there is plenty of capacity available to meet any increase in demand, or the expansion of demand is matched by the correct expansion of capacity, brought about by accurate expectations generating the correct level of ordering. The spikes are generated by events which are not completely anticipated by the market, and as noted earlier tend to be wars or war-related events which impact on the shipping markets.

A clear example of such a boom is that of the early 1970s. Growth in demand for shipping services was very high in the late 1960s and early 1970s, with one peak observable in 1970. World commodity prices rose sharply in the period up to 1973, and shipowners fell over themselves to order new vessels. Many of these were of the new large designs, as this was the period of rapid increases in the sizes of dry-bulkers and tankers. In September 1973 this all came to a halt with the six day Arab-Israeli war ending with the closure of the Suez Canal and the Arab oil embargo on countries seen as pro-Israel. The 400% rise in the price of crude oil delivered a huge shock to the Western economies that had been previously growing quite rapidly. Their economic growth faltered; the UK's real income fell in 1974. Lower economic growth means lower growth in the demand for shipping movements.

It is worth examining Table A5.1 (see Appendix to this chapter) in the context of the above comments, and relating the data to the information contained in Figure 5.6. The rate peaks of 1970 and 1973 correspond to two of the years of highest annual growth of tonne/mile demand, of 10.3% in 1970 and 15.2% in 1973. Note that demand actually fell by 2.3% in 1975. In 1985, demand grew at 7.1%, and as you can see from the data, this figure is well above those observed until 1999. Note that there is no peak in the rates in 1984. The difference in the two situations is simple. In 1970 and 1973, there was very little laid-up tonnage. In 1985, as can be seen from Table 5.1, over 20% of the fleet was laid-up. The increase in demand was easily met from existing capacity, and no peak in rates is observed.

These observations are consistent with the demand/supply model discussed above; in the first two peaks demand is at or near full capacity, so further increases help generate large rate increases as supply response is very small. But in 1984 and 1985, there was plenty of spare capacity and significant increases in demand was met with no corresponding rise in freight rates.

5.8.1 Historical developments

Figure 5.7 shows the behaviour of certain dry cargo rates over the period 1989-1996

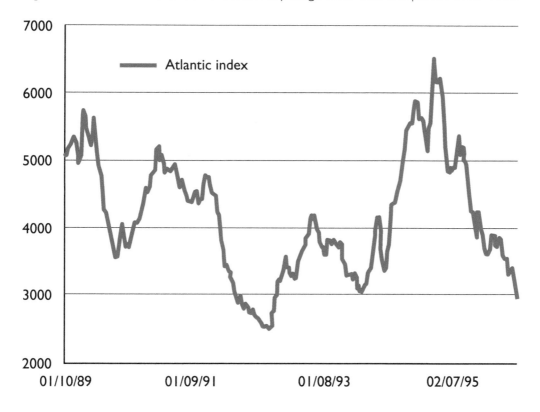

Fig 5.7 SSY Atlantic capesize Index, 1989-1996 (source: SSY Research Department)

Note: Base Index value = 5000

The SSY Atlantic index tracks the movements of freight rates on nine major routes on which Capesize tramp vessels operate and reflects their behaviour in index number form. The marked volatility of the index reveals just how sensitive rates are to current demand and supply conditions. The mid 1990s boom in the dry cargo sector is clearly reflected in the peak values of the index in the 1994 to 1995 period. Rates are clearly very responsive to changes in market conditions.

A more recent example of the same dynamic behaviour can be seen in Figure 5.8, which plots the movement of an index of dry cargo trip charters on a monthly basis from 2000. Note the index is based on 1985 =100, so the values have been kept in 'real' or 'constant' terms. A measure of the volatility of the index within the year has been provided, which confirms that the average rate has risen sharply since 2003, and with it, the volatility of the rate. In fact the volatility statistic shows just how dramatic the change in the market has been since January 2003. The intra-year volatility jumps from around 3% to figures which range between 14 and 33%

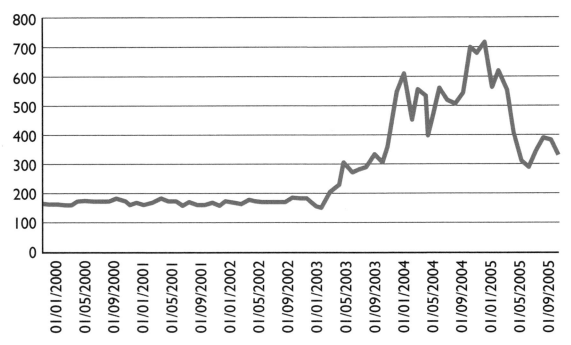

Fig 5.8 Dry Cargo Trip Charter Index, 2000 –2005 (Source: Derived from ISL data)

Intra-year Volatility %	
2000	3.7
2001	2.6
2002	3.2
2003	27.4
2004	14.4
2005	32.5

Table 5.2 Trip Charter Volatility, 2000 - 2005

Note: Measured as ratio of standard deviation of rate within year to year average rate

What has caused the dry cargo market to experience such a dramatic and sustained increase in freight rates and in their volatility?

There is a number of reasons, but they boil down to analysing demand and supply effects on the market. As Figure 5.8 and Table 5.1 show, tonne/mile demand has risen at a remarkable rate since 2003, with rates over 6% per year. If the fleet capacity does not grow as fast, ships have to work harder and rates will rise. The increase in rates will not solve the problem, but sends a signal to owners and investors that this segment of the shipping market is now worth investing in. Just how worthwhile investment is can judged by the report, which provides estimates of the daily operating costs of various dry cargo ship sizes and the time charter earnings they were negotiating in 2006. The daily operating expenses for a Capesize were put at $6,500 per day, $5,000 for a Panamax and $4,000 for a Handysize. Time charter equivalent earnings, that is, the spot rate converted into a time charter value, on a hire rate basis, were estimated at $50,000 per day for a Capesize, $30,000 for a Panamax and $24,000 for a Handysize in October 2006.

The time charter equivalent earnings are similar to those reported in Table 5.3.

year	Capesize 172,000-dwt	Panamax 74,000-dwt	Suezmax 52,000-dwt	Handymax 46,000-dwt
2002	11,918	7,725	9,309	7,978
2003	40,329	20,063	18,073	14,810
2004	69,002	35,725	33,508	28,191
2005	50,344	24,802	26,241	21,421
2006	45,139	23,778	22,420	20,940
2007	86,665	40,543	35,538	31,266

Table 5.3 Average Spot Time Charter Rates (Source: Galbraith's Weekly Report, June 2007)

As the charterer pays the voyage expenses in most trip charters, the gross profit margins in this sector are very large, especially for the years 2003-2007.

Such large earnings during this period caused the scrapping of dry cargo vessels to more or less disappear and generated a record number of newbuilding orders. Future rates are therefore being affected by the delivery of new tonnage and prospective future demand growth. It also affected the price of second hand tonnage, because the sellers would be giving up the rights to very large profit flows if rates continued at those levels. This means second hand prices become very high. Indeed, in certain cases a second-hand ship became more expensive than its newbuild equivalent, because the newbuild will not have been available for three years but the second hand one would have been earning profits in a few months. When rates are exceptionally high, it can be shown that this may make the second-hand price exceed the newbuild price. It is sometimes called the ready ship premium.

A number of factors have contributed to the demand growth and increased profits:

1. The rapid growth in world trade has stimulated increased manufacturing. Manufacturing requires industrial inputs. The demand for raw materials has risen as trade has been liberalised.

2. The China effect: China has become a major player in international trade. Its economy has grown at 10% per year compound for many years. With accession to the WTO in 2001 and demand for steel soaring, China is now the world's largest steel producer. This obviously increases demand for steel movements.

3. Steel requires iron ore and coking coal in its production. The demand for both commodities has risen dramatically. A major driver of this increase has been China, a country where reserves of high-grade domestic commodities are falling thus encouraging a rise in imports.

4. Other economies have grown rapidly as well, particularly India. India is another major steel manufacturer and the associated need for iron ore and coal derive from the same sector.

5. Shortages of suitable ships. Anecdotal evidence in 2007 shows that cargoes were being split into smaller lot sizes, because the largest size vessels were not available in sufficient quantities. This implied that demand cascaded down the chain as cargo demand was shifted. It also implied transportation costs would rise, as a given cargo quantity was carried in two ships rather than in one. So the dry cargo market, particularly the bulk sector, was transformed in the period 2002-2007.

5.9   DYNAMIC CONSIDERATIONS

The model employed so far has concentrated primarily upon current demand and current supply conditions. The only additional factor which has been discussed is the role of expectation. This helps determine owners' ordering, scrapping and operational decisions, because ships are long-lived assets and owners need to form a view about future market conditions as well as considering present ones.

To determine what shapes the expectations of shipowners for the future, one needs to look at past events. Historical data and recent trends can be projected forward to help shape their estimates as to future demand conditions.

The huge wave of ship ordering in the early 1970s can be seen as a response to the widely-held view that the market was going to continue to grow as rapidly in the second half of the 1970s as it did in the first three years. If one anticipates a prosperous period, one needs to order new vessels early, as they may take 18 months to two years to build. If these expectations are fulfilled, there will be no difficulties encountered; especially if demand grows as everyone expected it to, and the capacity is there to meet it.

But suppose the expectations turn out to be incorrect and the unexpected happens. New vessels have been ordered, and a large number of them have been delivered. Market conditions in the late 1970s became a nightmare for owners but profitable for charterers. The market was in turmoil, with large numbers of vessels and little growth in demand.

Trying to understand demand and supply conditions in the next decade would therefore make very little sense if one just examined demand and supply in the current year. The supply available is itself the consequence of past decisions by owners. It is this fact that leads to the conclusion that the market will generate its own dynamic behaviour over time, as it continually re-adjusts to new demand conditions as best it can.

The poor trading conditions of the late 1970s and early 1980s influenced newbuilds. Orders became relatively scarce. But if demand conditions alter for the better, this lack of new investment may itself generate another cycle in the market.

The fact is, dry cargo markets appear to move through cycles of boom, recession, slump, recovery, and back to boom again. These cycles are partly generated by the cyclical growth in demand, but are also a result of the fact that supply adjustment is a slow and often painful process in markets where assets are long lived, as they are in shipping. It may be more sensible to modify our demand and supply model to allow for the presence of such cycles of economic activity.

Some observers have suggested that there are cycles of different periods observable in the market, overlaying each other. For example, one might observe a seasonal pattern of demand as being the shortest cycle. On top of that, world demand growth appears to cycle over 5-7 years. Ship supply cycles are longer, on average 13 years. Finally, some observers such as Kondratieff have suggested very long cyclical patterns of around 50 years.

Whether or not one accepts the presence of all of these, it is undeniable that viewing the market as a dynamic one, as a process in which demand conditions and supply responses change over time, gives a much richer picture of the way the market operates. Unfortunately, it is also a more complex idea to grasp. But realising that ship supply responds to a change in demand, often spread out over several periods (even years)is a step in the right direction.

Figure 5.9 is a practical illustration of the potential link between freight rates and demand and supply conditions. Whilst the demand growth of 2000 is similar to that of 2003, the behaviour of prices is not. There is clearly a link, but the link is complex. One obvious factor is the issue of lay-ups or low utilisation of vessels, which would help to explain the difference in response in the two years. Another possibility is that the structure of demand changes, in terms of voyage distances and the trades affected may be different.

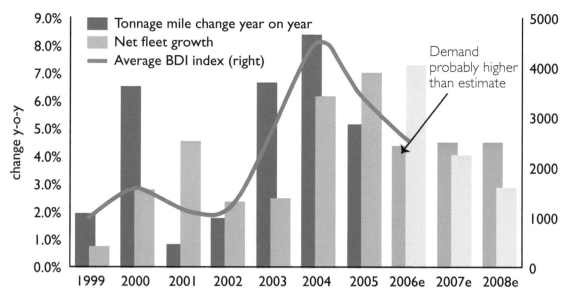

Fig 5.9 Supply and Demand Growth and Freight Rate Indices (Source: Fearnleys Research)

Note: BDI is the Baltic Dry Index

5.10 CONCLUSION

This chapter has examined the dry cargo market for tramp shipping in some detail. After examining the changing definitions of a tramp and the changing nature of the market, various aspects of the costs of operating as a tramp were explored. It was argued that the dry cargo market could be viewed as a highly competitive market structure, close to perfect competition. A model of the market was developed based on this assumption. Demand was always price inelastic, but supply elasticity depended upon the present level of fleet utilisation. The behaviour of market rates was examined and the data related to that provided in Table 5.1. Finally, the dynamic nature of the market was emphasised.

APPENDIX

The following table, published in earlier versions of this volume, is provided for a historical perspective on the development of the dry cargo fleet.

Year	Dry Cargo millions of tonnes	Annual % growth	Dry Cargo billions of Tonne / miles	Annual % growth	Average haul in nautical miles	Ore and Bulk Fleet in millions of gt	Annual % growth
1968	1,066		3,425		3,103	34.9	20.0
1969	1,157	8.2	3,761	9.4	3,213	41.8	18.0
1970	1,241	7.0	4,167	10.3	3,251	46.7	11.1
1971	1,260	1.5	4,275	2.6	3,358	53.8	14.2
1972	1,317	4.4	4,454	4.1	3,393	63.5	16.6
1973	1,544	15.9	5,187	15.2	3,382	72.6	13.4
1974	1,631	5.5	5,766	10.6	3,359	79.4	9.0
1975	1,630	-0.1	5,636	-2.3	3,535	85.4	7.3
1976	1,587	-2.7	5,874	4.1	3,458	91.7	7.1
1977	1,675	5.4	6,050	3.0	3,701	100.9	9.6
1978	1,764	5.2	6,388	5.4	3,612	106.5	5.4
1979	1,991	12.1	7,016	9.4	3,621	108.3	1.7
1980	2,010	0.9	7,372	4.9	3,524	109.6	1.2
1981	2,024	0.7	7,469	1.3	3,668	113.1	3.1
1982	1,921	-5.2	7,217	-3.4	3,690	119.3	5.3
1983	1,878	-2.3	7,022	-2.7	3,757	124.4	4.2
1984	2,065	9.5	7,778	10.2	3,739	128.3	3.1

Table A.5.1 Dry Cargo Seaborne Trade, Fleet and Growth, 1968 – 1984 (Source: OECD Maritime Review 1994, UNCTAD Review of Maritime Transport 1995)

Chapter 6
. . . .
COMPETITIVE SHIPPING MARKETS: TANKERS

The world's smallest banknote, issued in Morocco, was the size of a postage stamp.

A tanker may be defined as a vessel that is specifically designed to carry liquid cargoes. The most common types of cargo carried in such vessels are chemicals, wine, vegetable and other food oils, refined oil products and crude oil. This chapter will concentrate on the market for crude oil and refined oil tankers, as these are by far the largest. The markets for crude oil and refined products are often referred to as the tanker trades. Between 2002 and 2007, the tanker markets and freight rates have been at their strongest and fastest growing since the early 1970s. It is this growth that has raised the tanker industry to greater prominence within the oil sector, and also within the wider financial community as an area for potential equity investment. But a glut of newbuilding deliveries has since created downward pressure on freight rates.

Tanker trades are a subject that can be written about at great length; they are a fascinating subject in their own right. The principal reasons for studying them are:

1. The oil trades have grown enormously over the past 40 years; but they have also grown very unevenly. The success of the tanker industry over recent years cannot be understood without some knowledge of earlier periods.

2. The overall size of the tanker fleet has grown dramatically, especially in the 1970s and in the last few years.

3. Specialisation in tankers has also developed in the last twenty years, with more dedicated, specialised vessels appearing in the products trades.

4. Politics have played a special role in this sector, because of the strategic nature of the cargo and because of the huge macro-economic effects that the dramatic oil price changes have upon the world economy.

   Because of its extreme political sensitivity, tanker freight rates have exhibited sudden marked increases from time to time, usually associated with wars. While it is true that most commodity prices are sensitive to acts of aggression, oil prices and tanker freight rates appear to be especially affected. The most recent boom period is probably the first that has been triggered without a conflict.

5. As in other industrial sectors, quality has become a major feature of the tanker industry following major oil spills since the 1989 Exxon Valdez incident. More legislation has resulted in the phase out of single-hull tankers in 2010, which has implications for the tanker market and freight rates.

In this chapter, the reasons for the volatility of tanker rates will be explored. The essential explanation lies in the recognition of the fact that the tanker market, despite some appearances to the contrary, is a very competitive one; indeed, some sectors of it are more competitive now than they were 40 years ago. The competitive nature of the market, when coupled with its sensitivity to fundamental, strategic, and political issues, has made it an extremely volatile market in the past.

6.1 SEABORNE TRADE IN CRUDE OIL AND OIL PRODUCTS

6.1.1 The distinction between crude oil and oil products

The oil market is traditionally split between the analysis of unrefined or crude oil and the markets for refined oil or oil products. Each barrel of crude oil, when refined, yields different quantities of various products, ranging from naphtha to diesel, heating oil and kerosene for the lighter fractions, to fuel oil, bitumen and road surfacing material for the heavier fractions. Further processes at the refinery can then produce gasoline or petrol and take some of the heavier products and upgrade them to more valuable lighter fractions. Some of the lighter fractions are more volatile than the original crude oil, while the heavier ones such as bitumen have to be kept warm to prevent them from becoming almost solid.

The oil trades therefore consist of moving either the crude oil from its country of production to the international refining industry and the movement of refined products from the refineries to the final consumer. It should be clear that the location of the refinery is crucial in determining the relative balance of these two trades. In the 1950s, many refineries were built near final consumer markets, in both North America and Western Europe. This was for a combination of political and economic reasons. The political reason was to keep refinery capacity in countries that were economically stable. The economic reason was that transporting products involves smaller vessels, typically around 30-40,000 tonnes of cargo, whereas crude could be moved in larger vessels, carrying up to 300-320,000 tonnes. Moving the bulk of the cargo in crude form minimised the overall transportation cost to the consumer. Thus the crude trades evolved more rapidly, dominating cargo movements by volume. This pattern has changed slightly with the construction of refineries in the Middle East and the growth of Asian consumption, but it is still an accurate description of the main forces currently shaping the movement of crude and oil products. But the most recent wave of refinery investment took place in 2006-7. This resulted in the Middle East and India becoming even bigger product exporting regions.

The development of seaborne oil trades

Before the First World War, tankers constituted some 3% of the world fleet. By 1938 they had increased to 19% and by the late 1970s, just under 50% of the world tonnage. See Table 6.1 for the data. In deadweight tonnage terms, the world tanker fleet grew from 17m dwt in 1938 to 332m dwt in 1977, a spectacular increase. World oil production, which of course is a key driving force in the growth of the oil trades, rose from 258m tonnes in 1938 to over 15 times that in 2006 and is still growing.

The increase in world oil production has not, however, been even. It increased fourfold between 1938 and 1957, three-and-a-halffold between 1957 and 1977. Growth then slowed abruptly. Between 1977 and 1988 production hardly increased at all - from 2,915m tonnes to 3,050m tonnes. After 1988 production increased gradually, reaching a high of 3,281m tonnes in 1995. Since 1995, oil production has continued to rise and reached 3,914m tonnes in 2006, driven by China's continued rapid expansion, by increases in demand in the USA, the Middle East, and other Asian countries including India.

Oil consumption growth is the key to the trends in production, since the two will be very close over the longer term, with differences being accounted for by changes in oil stocks. Table 6.2 shows the annual growth rates of consumption over five year intervals from 1960-65 to date. It reveals significant differences in the growth pattern over this period.

In the period 1960-70, oil consumption grew at 7-8% per annum compound, a tremendous rate of growth. It slowed down in the 1970s and actually declined in the period 1980-1985, when consumption fell by 1.3% per annum as a consequence of the second oil price shock. The lowest point of the period was reached in the mid-1980s. Since then, consumption growth has recovered, with a small positive growth rate in the early 1990s, and a return to around 2% per year since 1995. Exceptional growth was seen in 2004 - three million barrels per day, a 4% annual increase, due to demand growth from China and USA.

While trends in oil production and consumption are reasonable indicators of the likely growth in demand for shipping crude oil and oil products, a much more accurate measure is that provided in Row 2 of Table 6.1, which shows the volume of oil shipped on an annual basis. Between 1967 and 1977 this volume doubled; 59% of all oil produced in the world was moved by sea in 1977. Note the change in the share - the increase in the share taken by seaborne oil movements over the previous decade means that the demand for shipping oil rose faster in this period than the growth in the demand for oil itself. Conversely, between 1977 and 1987, although oil production remained roughly static, the share of oil shipped by sea declined to 44%. A static level of production and consumption, combined with a falling share, means falling demand for shipping services in this sector, a classic example of derived demand at work. Indeed oil movements declined from 1,724m tonnes in 1977 to 1,279m tonnes in 1987, before beginning to recover. It was only in 1994 that the total oil cargoes moved by sea exceeded the 1977 level, and continued to do so in the late 1990s, when measured in tonnes of cargo moved. It is interesting to note that in 2006, the proportion of oil that is traded is at the 1977 level of 60%. This, together with the increase in oil production, implies a significant recovery in the demand for oil tanker services.

1960 - 1965	7.20	2000	1.29
1965 - 1970	8.20	2001	0.72
1970 - 1975	3.10	2002	0.97
1975 - 1980	4.00	2003	2.07
1980 - 1985	-1.30	2004	4.08
1985 - 1990	2.30	2005	1.29
1990 - 1995	0.30	2006	0.94
1995 - 2000	1.80	2007	1.57
2000 - 2005	8.62	2008	-0.27
2005 - 2010	2.97	2009	-2.20
		2010	3.06

Table 6.1 Oil Consumption Annual Growth Rates % per annum (Source: BP Statistical Review of World Energy 1995, 2011 ??)

Changes in tonne/miles and voyage length

The growth and decline of oil tonnage movements tells only part of the story of demand change. Demand can be measured in terms of tonne/miles, as well as in tonnage terms. Rows 5 and 6 of Table 6.1 are well worth studying. Between 1967 and 1977, while oil cargo shipments doubled, the tonne/miles transported nearly trebled from 4,130bn to 11,467bn. The difference in the two arises from the fact that the average length of voyage rose from 4,775 nautical miles in 1967 to 6,651 in 1977. A large part of the increase can be related to the closure of the Suez Canal in 1967, which did not reopen until 1975. As a consequence the laden distance between the major exporting centre (the Middle East) and two major importing centres (North America and West Europe) increased dramatically as vessels were being routed around the Cape of Good Hope.

This increase in the laden leg gave a dramatic impetus to the development of large tankers, as 100,000, 250,000 and even 500,000-dwt vessels were designed and built in the period 1967-1975.

Between 1977 and 1987 the average laden leg declined by nearly 50%. Note that this coincides with a decline in the volume of tonnage moved as well. Essentially demand for tanker services collapsed dramatically during this period, creating severe problems for tanker owners and operators. The market response to this will be considered later in this Chapter. Since 1987, average voyage lengths have fluctuated between 4,600 and 5,200 nautical miles, with changes in the balance of long haul and short haul cargoes affecting this figure.

Changes in the Regional Balance of Oil Consumption and Production

Everyone is well aware that the Middle East is the major source of oil exports. What is less well known is that its share of oil production has fluctuated quite dramatically in the past 35 years, but has stabilised recently. The relevant data for production and consumption shares are shown in Tables 6.3 and 6.4 below.

North America accounted for 39% of the world's oil consumption in 1965, and 30% of production. It therefore needed to meet its full consumption needs by importing. Western Europe accounted for 25% of world oil consumption in 1965 and had no oil production. It was even more dependent on oil imports than North America. The Middle East, on the other hand, accounted for 2% of the world's oil consumption and produced 27% of the world's oil, a smaller share than North America.

Year	World Production (mln tonnes)	Seaborn Trade (mln tonnes)	World Production %	Seaborn Trade (bn tonnemiles)	Average haul (n miles)1	World Tanker Fleet (mln DWT)	Tanker Productivity 2	World Merchant Fleet (mln DWT)	World Fleet %
1938	258					16.6			
1957	853					49.6			
1967	1,758	865	49	4,130	4,775	103.5	8.36		
1977	2,915	1,724	59	11,467	6,651	332.3	5.19		
1987	2,925	1,279	44	6,016	4,704	238.14	5.37	632.24	37.67
1990	3,179	1,526	48	7,821	5,125	235.79	6.47	629.98	37.43
1995	3,281	1,808	55	9,670	5,348	270.94	6.67	719.22	37.67
2000	3,611.76	2,435.42	67.43	10,265	4,215	283.07	8.6	793.77	35.66
2001	3,601.61	2,515.06	69.83	10,179	4,047	284.86	8.83	802.77	35.49
2002	3,584.23	2,505.18	69.89	9,898	3,951	286	8.76	822.01	34.79
2003	3,701.12	2,625.32	70.93	10,580	4,030	308.68	8.5	841.73	36.67
2004	3,877.03	2,767.80	71.39	11,235	4,059	320.66	8.63	863.67	37.13
2005	3,906.56	2,874.08	73.57	11,705	4,073	340.75	8.43	907.47	37.55
2006	3,916.25	2,951.52	75.37	12,151	4,117	356.11	8.29	965.01	36.9
2007	3,904.26	3,119.57	79.9			382.98	8.15	1,042.33	36.74
2008	3,933.74	3,067.48	77.98			407.88	7.52	1,117.78	36.49
2009	3,831.02	2,938.70	76.71			418.27	7.03	1,192.32	35.08
2010	3,913.65	3,004.78	76.78			450.05	6.68	1,276.14	35.27

Table 6.2 Development of the World Tanker Fleet, Selected years, 1938 - 2006
(Sources: Tutorship Manual 2001; BP Statistical Review of World Energy 2001 I ????);

Notes:
1 Year End figures from various sources. Numbers may not be exactly comparable as minimum sizes alter over time.
2. Defined as Tonnes Cargo moved per dwt of fleet per year
3. Average Haul defined as billion tonne/miles/million tonnes cargo.

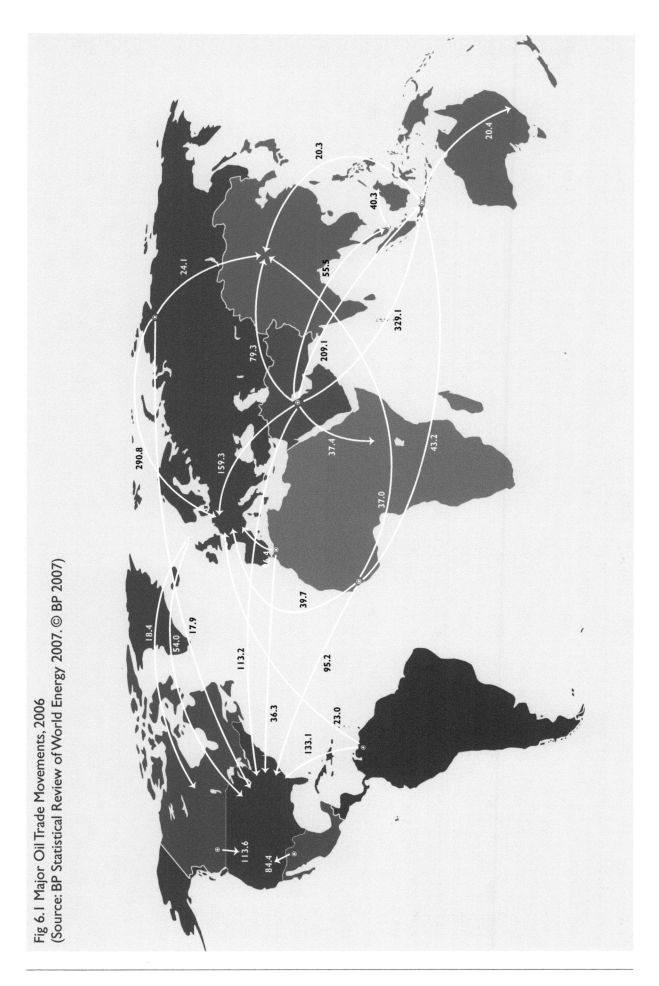

Fig 6.1 Major Oil Trade Movements, 2006
(Source: BP Statistical Review of World Energy 2007. © BP 2007)

Year	1990	1995	2000	2001	2002	2003	2004	2005	2006	2007	2008	2009	2010
North America	30.00	30.10	29.66	29.50	29.18	29.17	29.17	28.94	28.41	28.07	26.77	26.06	25.81
South & Central America	6.60	6.40	6.34	6.44	6.33	6.07	5.99	6.14	6.24	6.52	6.79	6.87	7.00
Europe & Eurasia	27.30	26.60	26.28	26.29	25.98	25.69	25.03	24.82	24.81	24.07	24.31	23.59	22.91
Middle East	6.30	6.30	6.69	6.76	6.95	7.10	7.23	7.38	7.66	7.84	8.38	8.81	8.94
Africa	3.30	3.30	3.27	3.29	3.32	3.33	3.33	3.44	3.39	3.51	3.67	3.86	3.86
Asia Pacific	26.60	27.30	27.75	27.72	28.23	28.64	29.24	29.28	29.49	29.99	30.08	30.80	31.47
World Total (mln tonnes)	3,153.80	3,263.90	3,571.61	3,597.25	3,632.25	3,707.44	3,858.74	3,908.47	3,945.33	4,007.29	3,996.49	3,908.65	4,028.09
OECD	62.40	62.20	62.07	61.59	60.79	60.48	59.27	58.94	58.04	56.80	55.31	53.59	52.48
Non-OECD	37.60	37.80	37.93	38.41	39.21	39.52	40.73	41.06	41.96	43.20	44.69	46.41	47.52
EU	19.90	19.50	19.58	19.63	19.34	19.06	18.60	18.50	18.37	17.68	17.74	17.15	16.45
Former Soviet Union	5.20	5.10	5.05	5.00	4.99	4.97	4.83	4.74	4.89	4.85	5.02	4.93	5.00

Table 6.3 Regional Shares of World Oil Consumption (Source: BP Review of World Energy 2011)

Year	1990	1995	2000	2001	2002	2003	2004	2005	2006	2007	2008	2009	2010
North America	20.70	19.70	18.02	18.10	18.42	18.10	17.21	16.52	16.51	16.41	15.75	16.50	16.56
South & Central America	7.20	8.90	9.56	9.44	9.32	8.60	8.72	8.88	8.81	8.52	8.53	8.83	8.94
Europe & Eurasia	24.90	20.40	20.07	20.73	21.93	22.13	21.93	21.63	21.66	22.03	21.63	22.36	21.80
Middle East	26.90	29.80	31.59	30.93	29.25	30.38	30.92	31.18	31.32	30.90	31.96	30.39	30.27
Africa	10.10	10.30	10.27	10.39	10.60	10.76	11.48	12.05	12.01	12.41	12.33	11.98	12.22
Asia Pacific	10.30	10.80	10.50	10.41	10.48	10.03	9.74	9.75	9.70	9.73	9.81	9.94	10.21
World Total (mln tonnes)	3,170.60	3,281.00	3,611.76	3,601.61	3,584.23	3,701.12	3,877.03	3,906.56	3,916.25	3,904.26	3,933.74	3,831.02	3,913.65
OECD	28.10	29.70	28.01	27.77	28.06	26.91	25.23	23.86	23.29	22.96	21.96	22.53	22.09
Non-OECD	71.90	70.30	71.99	72.23	71.94	73.09	74.77	76.14	76.71	77.04	78.04	77.47	77.91
OPEC	38.40	41.70	41.82	41.05	39.21	40.23	41.91	42.88	42.90	42.52	43.45	41.33	41.48
Non-OPEC	61.60	58.30	47.29	47.17	47.78	45.89	43.68	42.35	41.76	41.50	40.60	41.85	41.72
EU	3.80	4.80	4.60	4.32	4.41	4.00	3.55	3.22	2.93	2.90	2.68	2.58	2.37
Former Soviet Union	18.00	10.90	10.89	11.79	13.01	13.88	14.40	14.77	15.34	15.99	15.94	16.82	16.80

Table 6.4 Regional Shares of World Oil Production (Source: BP Review of World Energy 2011)

By 1980 several changes had occurred. North America's share of world consumption fell to 31%, although its total consumption had doubled from 1,565 to 3,222m tonnes. Its share of world production fell to 18% and it had become increasingly dependent on imports. Although North Sea oil had been discovered, it did not come on stream until the 1980s. Western Europe's consumption share of 23% was still dominated by imports. The Middle East's share of production now stood at 33%.

In the 1990s, the decline of output and prosperity in the former Soviet Union shows up clearly with its share of production falling to 11% in 1995, from 18% in 1990. Recovery in Russia's production has since taken place, to 15% in 2006. This is still below its 1990 share, but total volumes have increased. North America, Europe and the Middle East have all seen their shares rise over this period, with North America accounting for 28% of the market in 1996.

During the 1980s, Middle East production was seriously reduced due to the Iran-Iraq war. This shows up clearly in the data in Table 6.4, with the Middle East's share of world production falling to 18.5% in 1985. Note the corresponding increase in shares of North America and the rise in Asian and North Sea production.

Production shares altered in the 1990s, with the former socialist economies share decline being mirrored by increases in the regional production shares of the Middle East, rising sharply to 29%, with small increases in West Europe's share, from 6% to 9%. Other regions have remained broadly unchanged, with North America accounting for 20% of the world's oil consumption.

The major trading movements for 2011 are shown in Figure 6.1, derived from the BP Statistical Review of World Energy 2011. As the analysis of the share data suggested, the major exporters of crude oil are the Middle East countries, dominated by Saudi Arabia. With declining North Sea oil production, European countries have now sourced more of their import requirements from the Middle East and Russia. In Asia, 80% of oil imports are from the Middle East. Figure 6.1 also identifies the USA as a major importer, running at 671 million tonnes per year in 2006. This was sourced at roughly 110-120 million tonnes each from Canada, the Middle East, and South and Central America, together accounting for around half of all US imports.

Year	2000	2001	2002	2003	2004	2005	2006	2007	2008	2009	2010
Imports											
US	25.57	25.94	25.46	26.21	26.17	26.43	25.90	24.54	23.56	21.89	21.85
Europe	25.52	25.75	26.66	25.65	25.44	25.91	25.61	25.12	25.17	23.86	22.60
Japan	12.29	11.62	11.36	11.37	10.56	10.21	9.89	9.06	9.02	8.15	8.53
Rest of the World	36.61	36.70	36.52	36.77	37.84	37.46	38.60	41.29	42.25	46.11	47.02
Export											
US	2.05	2.03	2.03	1.97	2.01	2.21	2.50	2.59	3.60	3.72	4.03
Canada	3.93	4.03	4.39	4.48	4.36	4.30	4.43	4.42	4.57	4.81	4.86
Mexico	4.18	4.20	4.41	4.52	4.20	4.03	4.00	3.56	2.95	2.77	2.88
South & Central America	7.10	7.02	6.65	6.29	6.56	6.89	7.00	6.43	6.62	7.16	6.67
Europe	4.54	4.35	5.01	4.42	4.04	4.20	4.13	4.09	3.70	3.89	3.53
Former Soviet Union	9.85	10.45	12.04	12.84	13.06	13.82	13.61	15.00	14.98	15.23	15.97
Middle East	43.68	42.64	40.49	40.52	39.83	38.73	38.44	35.43	36.85	35.18	35.29
North Africa	6.30	6.08	5.87	5.81	5.92	6.00	6.14	6.00	5.97	5.61	5.36
West Africa	7.59	7.10	7.02	7.73	8.21	8.52	8.95	8.69	8.40	8.34	8.60
Asia Pacific	8.61	8.74	8.62	8.51	8.50	8.29	8.20	10.81	9.87	10.76	11.64
Rest of World	2.17	3.36	3.48	2.91	3.31	3.01	2.59	2.98	2.50	2.53	1.19

Table 6.5 Major Oil Trade Movements (% shares)

Notes: Before 2006, shares for Europe are for Western Europe only
China only shown separately for 2006. Europe shown separately for 2006 only
Before 2006, shares are based on crude and products. For 2006, share is based on crude trade only

Table 6.5 shows similar data as Figure 6.1, except the flows are expressed in shares for the years 1989, 1994, 1995, 2000 and 2006. In 2006, Europe and the USA accounted for 54% of all imports, followed by Japan (11%). China's significance is revealed with a share of 8%. On the export side in 2006, the Middle East dominates with 46%, the former Soviet Union countries accounting for 14%, West Africa 12% and North Africa and Latin America both at 6%. It is noteworthy that Japan, a major oil importer, has no domestic oil reserves at all.

Table 6.6 provides information on the total volumes of oil traded in 2006, split between crude oil and products. The USA imports more products than Europe. You should note that Europe exports more products than crude oil. In contrast, nearly all of West Africa's exports are crude. The interested reader may care to study these tables and link them to the flows observed in Figure 6.1.

	Crude Imports	Product Imports	Crude Exports	Products Exports
US	456.10	121.02	1.41	101.71
Canada	28.87	12.72	99.10	29.12
Mexico	0.37	30.07	67.84	8.47
S. & Cent. America	20.87	56.76	131.21	44.63
Europe	465.15	131.69	19.29	71.79
Former Soviet Union	0.00	4.85	317.97	103.25
Middle East	11.26	10.13	828.68	107.21
North Africa	12.31	11.95	112.56	29.19
West Africa	0.06	6.89	221.22	7.60
East & Southern Africa	5.05	7.26	16.22	0.43
Australasia	29.02	14.12	16.18	7.64
China	234.56	59.95	2.03	29.42
India	162.03	16.47	0.00	57.20
Japan	184.79	40.93	0.32	14.13
Singapore	39.86	100.08	2.09	65.83
Other Asia Pacific	225.47	131.68	39.66	80.16
Unidentified *	0.00	1.19	0.00	0.00
Total World	**1,875.78**	**757.75**	**1,875.78**	**757.75**

* Includes changes in the quantity of oil in transit, movements not otherwise shown, unidentified military use, etc.

Table 6.6 Oil Imports and Exports, 2010 (Source: BP Review of World Energy, 2011.)

This includes changes in the quantity of oil in transit, movements not otherwise shown, unidentified military use, etc. Note: Bunkers are not included as exports. Intra-area movements (for example, between countries in Europe) are excluded

To sum up, in 2010:

1. The USA accounted for 21.85% of world crude oil imports, and North America accounted for 16.56% of world oil production.

2. Japan has no indigenous oil reserves, and imported 8.53% of the world's traded crude oil.

3. China has no significant oil reserves, and in 2006 imported 12.5% of the world's traded crude oil.

4. The Middle East is responsible for 35.29% of all seaborne oil movements - but its dominance has changed, falling with rising oil production elsewhere.

5. Europe is still a large importer of oil, despite the exploitation of the North Sea, which is seen as having peaked in production in the 1990s.

6. Latin America and the Asian industrialised countries are strong growth areas for oil consumption. China and India have become significant consumers and are expected to become even more significant in the next decade.

6.1.2 The behaviour of the price of crude oil

Many of the events that drive the tanker market are bound up with both changes in the volume of oil moved and with its value. The decline in oil consumption and the fall in oil sea transportation that occurred in the period 1975-85 was itself triggered by the dramatic changes that happened in the world price of crude oil.

Figure 6.2 shows the behaviour of the price of Arabian Light Oil, one of the reference markers over the past thirty years. After averaging around $1.80 to $2.00 per barrel in the 1960s, the Organisation of Petroleum Exporting Countries (OPEC) raised the world price in 1970 to $4.00. In October 1973, following on the Arab-Israeli six day war, OPEC raised the price until it reached $9.00 by the end of that year, as well as threatening oil embargoes on countries that were viewed as Israel's allies. This fourfold increase in the price of a major strategic commodity generated three immediate effects:

a) it triggered a huge economic recession in many Western economies, leading to lower rates of economic growth. In some countries, such as the UK, real incomes fell in 1975 as a result.

b) it generated an international banking crisis, as many oil exporting countries suddenly found themselves with large current account surpluses on their balance of payments, while many oil importing countries grappled with large deficit problems.

c) it generated a sudden and dramatic stop in the growth of the tanker market, which had experienced two booms in rates in 1970 and in 1973. These booms were generated by the huge growth in demand volumes at the time, which had also created a very rapid expansion in the tanker fleet.

The rest of the 1970s were characterised by a steadily rising nominal price of oil to about $12 a barrel. In the wake of the Iranian revolution of 1979, the OPEC price peaked at around $40 a barrel or $90 at 2006 prices. This was the result of OPEC trying to maintain the price of oil in real terms. This in effect meant that whenever the dollar devalued against other currencies, the $ price of oil was increased to compensate OPEC members for the loss of the dollar's earning power.

This policy was can be seen as counter-productive since it helped create a cycle of low growth. The USA tried to offset its deficit and restore the dollar by recessionary policies, leading to low growth, falling demand for oil and stagnation of oil exports.

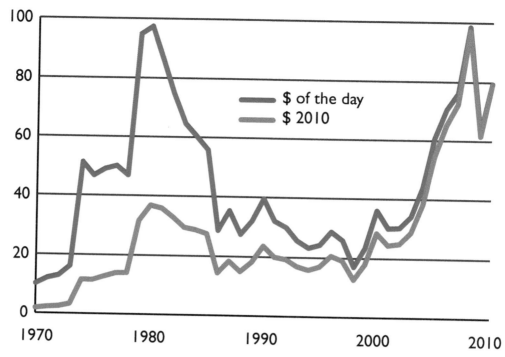

Fig 6.2 The Development of Oil Prices 1970-2006 (Source: BP Statistical Review of World Energy 2011)

In the mid-1980s, Saudi-Arabia and other OPEC members altered their pricing policy to match that set by Mexico, which had become a significant oil producer but was not a member of OPEC. This change in policy coupled with rising output from Non-OPEC producers forced a decline in the oil price. Saudi-Arabia, for example, introduced Netback pricing for its crude, which was determined by the selling prices of the refined products at the point of final consumption less the transport and refining costs. This policy emphasises the fact that the crude oil price is driven by consumer demand for the products and the price obtained in the retail market.

As can be seen from the diagram, the last major price rise was in 1990, triggered by the Iraqi invasion of Kuwait. But Middle East oil production was no longer as dominant as it had been and the increase was short lived.

Indeed, in real terms and allowing for the decline in the purchasing power of the dollar over time, the 2006 price of crude oil is about the same as it was between 1979 and 1982, but has not yet reached the same peak values. In the period after 2002, prices rose sharply, driven by demand growth. In 2006-7, prices were quite high in real terms, reflecting the balance of strong demand growth against the current refinery capacity levels.

OPEC as a cartel

The principal economic reason for the dramatic rise in the price of crude oil in the early 1970s was the ability of OPEC to regulate the world supply of crude oil, with all members agreeing to set common prices and, just as importantly, set production quotas to limit supply and raise prices.

The ability to restrict prices depends heavily upon the quotas being adhered to. In the 1980s several countries began to break ranks, undermining this power. Nigeria for example regularly exceeded its quota. In addition, rising production from non-OPEC countries helped to undermine its monopoly position. The increase in OPEC market share since 2000 may again help to establish greater dominance, but its pricing policy is now very different from that of the 1970s. Consequently, this may not be such a threat to global macro-economic stability.

After this discussion of the oil market and changes in demand, attention is now turned to the behaviour of the tanker sector.

6.2   CHANGES IN THE TANKER FLEET

At its peak in 1977 the world tanker fleet accounted for 45% of all world shipping tonnage, having climbed steadily in the previous decade. Following on from the events described above, this trend was reversed, with the share declining steadily, reaching 30% in 1994. This was most marked in the period 1981-1985, with a fall in tanker tonnage.

The stock of tanker tonnage has therefore broadly followed the pattern of demand, rising rapidly until the early 1970s, stalling, and then declining in size until 1988, since when it has begun to grow again. This long run adjustment of supply to the level of demand has often been a painful process in particular periods.

Period	GT	DWT	Tonnes Demand	Tonne/mile Demand
1963-68	8	n.a.	n.a.	n.a.
1968-73	10.8	n.a.	13.6	21.4
1973-78	8.7	12.3	0.0	0.0
1978-83	-2.2	-1.9	-5.6	-9
1983-88	-4.1	-4.0	3.5	3.4
1988-93	2.4	1.8	5	8.2
1990-94	1.8	2.3	3.6	3.8
1995 - 2000		1.3	3.6	6.0
2000 - 2006		3.0	1.2	2.8
1977 - 2006		0.1	-0.8	0.2

Table 6.7 Annual Average Percentage Changes of the Tanker Stock and Changes in Demand (source: Tutorship Manual 2001 Table 6.1)

An indication of the uneven development of the tanker fleet can be seen in Table 6.6. It is well worth careful study. It is clear that even with five year averages, demand growth leads to supply response. In the early 1970s demand growth outstripped supply but then demand growth collapsed to zero, while supply expanded by 8-10% per year. This created a huge problem of adjustment in the tanker market, which was only resolved by the late 1980s. This adjustment problem is well illustrated in Figure 6.3 below.

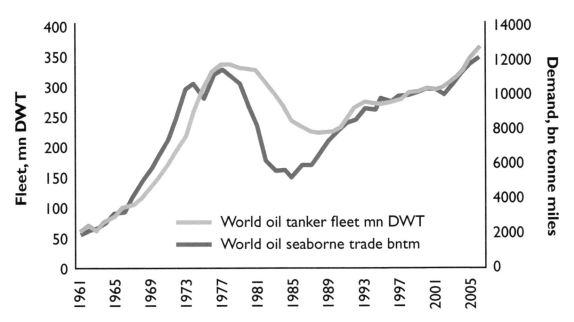

Fig 6.3 Growth of World tonne/mile Demand and World Tanker Fleet (Source: Fearnleys Annual Reviews, UNCTAD Maritime Review, various issues)

The same picture emerges from inspection of the graphs provided below. Figures 6.4-6.6 show the movement of tanker orders, scrapping and lay-ups plotted against the prevailing level of spot rates, measured in Worldscale. What should be apparent is the close correspondence that exists between high rate levels and rapid demand growth, and between low freight rates and the low levels of demand relative to supply. It must be remembered that the stock of vessels (supply) alters all the time, slowly adjusting to the shifts in demand, as shown in Figure 6.3.

Worldscale and its successor, New Worldscale are tanker industry conventions designed to generate a uniform scale, or index, for tanker rates. Each route is calibrated for an assumed vessel size and cost structure. The calculated rate is set at Ws100 for that route. All fixtures are then quoted relative to this rate. Large vessels will generate a Ws rate of say, Ws50, small vessels Ws120 say, because their operating costs are so different from the assumed size in the model of 75,000-dwt.

Figures 6.4-6.6 also bring out the volatility of the spot rate itself, even on an annual basis. The peak level is Ws258 in 1973; in fact, in one particular week, they reached Ws435 or so.

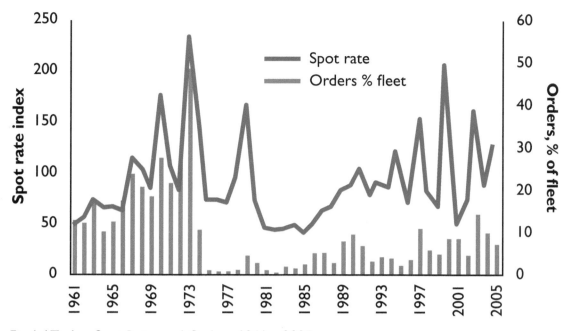

Fig 6.4 Tanker Spot Rates and Orders, 1961 – 2005

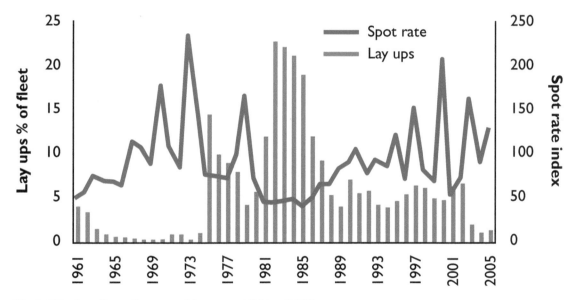

Fig 6.5 Tanker Spot Rates and Lay-ups 1961 – 2005

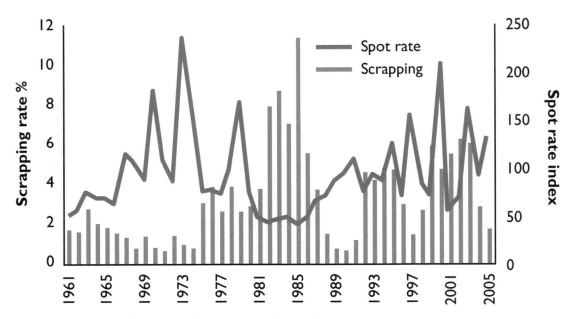

Fig 6.6 Tanker Spot Rates and Scrapping, 1961 – 2005

Note: Sources for Figures 6.4 to 6.6: 1960 –1995, Fearnleys Annual Reviews. 1995 on, UNCTAD Maritime Reviews

6.3   THE RELATIONSHIP BETWEEN TANKER AND DRY CARGO MARKETS

Although most analyses of the tanker market treat it as an independent sector, examination of the movement of dry cargo and tanker rates over long periods of time reveals that they tend to move together. As has been pointed out, the tanker freight rate is the more volatile of the two, but there is a good correspondence between peaks in one sector and peaks in the other. The exception to this appears in the 1980s, when the dry cargo sector continued to grow while the tanker trade suffered a decline.

There are a number of reasons to explain the correlation related to the concept of substitution in economics. Separate markets are more closely related. The higher the degree of demand substitution between the two sectors (due to the substitution between oil and coal), the higher the level of supply substitution between them.

The tanker and dry cargo markets share the same key drivers. When world trade grows it tends to create good conditions in both markets segments. Hence there is still a long term link. For example, China's economic growth has generated significant increases in the demand for imported oil and gas and, at the same time, its demand for iron ore and coal has also increased. This has led to record rates for Capesize vessels. The growth of Chinese oil consumption and import demand has helped to raise the demand for shipping oil.

There is one other way in which freight rates between oil and dry cargo can be theoretically linked. High freight rates mean high profits, which create high second hand prices for the assets, the ships themselves. Shipowners rush to order more ships. But berth capacity is finite, so in a boom, one way of building more dry bulk vessels is to build fewer tankers. If new tankers become scarcer relative to demand, the newbuild price will rise and, implicitly, so will future tanker operating costs. This will raise freight rates in the tanker market. The limitation of shipbuilding capacity thus creates a potential link between freight rates. Note that this model assumes that shipbuilding capacity is fully utilised at all times. If not, extra dry bulk vessels can be built without reducing tanker newbuild capacity, and the above argument carries less force.

6.4 THE STRUCTURE OF THE TANKER MARKET

In the past, the oil industry was dominated by the major multi-national oil companies. Indeed, in the 1960s, they became known as 'the Seven Sisters' - seven large companies (Exxon, Gulf, Shell, Chevron, Texaco, BP and Mobil). These companies appeared to dominate many of the national domestic markets for oil and oil products, giving the impression of a highly concentrated market driven by a few large players.

It appeared that such a structure would dominate all markets including the tanker market. In the 1960s, the major oil companies owned one third of the world's tanker tonnage and chartered another third on long term timecharters. This left only one third of the world's tonnage to trade in the rest of the market. If the big oil companies controlled up to 70% of the tonnage, it suggests that the tanker market was akin to an oligopoly rather than a perfectly competitive market.

In an oligopoly, price competition becomes less likely. There may even be periods of collusion between the major companies, leading to price rigging. Indeed, in the UK market for petrol, there have been a number of inquiries by the Competition Commission, investigating the degree of competition that exists between UK oil and petrol companies.

However, appearances can be deceptive. The general consensus amongst scholars of the tanker market is that it is extremely competitive. Moreover, the trends over the past twenty years have made the market more competitive than it was, especially in the crude oil sector. On the other hand, the continuing development of specialist vessels (such as LNG and chemicals tankers) has meant that some of the segments may be potentially less competitive than when the market was less fragmented.

The two major contributors to the academic study of the tanker market are Koopmans (*Tanker Freight Rates and Tankship Building. Haarlem*) and Zannetos (*The Theory of Ocean Tankship Rates. MIT Press MIT*). A number of other studies appeared subsequently, but they have tended to accept the views put forward in the above texts. Basically, both authors have argued that the tanker market is perfectly competitive.

The basic properties of a competitive market are:

1. All owners seek to maximise profits;

2. There is a large number of buyers of the service;

3. There is a large number of sellers, but none big enough to influence price;

4. The product is homogeneous;

5. There is complete freedom of entry to, and exit from, the market;

6. Full information on market conditions and rates is available to all participants.

6.4.1 Large numbers of buyers and sellers

Even in the 1960s when the 'Seven Sisters' were at their peak and large oil companies controlled significant proportions of the word's tanker tonnage, there were still many independent oil companies that needed to ship cargoes of oil. Since the 1970s, the economic share of the oil majors has declined significantly for a number of reasons. Firstly, the rise of State-owned oil companies in the Middle East and elsewhere, reducing the share of the big seven. Secondly, the development of a large spot oil market in Rotterdam from the early 1970s has meant that a ship's cargo may go through many owners before it reaches its destination. The rise of the oil trader has led to an increase in the number of independent charterers of ships.

The rise of the Rotterdam spot market coincided with the loss of market power by the oil majors during the 1970s and 1980s as independents opened up new distribution channels in many countries. The ramifications spread to the tanker market where the oil majors reduced the amount of tonnage held on long term charter, in response to the oversupply situation of the mid-1970s. They also began to reduce their direct ownership of tonnage, partly in response to the introduction of Oil Pollution Act 1990 (OPA90), which made the owner of any vessel polluting the US seaboard liable for unlimited damages.

These changes in ownership have led to a substantial reduction in the relative importance of the oil companies total tonnage, as can be seen in the data displayed in Figures 6.7 and 6.8 below,

The independent owners' share of total tonnage has risen from 70% in 1996 to a staggering 97% in 2007. The top ten independents account for 83m dwt or 14% of the world fleet. This implies that thousands of other independent companies control the other 86%. The largest independent tanker owner in 1996 was Worldwide Shipping with 5.9m dwt, or 2.1% of the world fleet. The largest oil company fleet is Vela, the Saudi Arabian oil company which represented 2.5% of the world tanker fleet. In 1996, the largest tanker operator was responsible for only 2.5% of the tanker tonnage. The largest independent tanker owner in terms of dwt is now Frontline and Ship Finance International, with 12m dwt. This represents 3.4% of the world fleet. The largest oil company fleet is now BP, with 3.3m dwt, less than one per cent of the world fleet.

Figure 6.7 shows the percentage share of the 83m dwt of tankers owned by the ten largest oil majors, ranked by tanker tonnage. The data shows that the top ten independent companies owned 14% of the world fleet. Figure 6.9 presents the shares of the largest oil companies. In 1966, the top 5 oil majors owned 23% of the fleet. In 2007, the top ten oil companies' share was a mere 3.4%, representing a grand total of 12.1m dwt. This is a clear decline in the relative importance of these companies.

In 2007, the twenty largest tanker operators by dwt accounted for only 37% of world tanker tonnage, and the ten largest, 24%. These are very low figures for industrial concentration, and suggest that properties two and three are appropriate in the context of the tanker market.

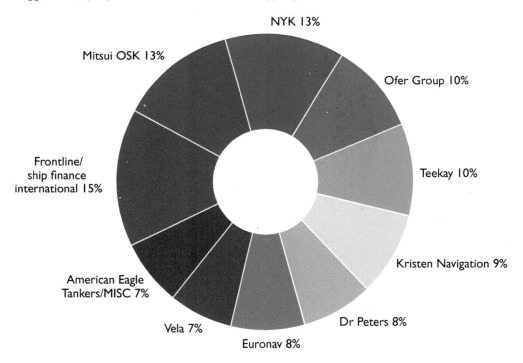

Fig 6.7 Independent Owners, 2007, Top 10 (Source: Gibson Shipbrokers Ltd)

Notes:
1. Top 10 Independents owned 83.1m dwt.
2. Shares based on this figure.
3. World fleet estimated at 349m dwt in July 2007

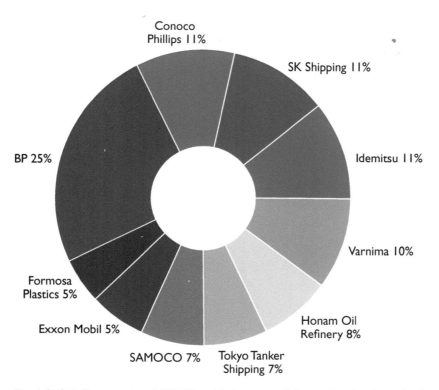

Fig 6.8 Oil Companies, 2007, Top 10 (source: Gibson Shipbrokers Ltd)

Notes:
1. Top 10 oil companies owned 12.8m dwt.
2. Shares based on this figure.

There is also a great deal of trading between the oil companies, because different regions produce different grades of oil. Demand fluctuations generated by seasonal changes also lead to a need to trade between each other.

6.4.2   Identical service

Although oil itself might appear to be a homogeneous product, it does in fact vary in terms of its sulphur content and viscosity. Some of the trade involves the movement of different qualities of oil to be blended at refineries, as different blends meet different market needs.

In fact, the key feature lies in the nature of the transportation of oil, not oil itself. It is clear that the transportation of oil is very homogeneous, since the service provided by one crude oil tanker is pretty much identical to that provided by another, assuming that delivery times, vessel reliability and so on are similar. The economic assumption that the product is homogeneous can therefore be maintained.

6.4.3   Freedom of entry and exit

The main factor determining ease of entry is access to capital to pay for a new or second-hand vessel. It is worth noting here that the purchase of a second-hand vessel may mean the entry of a new company, but it is usually at the expense of an existing operator: tonnage supply has not increased overall. Since the financial crisis of 2007/2008, obtaining the necessary funds from a bank or other financial institution can be much harder and at higher rates than before.

Many countries provide tax relief for investing in shipping. Many of these investments are made at the top of the shipping business cycle, when freight rates and time charter fixtures are relatively attractive. This encourages shipowners to invest in more ships and banks to lend more money in the expectation that rates will be high in the future. On the other hand, when spot and timecharter rates are low, banks are less willing to supply finance, but of course there are fewer owners willing to risk the purchase of a new vessel.

Exiting the market may be by scrapping the vessel or, for an individual company, selling to another operator, although the latter does not reduce the tonnage supply overall. In some industries, exiting is very difficult. For example, £8 billion has been committed to the Channel Tunnel, yet if the owners of Eurotunnel wanted to leave, they could not convert their capital into cash. The assets would have to be sold at the market value, which might be well below the initial cost of building the tunnel. In this case, the company would find it very difficult to leave the industry, in terms of getting out with its capital intact. In the tanker industry, this means of exit is much more likely, since there are many buyers and sellers. Only in exceptionally bad market conditions might there be a problem with exiting the market.

The physical mobility of the vessels themselves means that the large proportion of capital invested in this sector is literally mobile. This means that any regional demand imbalances can be quickly rectified by a shift in relative supply. This statement must be qualified by the fact that the development of very large crude carriers means that some segments of the market are less flexible than others. VLCCs are excluded from some trading routes by either port or draught restrictions. For example, the very largest vessels cannot trade into the US East Coast ports because of shallow waters. Furthermore, the largest vessels cannot use the Suez Canal when laden because of the draught. These characteristics mean that in some trades, Suezmax tankers are more flexible than bigger vessels.

Despite this qualification, the substitutability of one tanker for another on most routes or trades means that all sectors tend to move together. Supply can be very flexible in the short run, as Table 6.9 reveals. The existence of a fleet of laid up tankers meant that the increase in demand was easily be met by a sharp fall in lay-ups. Once lay-ups had fallen to 1%, such a response would not be available and only new capacity would increase supply in such a situation. But it is worth noting here that the general global tanker inspection and approvals regime does not encourage owners to lay up their ships unless market conditions and outlook are poor.

6.4.4 Full information

The market is extremely well served by the specialised shipbroking companies which keep in constant contact with both owners and charterers on a 24-hour basis all around the world. Many shipbroking companies have offices in strategic points around the globe to offer this service. London plays a crucial role, because it is located in a time zone which can trade with the Far East on the same day as trading with New York.

In addition, there are many specialist companies offering consultancy services to the industry.

All this activity means that charterers and owners are continuously informed of current events and prices. Many fixtures are publicly reported, with all salient details available. This makes the provision of market information relatively cheap and very efficient and it provides a benchmarked market.

The emergence of publicly quoted tanker companies, whose shares are traded on the world's stock exchanges, also means that information becomes more readily available as these companies must file accounts and provide information to shareholders.

Overall then it would appear that all the fundamental properties of a perfectly competitive market are fulfilled when the tanker market is examined. This means that modelling its behaviour using demand and supply analysis can be justified.

6.5   SEGMENTED SUPPLY

Studies have shown that different tanker sizes have different own-price and cross-price elasticities of demand with respect to freight rates. This implies some degree of differentiation in the market. A study of tanker profitability in the 1970s showed that the gross profit margins varied widely between sizes and that large tankers had significantly greater variability in those margins. If tankers were all in the same market, the variability should have been the same. Kavussanos *Price Risk modelling of different size vessels in the tanker industry Logistics and Transportation Review, vol 32, pp. 161-176.*, using a technique borrowed from the world of financial analysis, also arrived at the same conclusion, by showing that the conditional volatility of tanker freight rates differed across ship sizes.

The question arises; does this mean that the tanker market has become less competitive? It can be argued that the answer is a resounding no, because although the segments within the tanker market may have become more distinct, allowing them to behave differently in the short run, it does not follow that they are unrelated in the long run. This is because shipowners have the choice of investing in all of these segments, none is closed to them. Free entry and exit exists in all parts, so that market imbalances may exist for a few years, but will be self-corrected by different rates of entry and exit in the sectors. If the market for VLCC's is badly hit, this sector will have very high lay-ups, higher than average scrapping rates and few new orders. Owners will be concentrating on the sectors that are relatively more profitable, until the excess supply problem is resolved.

In the long run, one would expect to see the same common factors driving each of these sectors and common trends appearing.

6.6   MODELLING DEMAND

It should be clear from the above discussions that the demand for oil transportation is likely to be extremely price inelastic. Remember it is a derived demand and the freight rate elasticity of derived demand depends on:

1. The own-price elasticity of demand for the final product;

2. The ease with which shipping can be substituted by other modes of oil transportation (cross price elasticity);

3. The share of freight costs in the final delivered cost to consumers;

4. The elasticity of supply of tanker transport services.

The lower the price elasticity of demand for the final product is, the harder shipping can be substituted and the share of the freight costs in the final delivered cost to consumers.

In normal conditions, with spare tonnage laid-up, one would expect the own-price elasticity of demand for tanker freight services to be very inelastic. This is because:

1. The own-price elasticity of products derived from crude oil are very low, because:

    a) there is limited technical substitution, for instance one cannot readily put methane in a petrol engine;

    b) there is limited substitution for oil as an energy source in the long run. One estimate gave a value of -0.17. This is very inelastic.

2. Ocean oil transportation is highly specialised. Oil pipelines act as substitutes for some trades such as North Sea oil fields, but in other areas there is no practicable alternative;

3. The share of freight costs in the retail price of petrol in the UK is about 2%, say 2p on 97p. Oil products are often highly taxed at the retail end because of the low price elasticity;

4. Supply elasticity is usually quite high, but can fall to zero in extreme booms, assuming a moderate value is not unreasonable.

All the above points lead to one conclusion. The responsiveness of demand to changes in freight rates can be regarded as close to zero, i.e. extremely inelastic.

Although demand is very inelastic with respect to the current freight rate, it is very sensitive to the level of economic activity, as seen in earlier sections. Demand might be represented as more or less vertical when plotting the quantity demanded in tonne/miles or tonnes of cargo, against the freight rate, for a given level of economic activity. When the rate of economic activity increases, the entire schedule can shift very rapidly. It will shift to the right in booms and to the left in recessions.

6.7 MODELLING SUPPLY

The supply schedule for the market as a whole is assumed to have a shape that is very similar to that developed on the Dry Cargo Market. It will be elastic when there are significant amounts of tonnage laid-up, as this tonnage is readily available to increase the size of the active fleet. But one must remember the oil company approval regime mentioned earlier. As the laid-up proportion falls, the sources of extra short run supply become more limited, so that the elasticity declines. This shape is shown in Figure 6.9 below.

The 80:20 split is based on the analysis by Platou of tanker rate volatility. It argues that practically all variations that are observed in the tanker market are observed when the utilisation of the fleet was in the last 20%. This is consistent with the shape of the supply curve below, elastic over the 80% range, but becoming less and less elastic until full capacity utilisation was achieved.

It is important to remember that this is a model for the short-run supply of shipping. The assumption is being made that the tanker tonnage supply is unchanged, with variations in tonne/miles produced generated by variations in lay-ups, storage, ship speed and delivery.

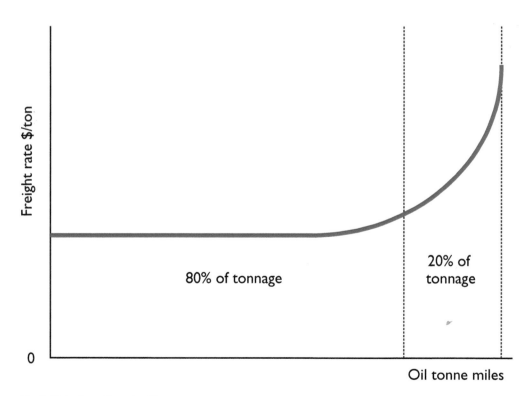

Fig 6.9 Tanker Supply Curve

6.8   THE MARKET MODEL

Putting the very inelastic demand schedule together with the varying elasticity supply schedule generates a model of the equilibrium spot freight rate for tanker services (Figure 6.10).

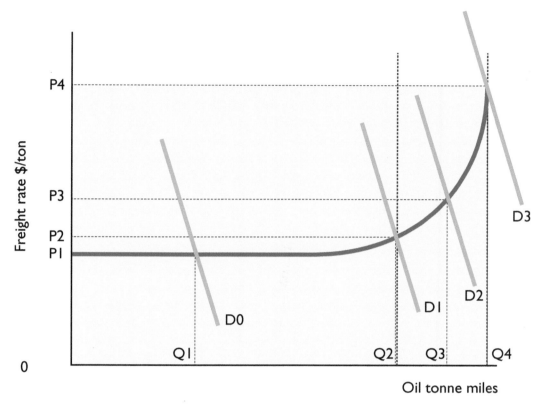

Fig 6.10 Modelling Demand and Supply in the Short Run

D0 - D1 Large shift in demand, but lots of spare capacity; little effect on rates. Freight rate moves from P1 to P2, while tonne/miles increased from Q1 to Q2.

D1 - D2 Smaller shift in demand and capacity is less readily available; larger increase in rates. Freight rate rises from P2 to P3, and tonne/miles increase from Q2 to Q3.

D2 - D3 Supply nearly perfectly inelastic; small shifts in demand can generate large increases in rates. Freight rate rises rapidly from P3 to P4; tonne/miles performed rise slightly from Q3 to Q4.

The above model is consistent with:

a) great rate volatility (at the higher demand end of the model);

b) the possibility that rate increases do not increase the short-run supply at all, once full utilisation of the existing fleet is achieved. The model is very similar to the one developed for the dry cargo sector, because both are very competitive sectors.

6.8.1   Tanker and dry cargo rate volatility compared

The observed higher rate volatility in tanker markets compared to dry bulk markets can be explained by the following points:

1. The dry cargo market is, in fact, not a single market at all. It consists of several major bulk trades plus large numbers of other commodities being transported on a tramp basis. This means that if one sector of demand grows while another declines, tonnage can be shifted from the declining sector to the growth sector. But this process keeps rate volatility in check in the individual markets.

2. The average size of dry cargo vessels, even the bulk ones, is smaller than that for tankers. There is a direct link between rate volatility and vessel size, which can be explained in common sense terms. Large vessels generate economies of scale, so that the average rate is lower than those for smaller vessels. The same size increase in rate for both sectors will generate a larger proportional increase for the lower initial rate, i.e. for the larger vessel. Thus rate volatility might be higher because of the differences in average vessel size between the two sectors.

3. The oil industry has a special place in Western economies. As well as being indispensable to the transport sector, oil is an important energy source for factory power and for the chemical industry. The plastics industry is based on oil derived products. As has been shown, the principal export region is the Middle East. The West's strategic control over this region declined sharply in the 1960s, with the rise of Arab Nationalism and the Arab-Israel conflict. Practically every significant spike in tanker rates has been associated with an event in this region. The 1956 closure of the Suez Canal, the 1967 six-day war, the 1973 Yom Kippur war, the 1979-84 Iran-Iraq war and the 1990 Iraq-Kuwait war can all be observed in the tanker rate data. This relationship may change in the future, but is not likely. Although growth in the period 2002-2007 has been driven by market fundamentals. The fact that the Middle East is likely to loom large as a supplier in the future means the chances of further price changes due to political instability must be quite high.

The reason for the early spikes is easy to see. The large multi-national oil companies ordered as much oil as possible to be extracted from the Middle East as soon as tensions flared but this was not associated with extra supply, hence the rates went up. It is also important to note that rate increases, such as occurred in 1990, appear to be much more short-lived. The Middle-East was no longer quite as dominant in export shares as it had been in the early 1980s and oil companies are not so vertically integrated. In 1990, Saudi Arabia's reaction was also quite different. Fearing invasion from Iraq, it co-operated with the western military forces and also deliberately increased its own oil production to compensate for the loss of Kuwaiti output. The price of crude oil fell and until the last quarter of 1996 was trading around $20-25 a barrel. No stock building surge was experienced so freight rates also declined after the initial scare. High prices observed for oil in recent years are related to demand levels reaching refinery capacity levels, rather than due to political events. Whether western economies were quite so dependent on oil in 2000 is less clear. Certainly the UK economy appears to have absorbed the price increases with much less impact on domestic inflation than occurred in the 1970s. The French economy now generates 70% of its power from nuclear sources. The reduced share of manufacturing in the economies of the developed countries means that energy price changes have less impact on domestic inflation than 30 years ago.

4. The role of expectations. It has been suggested that tanker rates were affected by what was called price elastic expectations. That is, the higher the rate, the more sensitive the market became to rates themselves and the market raised its expectations about future rates by more than was warranted. But this new level of expectations would cause a shift in the current demand curve, which would raise prices, until unsustainable levels were reached. It is very like a speculative bubble occurring, where all traders know the price is not related to economic fundamentals, but everyone is making so much money out of the perpetual rise in prices that no-one really asks whether the process can continue indefinitely.

The answer is that it cannot. A modern version of this idea is called rational expectations in market behaviour. The movement of tanker prices is driven as much by what we expect to happen to future tanker rates and future profitability, as it is by anything else. If the market is efficient, then all known information about such a market is argued to be captured in its present market price, freight rates or second hand tanker prices. Changes in expectations about the future will then automatically alter current prices. A war in the Gulf will send both oil prices, freight rates and second hand tanker prices up immediately because the likelihood of greater profitability is a consequence. Recent research has suggested that the rational expectations model of tanker market behaviour is not a good explanation of observed events. Researchers suggested that this was because the model assumed that everyone in the markets had identical expectations and the evidence suggested that this was not the case.

6.9 FLUCTUATIONS IN MARKET FREIGHT RATES

The actual behaviour of spot tanker freight rates was illustrated for annual average data in Figures 6.4-6.6. They illustrate peaks in 1967, 1970, 1973 and 1979, all years associated with wars in the Middle-East. Examination of rates over quarterly, monthly or even weekly time periods would generate even more variation. For example, tanker rates reflect the seasonal increases in demand generated in the West for oil in the winter months or the effect of the USA's summer driving season on the demand for transport fuel in the summer months. Figure 6.11 shows tanker freight rates for crude oil transport for three ship sizes, measured in current Worldscale.

6.10 ENVIRONMENTAL ISSUES

In the past decade, environmental issues have come to the fore and have helped raise the quality of the services provided by tanker operators. One might argue that some of the improvement has been generated by political and public reaction to major oil spills, but there also appears to be a growing emphasis in the industry itself on both the quality of the ship and of the crew which operates it.

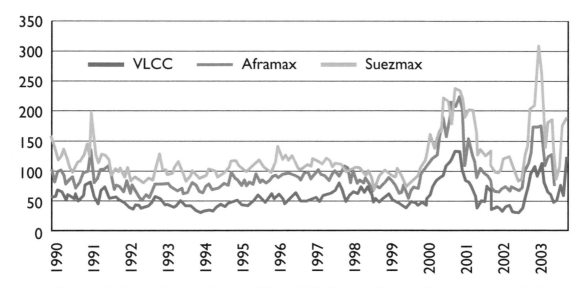

Fig 6.11 Monthly Tanker Freight Rates, 1990 – 2003 (Source: Derived from data supplied by Gibsons Shipbrokers Ltd.)

The principal driver of this change was originally the American reaction to the *Exxon Valdez* pollution incident in Alaska in 1989. In the USA, the Oil Pollution Act was passed in 1990, under which doubled-hull tankers were to become mandatory for vessels trading to US jurisdictions. The US led the way at the IMO and the phasing in of double-hulled vessels for all operators by 2015 was agreed. After the incidents of the *Erika* in December 1999, and the *Prestige* in November 2002, the EU proposed an accelerated phased withdrawal of single hull vessels by 2010, instead of 2015. Despite the longer term structural concerns for the integrity of double-hull vessels, this became the only viable solution to reducing the spill potential in the event of a tanker accident.

The introduction of double-hull technology provided a major spur to tanker investment, transforming the fleet. Whereas in the 1990s VLCCs were largely ageing vessels, the sector was transformed by the renewal program. So too have the other segments, creating younger, more efficient and safer oil transportation.

There is evidence that oil pollution from tanker accidents or operations is now significantly lower than it was in the 1980s and 1990s. In addition, the introduction of the ISM code in 1998 has transformed attitudes to safety in the shipping industry. State port inspections have kept shipowners on their toes in terms of operational quality.

Finally, the standardising of crew certification through the STCW system has probably helped raise the standard of training of crew. This standard became mandatory in 2001. These processes have all helped to raise the standard of shipping quality and contributed to the reduction in pollution incidents noted earlier.

6.11 CONCLUSION

After reviewing the driving force of tanker demand, changes in regional production and consumption patterns, the principal factors affecting the growth of oil tonne/mile demand was outlined. The price of oil played a key role, not directly, but because of its macro-economic effects on world economic growth rates over the period 1970-1990.

The structure of the tanker market was examined and it was shown that it has become even more open and competitive than in the 1960s, when it was already considered by many to be competitive. The possibility of market segmentation was briefly discussed and a model of freight rate determination was introduced. Factors that made tanker rates more volatile were examined in the penultimate sections.

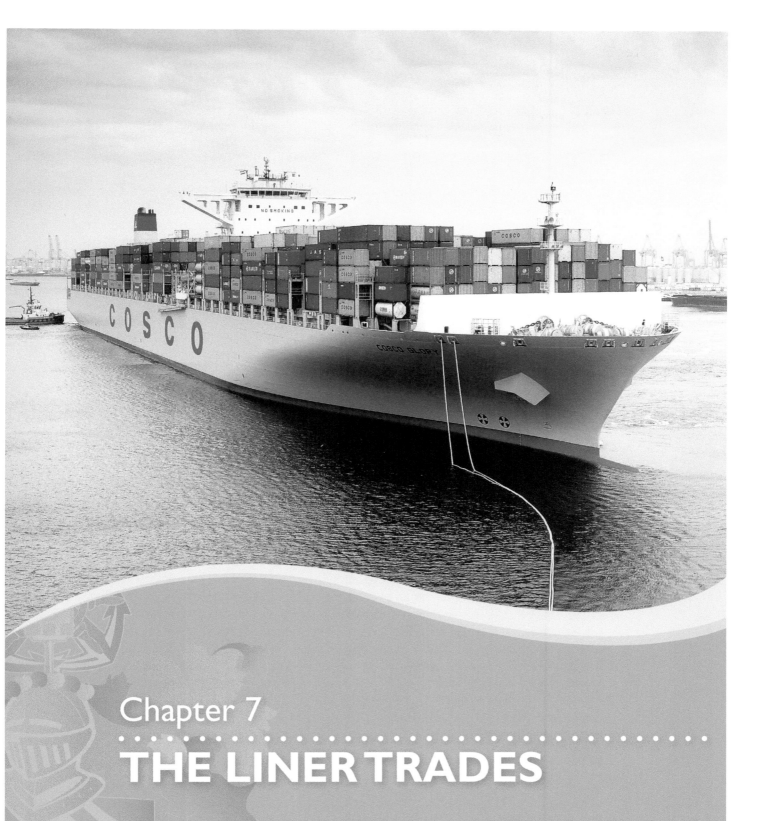

Chapter 7

THE LINER TRADES

The largest bank note was the Chinese 1 Kwan, printed in the 14th century, measuring 9 X 13 inches.

7 INTRODUCTION

In this chapter the development of another important sector of the shipping markets, the liner trade, is reviewed. In contrast to the bulk trades considered in previous chapters, there are many significant differences. They vary both in terms of the nature of the service being offered and the consumers and in the way the service is provided by liner shipping companies. Essentially, liner trades may be viewed, in economic terms, as being an oligopolistic market structure, in contrast to the competitive markets so far considered. But it must be emphasised at the outset that this does not mean an absence of competition in this market. It means that the forms of competition that are present are not simply observable by market price. Perfect competition implies that operators compete solely on a price basis, but once market structures alter, many other types of competitive behaviour between companies can be observed and this is true of the liner trade.

The second point to note is that liner trades have been revolutionised by the widespread introduction of containerisation. Some of the early classic analyses of liner trades, widely referred to in the literature, are now very dated in terms of the technology that they describe. Nevertheless, the economic organisation of these trades cannot really be understood without some knowledge of the historical development of the trades and an important institutional arrangement that still exists today, the liner conference. Knowing the history and the effects of containerisation on this sector helps to explain the current developments in this rapidly growing sector of shipping.

7.1 DEFINITION OF A LINER SHIPPING SERVICE

The liner trades differ radically from other sectors of the industry. It cannot be defined on the basis of the individual specialised technology of the vessel such as a tanker. Rather, liners consist of a group of widely differing vessel types. It is therefore more appropriate to seek a definition in terms of operational characteristics rather than technology used. The key feature distinguishing liners from other sectors is that they are engaged in the provision of scheduled services between specific ports. Scheduled services are those operating at a regular frequency on a particular trade route according to a published timetable. According to Bennathan and Walters in *The Economics of Ocean Freight Rates Praeger: New York, page 2-3, 'The main operating distinction between tramp and liner is that the latter runs on regularly scheduled services advertised in advance, whereas the former has no schedule and picks up traffic where and when it can profitably compete: A liner service is in quite a different class from a tramp carrier. The value of the service may be reflected in the fact that it is available at regular intervals, whether it is used or not. The shipper, therefore, may regard the availability of a regular service as being of considerable value to him.'*

Two points arise, which are still relevant today.

Firstly, the service being provided has to be regular and scheduled. Users of the service know that sailings to a certain region or set of ports will take place on a certain day at a certain time, week in, week out. Shippers can therefore rely on their goods being delivered to the destinations within a very narrow time frame.

Secondly, the availability of cargo space. The port of Hamburg claims to be able to load a containerised cargo onto a vessel with just 20 minutes notice. While this claim may be exaggerated, it emphasises the fact that there must be capacity on the vessel to accept such cargo at such a short notice, there must be available carrying capacity on the vessel or vessels.

C. E. Fayle, in an earlier work, *A Short History of the World's Shipping Industry*, provides another definition which is still relevant today. *'Strictly speaking, a liner service implies today a fleet of ships, under common ownership or management, which provides a fixed service, at regular intervals, between named ports and offer themselves as common carriers of any goods or passengers requiring shipment between those ports and ready for transit by their sailing dates. A fixed itinerary inclusive in a regular service and an obligation to accept cargo from all comers and to sail, whether full or not, on the date fixed by the public schedule. These, and not the size and the speed of the ship, nor the number of vessels in the fleet, are what distinguish the liner from the tramp seeker or general trader. The ship which can be hired as a whole by the voyage or by the month, to load such cargo and carry it between such ports as the Charterer may require.'*

This definition is worth reading several times. The following points are worth emphasising.

1. Fleet of ships under common ownership or management;

2. fixed service at regular intervals;

3. between named ports;

4. common carrier obligations;

5. vessels sail whether full or not.

7.1.1   Fleet of ships under common ownership or management

The typical liner service requires the use of several vessels if it is to provide a regular frequent service. Normally most liner services are defined on a minimum frequency of 14 days, as for example, in the USA's Federal Maritime Commission (FMC) determination of a liner operator for the purposes of the 1984 US Shipping Act. Table 7.1 below shows a representative sample of two modern liner companies providing a service between North Europe and the Far East, with Ports of Call and number of vessels. At least eight largish container vessels are used to provide a fortnightly service calling at each port.

The examples in Table 7.1 indicate that this type of service is operated by alliances of liner companies; they have pooled their shipping resources to provide a jointly-operated liner service from North Europe to the Far East and back again. Although the vessels are not under a single owner, they are in effect being managed by one, namely the alliance. Note also that the two services quoted overlap in several ports, but provide a specific access to others. This is a common feature in liner services.

7.1.2   Fixed services at regular intervals

Another key feature of the definition is that the service is guaranteed to shippers. The vessels will sail according to the timetable. This means that shippers can rely on a steady flow of cargo to their warehouses or customers, which is increasingly important now that manufacturers use 'Just-in-Time' production methods to minimise inventory costs. JIT depends upon reliable and regular delivery services at all stages of the supply chain.

Operator	Ports of Call	Vessel Nos.	Vessel Capacity teus
Maersk/Sea-Land	Gothenburg, Rotterdam, Southampton, Algeciras, Singapore, Hong Kong, Kaohsiung, Kobe, Nagoya, Yokohama, Kaohsiung, Hong Kong, Singapore, Rotterdam, Hamburg, Gothenburg	9	3,500-6,000
YangMing/K-Line	Hamburg, Felixstowe, Le Havre, Hong Kong, Kaohsiung, Kobe, Nagoya, Tokyo, Kaohsiung, Hong Kong, Singapore, Rotterdam, Hamburg	8	3,456-3,502

Table 7.1 (Source: 'Europe/Far East Trades under pressure', Lloyd's Shipping Economist, October 1996, p13)

7.1.3 Vessels sail, full or not

The liner vessel is obliged to sail according to the published timetable. Shippers expect their cargoes to be delivered to the correct port at the correct time, so reliability and running-to-time are paramount. The obligation to maintain the schedule means that vessels may often sail with less than a full cargo load. This is especially likely to occur if trade volumes are unbalanced between outbound and inbound legs of a route, since the capacity required will be determined by the volume on the busiest leg. This means that the thin leg will operate with vessels trading at low levels of space utilisation. It follows that one of the prime concerns of the liner operators is to ensure that cargo carrying capacity is utilised to the maximum. Many of the distinctive features of liner tariff structures flow from this concern.

One final point to be noted is the mention of passenger traffic. The decline of passenger liners coincided with the rise in international air travel, which became a cheaper and much quicker alternative. Passenger traffic is still important in two sectors, the short sea ferry trades and the cruise market. While there are still vessels designed to carry some passengers and freight, numbers are greatly diminished and they are not a significant part of the market. (See Table 7.2 for numbers)

In general, the market has shown signs of increased specialisation, as vessels are designed to meet the specific requirements of market niches. Figure 7.2 below highlights this, by indicating the way that the Passenger and Cargo Liner trades have evolved into a number of segments, reflecting changing market conditions over time. The specialist vessels indicated in Figure 7.2 are not comprehensive, but the diagram clearly indicates the way in which the traditional all-purpose vessel of sixty years ago has evolved in specialised sectors.

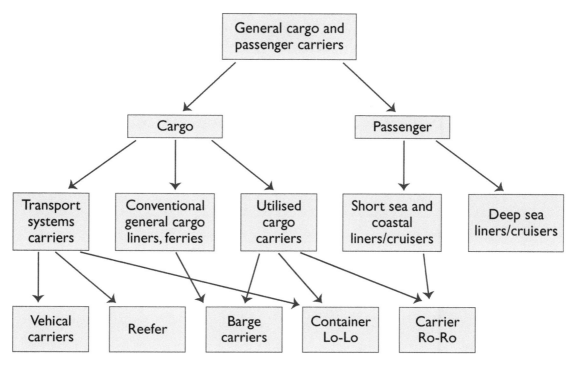

Fig 7.1 Development of Modern Liner Services

7.2   SHIP TYPES SERVING IN THE LINER TRADES

Figure 7.1 revealed the evolution of vessel types meeting a variety of needs gathered under the term General Cargo. Table 7.2 shows how the major components of these ship types have evolved from 1980. The table provides data on gross tonnage, numbers and average ages of the vessels in that sector. Note that the minimum size of vessel included in the data reduced from 300-gt to 100-gt from 1995. This explains the big jump in ship numbers between 1990 and 1995. For this reason, average growth rates for the recent period are calculated using data from 1995 onwards. A number of points are worthy of note.

1. For the period 1995 – 2006 the annual average growth of container vessels, both lift-on lift-off or lo-lo in gt was 9.6% compound, with the average age of vessel remaining constant at 10 years. This is well below the average ages seen in the rest of the Table. The average size has increased from 22,000-gt to 28,000-gt. This trend of rising numbers and increasing size will continue. In 2006 - 2007 several vessels of 11-12,000-teu were taken into service and the ship-builders order books were bulging. Container vessels now became the dominant sector by dwt and gt. The increase in share captured over the past decade is well clearly illustrated in Figure 7.2.

2. Both general cargo vessel numbers and gt have continued to remain stable or decline slightly, a trend that has been noted since 2000. Numbers fall from 17,180 in 1995 to 16,479 in 2006, an annual average decline of 0.6 per cent. Average size declined from 3,300-gt to 3,200, while average age rose from 21 to 24 years. Declining numbers and rising age imply a fall in the relative importance of the sector. This is clearly brought out in Figure 7.3. It is clear that as containerisation extends its reach to trades not previously large or important enough to be unitised, the market share of these vessels will continue to decline. It must be noted that this does not necessarily imply that they will completely disappear, since growing total trade volumes combined with falling market shares may still mean that demand volumes can increase. There will always remain trades where volumes are too irregular or cargoes too specific for the liner services to capture the business.

3. The number of specialist vessels has also increased. Roll-on roll-off (RoRo) cargo vessels have become more popular, reaching 35.3 million-gt in 2006, and growing at 5.0% per year since 1995. These vessels serve short sea shipping and with greater use of containers on many services,

integration into the logistics chain requires more of these vessels. Some services carry cargo only and these ships are ideal for this kind of service. Refrigerated cargo ships and reefers, have suffered a different fate. Reefer numbers increased from 336 in 1980 to 529 in 1996. From 1995 to 2006, numbers declined and gt fell by 0.8% per year. Average size has hovered around 6,500-gt and age rose. Reefers have faced competition from refrigerated containers being carried in Lo-Lo vessels. For example, more bananas are moved by refrigerated container than by reefer. This substitution process restricts the potential for reefers. The globalisation of manufacturing trade, particularly the car industry, has created a market for dedicated car carriers moving completed vehicles from production country to distribution centres.

4. Another specialist sector which shows considerable expansion is the Cruise Liner business, which grew at 4.8% compound over the period 1980 -1996 in gt terms, or by 1.8% per year in number terms. Over the period 1995–2006, the sector accelerated its growth to 8.3% per year in gt and now there are 12.6m gt of cruise vessels, dominating the passenger sector. The period has seen younger age groups going on cruises and larger and larger vessels being introduced. The *Allure of the Seas*, and the *Oasis of the Seas* are at present the largest. These sister ships are 225,000-gt and carry around 6,200 people onboard. It is interesting to note the high average age of these vessels, ranging from a youthful 22 years in 1980, to 25 in 1987, to its present 24 years.

5. The Passenger/General Cargo sector, with numbers falling from 351 in 1995 to 347 in 2006 and with gt stagnant. This sector is clearly the one that may well have only a limited long term future, so the twin pressures of unitisation and specialisation may limit the opportunities for this ship type in the future.

6. Overall, the average compound growth rate for all vessels over the period 1980-1996 was 2% per year, when measured by vessel's gt, using the data for ships greater than 600-gt . For the data shown in Table 7.2 for the period 1995-2006, the growth rate in total gt is 4.8% compound. It would appear that the liner trades have enjoyed a better period in the past 15 years than they did in the period 1980 – 1996.

Three clear trends can be identified from Figure 7.2 and Table 7.2.

1. The rise of the container ship as the most common form of liner cargo transportation.

2. The separation of passengers from cargo, as vessels specialise in one or the other of these now distinct market sectors of deep-sea shipping.

3. The decline in the importance of the general cargo vessel which is clearly being substituted by other ship types, but will retain a niche, serving trades without container equipment at ports.

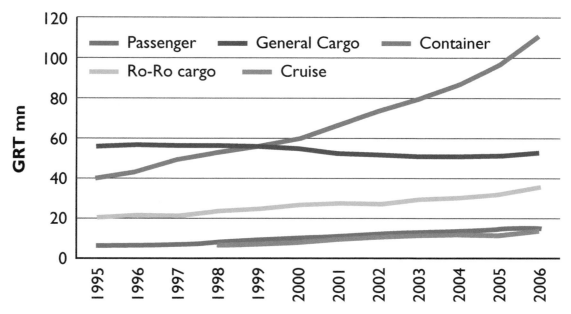

Fig 7.2 Liner Cargo Fleet Trends, Selected Ship Types, 1995 - 2006 (Source: Derived from Table 7.2)

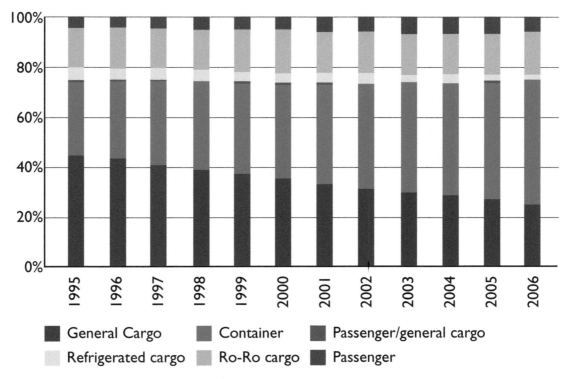

Fig 7.3 Ship Type Shares of Liner Trades 1995 - 2006 (Source: Derived from Table 7.2)

Note: Shares relative to total of ship types shown in Table 7.2

		1980	1985	1990	1995	1996	1997	1998	1999	2000	2001	2002	2003	2004	2005	2006
General Cargo	No.	4857	4123	3323	17180	17511	17467	16842	16880	16755	16466	16448	16253	15859	16086	16479
	GRT.	47.7	43.4	36.9	56.8	57.2	56.6	55.8	56.0	54.9	53.2	52.1	51.2	50.8	51.9	53.1
	Age	13	14	15	21	21	21	20	21	22	22	24	23	24	24	24
Passenger/ General Cargo	No.	74	41	28	351	346	342	340	348	347	339	342	340	339	329	347
	GRT.	0.8	0.4	0.3	0.7	0.6	0.6	0.6	0.6	0.7	0.6	0.6	0.6	0.6	0.6	0.6
	Age	25	24	24	29	29	30	3.1	31	31	31	33	33	33	34	33
Container	No.	575	935	998	1763	1949	2187	2382	2457	2590	2756	2918	3055	3238	3531	3904
	GRT.	12.8	19.0	24.9	38.7	43.1	48.9	53.2	55.3	60.2	66.8	72.9	78.4	85.8	96.3	110.7
	DWT					48.6	55.5	61.0	63.4	69.1	76.6	83.9	90.5	99.2	111.7	128.3
	Age	8	8	9	10	10	10	9	10.0	10	10	11	10	10	11	10
Refrigerated Cargo	No.	336	407	473	1446	1441	1443	1441	1415	1414	1407	1334	1272	1242	1236	1231
	GRT.	3.0	3.7	4.3	7.2	7.2	7.1	7.2	7.0	7.0	6.9	6.7	6.4	6.2	6.2	6.6
	Age	9	10	11	16	16	17	17	17	18	19	20	19	20	21	22
Ro-Ro Cargo	No.		7	7	1673	1711	1742	1769	1844	1882	1871	1904	1921	1959	2092	2300
	GRT.	0.0	0.3	0.3	20.4	21.3	22	23.3	25.3	27.1	27.5	28	29.1	30.6	32.8	35.3
	Age		0	5	15	13	16	16	17	17	17	19	18	18	18	18
Passenger	No.	232	237	264	2613	2720	2828	2833	2940	3019	3082	3165	3265	3314	3414	3489
	GRT.	2.6	2.9	3.6	6.2	6.8	7.1	7.8	8.5	9.3	10.3	11.3	12.1	12.9	13.4	14.1
	Age	22	24	24	18	19	19	19	19	20	20	22	21	22	22	23
Of which Cruise	No.							337	345	357	372	392	432	441	456	465
	GRT.							6.5	7.2	8.0	8.9	9.9	10.7	11.5	11.9	12.6
	Age						24	24	24	24	23	24	22	21	22	22
Total GRT		**66.8**	**69.7**	**70.4**	**130.0**	**136.2**	**142.3**	**154.4**	**159.9**	**167.2**	**174.2**	**181.5**	**188.5**	**198.4**	**213.1**	**220.4**

Table 7.2 Development of Ship Types in the Liner Trades
(source: World Merchant Fleet Statistics, Lloyds Register of Shipping, various years: ICS Tutorship Manual 1997)

Notes: 1. Age measured in years. 2. GRT is in millions. 3. Some series are for 300gt or more for 1980 – 1990; 100gt or more for 1995 on.

7.3 THE NATURE OF DEMAND FOR DEEP-SEA LINER SERVICES

Thousands of different cargo types are moved by liner services, with many different products being carried in the same vessel. This makes discussing the demand for liner services qualitatively different from the dry bulk and wet trades, where cargoes are of one type and carried for one charterer in a privately chartered vessel.

The huge variety of products are carried under the liner's common carrier commitment. This means that the carrier is obliged to carry anything legally offered by the shipper, subject to the usual health and safety regulations.

Cargoes carried range from personal computers, electronic components, hi-fi, textiles, tea, coffee, cement, plastics, cooled cargoes, fresh and processed fruit, wool, hides, agricultural and industrial machinery, cars (both components and assembled), broken glass and many others. Note that the majority of these products are relatively durable, especially when stored under controlled conditions, so that shippers are interested in the regular delivery of their shipments, to match anticipated consumption in the destination country.

As a result of dealing with so many cargoes, liner companies have evolved a highly complex structure of pricing with tariffs for classes of commodities. Essentially, every potentially-transportable commodity is allocated a product group or class and charged accordingly. The structure of these prices will be explored in a later section of this chapter.

Although little can be said about the precise type of cargo carried because of the huge diversity, there are some essential characteristics common to all cargoes moved by the liner trades. These are to be found in the nature of the service offered to shippers by the liner companies. Alderton, in his *Reeds Sea Transport: Economics and operations 5th edition*, quotes the results of a survey of a number of American shippers who were asked to rank the relative importance of a number of features of the liner service. The results are displayed in Table 7.3.

The table highlights the importance placed upon timeliness and delivery, with price coming third. Note that Ford, as a shipper of cars, puts safety record above price, and also emphasises the financial stability of the supplier. It does not want to commit itself to suppliers who may go out of business and disrupt its logistics supply chain in the process.

This emphasis on reliability has become more and more important over the past twenty years as shipping companies become more intermodal in their operations. Many large liner companies now offer integrated door-to-door freight services to shippers, having diversified into land-based transport operations. This level of integration requires:

1. Land transport from factory to terminal;

2. movement from terminal to port, if cargo consolidation takes place off port limits;

3. port terminal operations, transfer to vessel;

4. vessel movement to destination port;

5. movement from destination port to shippers final destination.

	What Shippers Want		What Ford Wants
1	On-Time Delivery	1	Safety Record
2	Overall Responsiveness	2	Price
3	Price	3	Financial Stability
4	On-Time Pick-Up	4	Transit Performance
5	Transit Time	5	Handling of Damage Claims.
6	Service Territory	6	Equipment avail/suit.
7	Billing Accuracy	7	Equipment Condition
8	Correct Equipment	8	EDI Capability
9	Degree of Control	9	Ease of Doing Business
10	Claims Processing	10	Innovative Initiative
11	Tracing Capability		

Table 7.3 Ranking of Service Characteristics by Shippers (Source: Alderton (2005), quoted from American Shipper Survey, 1990)

Efficient use of these elements has led to the processes being increasingly integrated. One significant innovation which has materially helped in this process is the use of containerised cargo for freight. This is briefly discussed in the next section.

7.4   THE CONTAINER REVOLUTION

In 1966, the first deep-sea container service was started by Sea-Land, a company set up by Malcolm Maclean, based on his innovative development of containerised truck freight in the USA. The system used 20'x8'x8' metal boxes, or containers, which were transported to and from the port using trucks and chassis. The containers were stored on the chassis, and then loaded onto a dedicated vessel for sea transport. The vessel was fitted with cell guides to locate and secure the containers, which were lifted onto and from the ship using large gantry cranes.

This system of cargo handling revolutionised the liner trades. Traditionally, general cargo vessels spent a large proportion of time in port, being loaded and unloaded by gangs of stevedores. Cargo handling was slow, prone to high rates of pilferage and was a peculiar art, since cargo had to be packed and secured safely. But it also had to be stowed in the right location for retrieval at its destination. The development of a standard unit has transformed all this. The large dock labour component has been swept away, replaced by large capital investments in sophisticated ships, strengthened quaysides for container storage, container storing, stacking and retrieval systems, and container stuffing services, which are now often in the secure arena of the shipper's own premises. Very little container filling is carried out at the port or terminal.

The huge capital investment required was repaid with a dramatic increase in productivity. Container ships now spend little time in port - they can be loaded and discharged in a matter of hours, rather than weeks. A 1970 study by Lambert Brothers showed that one new container vessel was likely to displace up to five conventional cargo vessels in terms of cargo moved per year. Container movements per hour are such that the tonnes of cargo moved per hour has grown tremendously.

The investment effort required to develop the system has also created fundamental changes in the structure and organisation of liner trades themselves. In the 1970s, a new form of shipping organisation emerged, the consortia. A number of UK shipping lines, which included Ocean Steamship Company, P&O, Shaw Savill & Albion and the Cayzer Group merged to form Ocean

Containers Limited or OCL. They needed to do this to become large enough to finance investment in new technology as well as to create enough trade volume to make the investment worthwhile. This organisation later became P&OCL (O), which itself merged with NedLloyd in 1996 to form a new joint company, P&O/NedLloyd. This was taken over by Maersk in 2004, reflecting the continuing evolution of the industry. The process of change and concentration into larger shipping companies still continues. Recent developments in the nature and structure of liner organisations are discussed in Section 7.9.

7.5 PRICING BEHAVIOUR IN THE LINER AND TRAMP TRADES

The dynamic behaviour of freight rates in the bulk dry cargo trades has been covered in chapter 5. A characteristic feature is the high level of volatility of the rates on a monthly or daily basis. This was explained by the competitive nature of the sector, creating a situation where the market rate was determined by the interplay of demand and supply. Consider the data shown in Figure 7.2 below. Lloyd's Shipping Economist (LSE) data shows the behaviour of freight rates in the dry bulk trades for the year of 1995-6. The other information on the graph shows the rates charged on a number of unitised conference routes, that is, the average rates charged for the shipment of a standard 20-foot container. The data has been converted into index number form for ease of comparison.

The striking feature of the rates charged on the unitised routes is constancy over the period. There is no variation whatever in the rates quoted by the LSE on the conference routes over the period, in contrast to the single voyage dry bulk rate.

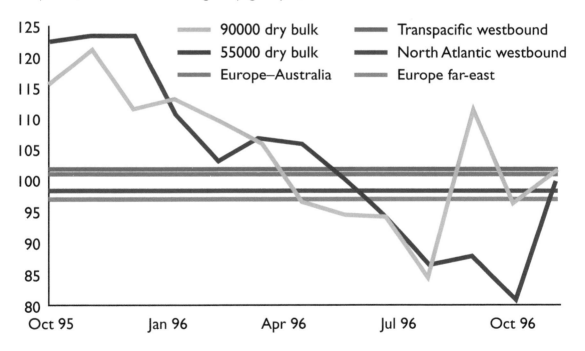

Fig 7.3 Relative Behaviour of Liner and Tramp Freight Rates 1995 (Source: Rates and Prices Data, Lloyd's Shipping Economist, February 1997)

Note: Data converted to index form. 1993 average is used for each of the rates as the base value.

The interesting question which arises is: Why are there no variations in the rates for containerised cargo over the year?

It is very clear that there is a trend decline in the dry cargo bulk rates, with quite large variations on a monthly basis. If demand and supply works in the bulk trades, why are there no corresponding variations in the market rate for unitised cargoes?

There are two answers to this. The first is to use an economist's concept of administered prices. This term captures the idea that in certain market situations the market price does not reflect the daily fluctuations in demand relative to supply. Administered prices are common in markets where supply is controlled by the main company or group of companies providing the product, which is a feature of oligopolistic market structures explained as competition among the few. Many industrial markets have this characteristic. For example, car prices in many European countries remain the same for a year, and are adjusted annually, to reflect changes in costs, not changes in demand conditions. Competition is fierce in the car market, but it is fought mainly on non-price terms, via styling, accessories, location of dealerships and quality differentiation. Price competition, in the sense of a weekly variation in the price to reflect present demand conditions, is notably absent.

Administered prices may exist either if it is expensive to alter them on a frequent basis or if the supply companies co-operate to regulate tariffs charged by all companies operating similar services on a particular route. There is an element of truth in both of these explanations.

The liner trade carries thousands of cargo types. The prices book runs to several volumes. In a pre-computer era, the labour required both to update these prices on a weekly basis and to keep the shippers informed was significant. The administrative costs imposed on the firm would be huge. A far cheaper alternative is to regulate the tariff structure, altering rates less frequently at perhaps three monthly or six monthly intervals. This also has the merit of providing shippers with some degree of certainty as to the level of freight charges that they face over the next few months. One explanation of rate stability may lie in the fact that the transaction costs, or menu costs, of altering prices were too large for anything other than intermittent price changes.

Stability of one liner organisation's rates may save administration costs, but these can be negated if rival liner services try to compete by price. This in fact was a problem of the early liner services, in which there were marked cycles of boom and bust for shipowners in the 1860s and 1870s. But if liner companies go bust, they fail in their obligation to provide a common carrier service to shippers. Shipping companies importing tea on the UK-Calcutta route agreed to set up a conference of shipping lines, who would agree to offer a regular service in co-operation with other conference members and who agreed to charge a set of common tariffs to all shippers. The conference system was born and despite rumours of its demise, there are several hundred still active today. It is good to bear in mind that since October 2008 the European Union holds a ban on Liner Conferences to and from the European Union.

This is the second element of the explanation; many liner routes are still characterised by the presence of a conference organisation, which organises and co-ordinates the economic activities of its members. In economic terms, such collusion usually means less competition, more profits for the shipping lines, less innovation and dynamism than in a competitive industry. The conference system is explored in the following section.

The pricing examples given above are perhaps a little forced. While the LSE data on published rates is accurate, the key rates are not the published tariffs, but the rates negotiated between the liner company and the client, be it Ford, GlaxoSmithKlein or a large freight forwarder. The actual rates agreed between the two parties are confidential. 'Containerisation International' publishes estimates of market rates and these do show greater variability than the published rates, but still much less variability than those observed in dry bulk and tankers. One study, by Oksana Bateman (*Are Liner Conferences a necessary institution in modern shipping? MSc Dissertation, London Metropolitan University, London*) tested this formally, by using a measure of the conditional variance of liner and dry cargo rates. Using the statistical measure of the variance does not allow for the average value of the series, but the conditional variance does. It permits meaningful comparisons across different series.

	Coefficient of Variation
Eur/US WB	0.055
US/Eur EB	0.012
Asia/Eur WB	0.116
Eur/Asia EB	0.109
Asia/US EB	0.123
US/Asia WB	0.113
HandySize	0.211
Suezmax	0.248
VLCC AG-Japan	0.309
Dry Cargo 120,000-dwtT	0.254

Table 7.4 Coefficient of Variation Values for Selected Routes/Types (source: Bateman (2004), Table 7, p. 59)

Note: Data for period 1993–2003

Bateman showed that in nearly every case in the sample period chosen, dry cargo and tanker rates were much more volatile than those in the liner sector. Table 7.4 shows that the most volatile liner trade route is only half as volatile as the least volatile series in the dry bulk and tanker segments. The lack of volatility is clearly seen in Figure 7.3

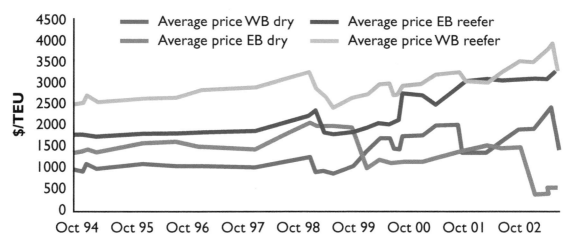

Fig 7.4 Published Ocean Freight Rates for TACA (source: Bateman (2004) op. cit. Graph 4 p38)

Note: TACA is the Trans-Atlantic Conference Agreement

7.6 THE CONFERENCE SYSTEM: KEY INSTITUTIONAL ELEMENT OR HISTORIC THROWBACK?

After the inauguration of the UK-Calcutta conference in 1875, many other conferences came into being. In their 1973 study, Deakin and Seward claimed that there were 360 active deep-sea conferences, with memberships ranging between two and 40 lines. This statistic was repeated regularly over the next 25 years, many comparatively recent texts still quote this 30-year-old figure. An OECD study into the liner trades estimated that 150 were still active in 2001, with membership also ranging from two to 40 lines in different conferences. Some are well organised, with offices, meetings and a secretariat, such as the Far East Freight Conference (FEFC) based in London, others less so.

In essence, a conference becomes a monopoly supplier of the shipping capacity on that route, if it is able to enrol all liner companies serving a particular trade between named ports. It is important to note that this monopoly is only over the liner service component of the trade. Liner conference members still face competition from tramp operators and from air transport, for certain types of cargoes to be moved between the two ports. But the key element in the conference is that its members limit the degree of internal competition between themselves.

This limitation of competition is achieved by entering into various legal agreements. The main areas covered are:

1. Agreements on common tariffs to be charged to shippers;

2. cargo allocation arrangements;

3. revenue pooling arrangements.

These arrangements can become very sophisticated and require monitoring by the conference organisation. A simple model of a profit maximising cartel, developed in Appendix 1 of this chapter, shows why such arrangements might be needed. It is often insufficient to regulate prices alone, because competition is then diverted into other forms, such as over-expansion of the tonnage supply or by individual lines undercutting on their partners by offering secret discounts on the official tariff rates to key shippers.

Deakin and Seward pointed out that many conferences organised sophisticated cargo allocation schemes under which certain lines were allowed to load and discharge at certain specified ports. Sailing frequency was regulated or limits set on the amount of cargo that they could lift. Conferences spread rapidly after their 1875 inauguration. Jansson and Shneerson in *Liner Shipping Economics Chapman and Hall: London* state that: *'There is no accurate figure available for the total number of conferences in operation'*. They go on to state: *'Anyway, conferences exist in most liner trades and in practically all intercontinental trades'*.

Two very important trading routes for liner shipping are the Europe/Far East and trans-Pacific trades. In 1996, for the Europe/Far East trade, conference lines held 67% of the Eastbound slot capacity and 65% Westbound, with non-conference lines accounting for the remainder. Conference members held a much smaller proportion, 56% for the trans-Pacific. These shares are still large enough for the sectors to be classified as an oligopoly or monopoly under present UK competition law.

Since the abolition of the block exemption for Liner Conferences by the European Commission in October 2008, the trade to and from the European Union can no longer be handled by a liner conference. However, other forms of co-operation between liner companies are still allowed as long as they do not include tariff agreements (e.g. alliances).

7.6.1 Activities of the conference organisation

Conferences essentially provide a means for member lines to co-ordinate and run joint services and co-operate with each other. These functions may appear to be inconsistent with normal competitive behaviour where rivals act independently in all key decisions. Conferences also agree with other conferences where their geographic range starts and ends, in effect dividing the total market into distinct sectors.

The degree of co-operation starts with setting agreed common tariffs for shippers and progresses into more sophisticated arrangements covering tonnage provided, cargo lifting/discharge rights and, ultimately, revenue pooling.

7.6.2 Types of conferences

Two principal types can be observed: Open and Closed.

A closed conference was the original type. Essentially the liner companies would provide a monopoly service between two ports, with entry by other lines being permitted only by the unanimous agreement of its members. Since the existing lines would lose market share to any new entrant, this inhibits competition. Such conference structures became the subject of a number of government studies in the UK and the USA during the early 1900s. As a consequence of the 1916 US Shipping Act, later updated in the 1984, US Congress agreed that conferences would be exempt from the Anti-Trust legislation provided that such conference arrangements, which involved trading into and out of US ports, permitted the free entry of any company wishing to operate a liner service that agreed to be be bound by the rules of the conference.

Open conferences

As might be inferred from the previous paragraph, an open conference tries to regulate tariffs and capacity on a particular route, with new members free to join in the service provided they satisfy the rules and obligations of membership. The 1984 US Shipping Act states that such a commitment means the liner company being willing to operate a scheduled service with a minimum frequency of 14 days. Providing that condition is met, existing members cannot prevent entry to any trade operating to or from a US Port.

The 1984 Act also has another important clause. The clause states that *'Each conference agreement must provide, that any member of the conference may take independent action on any rate'*. This gives to any member of a US related conference the right to compete by cutting rates, which of course defeats the principal object of a conference.

One other point that applies to all conferences operating under the jurisdiction of the US legal code is that the 1984 Act expressly requires that freight rates must never be less than the marginal cost. One way of seeing the importance of this clause is how it relates to the ability of members to vary the rate. The US government has tried to limit the potential damage to liner operators that might be triggered by a rate war by laying down a lower limit for the rates.

7.6.3 The UNCTAD liner code

The emergence of new national shipping lines from the developing countries in the 1970s led to an international debate concerning the difficulties they faced in entering the conferences that often dominated trades. The code tried to regulate these trades by insisting on a 40-40-20 rule for cargo allocation, 40% each for the companies at the origination and destination areas and 20% for cross-traders. At the time the agreement was negotiated, an important agreement, known as the Brussels package, was introduced. In effect, it made the new code inapplicable to trades to and from Europe. The USA has never signed the Code. These two events prevented the code from being enforced on many major trades and it is now completely ineffective.

7.6.4 Conference pricing of cargoes

There are essentially two distinct issues to consider when exploring the structure of tariffs in the liner trades and inside conferences in particular. Firstly, no discussion is complete without a discussion of the way that conferences set their tariffs. Secondly, conferences have developed certain methods that are designed to limit competitive pressures on the market. These two aspects will be considered in turn.

Basis for charging

Delegates at the 1941 Inter-American Maritime Conference identified 27 different factors which were felt to influence the structure of freight rates charged in the liner trades. A study by the

Economic Commission for Latin America (ECLA) tested these factors against real world data using regression analysis. The study found that it could reduce these factors to two key determinants of the rate structure, namely the unit value of the commodity and the cargo stowage factor. An econometric model of the freight rates set for companies operating on UK related conferences found similar results, with demand based unit value accounting for $2/3$ rds of the explained variation in rates and cost related factors, primarily the stowage factor, the other third.

Table 7.5 clearly shows the large variation in the rate that was charged for moving containers of different commodities between Germany and Israel in 1985. Note the highest rate is for alloyed metals, followed by pharmaceuticals. These are both high unit value items. Wood, paper and machinery are priced much lower.

It should be noted that such pricing structures are continually evolving as new products are invented and old ones die away. The conferences used to regard the rate books, which were often massive volumes, as highly confidential documents to be kept in a very secure environment. While rate structures have been simplified, the essential characteristic still remains, which is to charge different prices for different commodity types, even though they now mainly all go by container.

Commodity Type	Price $
Food	4,225
Chemicals	4,400
Pharmaceuticals	4,665
Alloyed Metals	7,480
Wood and Paper	3,860
Machinery and Tools	3,620

Table 7.5 Tariffs per -teu by Commodity Type – Germany to Israel (Closed Conference) 1985

A number of commentators have suggested that since it costs the same to move a box, irrespective of what it contains, rates should be set at the same standard value, irrespective of content. This is known as FAK, or Freight All Kinds. Although there appears to be some merit in the argument, from an economics viewpoint, it can be said to be fallacious. Companies are quite right in charging by unit value as long as differences in unit value reflect differences in the underlying price elasticity of demand for the commodity. This point is explored in more detail below.

Limiting competitive pressures

There are two sources of competitive pressure; external and internal.

External pressure is brought to bear from

1. Air freight competition;

2. tramp shipping.

Air freight puts a limit on the rates that can be charged for high unit value, low weight cargo types. Air freight has grown steadily in the past decade and its major advantage is in moving items very quickly. Perishable high value items such as cut flowers or foodstuffs are often moved this way. The high transport cost is still a small proportion of the retail price of the cargo and it is essential that its freshness be preserved. Air freight still carries a small proportion of the total, because in many cases speed is not critical. Nevertheless, the existence of a substitute implies that the price of moving certain commodities will be more price sensitive as a result.

Large volume, low value, high weight cargoes can always be moved by tramp operators. Tramps have no common carrier obligation, nor do they need to keep to a published timetable. As a result, the operating costs may be lower than a liner's for certain volumes of cargo. In order to prevent tramps from gaining business, conferences have set low prices for the bulk commodities in which tramps have a potential advantage. These rates may indeed not cover the long-run average cost of providing the service but, in line with the 1984 US Shipping Act, they do cover the average incremental cost or marginal cost of lifting and moving that cargo.

Competition from air freight and tramps helps to determine the nature of the tariff structure set in the liner trades. It also implies that demand might be price sensitive at the top end, price insensitive in the middle and again price sensitive at the low unit value end of the market, given the competition from air freight and tramps.

In addition to the tariff structure, conferences often provide one of two types of tariff rebate scheme, which have the effect of increasing shipper loyalty. These are known as the deferred rebate scheme and the exclusive contract scheme. The deferred rebate operates by the conferences offering a refund on the published tariff rate to a shipper if they can show that over the previous six months they have not used a non-conference member's services to move their cargoes. Once the shipper has entered such a contract, this sum is in effect a fine to be imposed, should that shipper renege.

Under an exclusive contract scheme, the shipper agrees to send all their cargoes on conference member vessels, in exchange for a lower tariff. In this case, the tariff applies immediately.

Both of these schemes try to tie in shippers to conference members and thus reduce the potential loss of trade that might be caused by tramp and air freight competition.

Internal pressure

Internal pressure arises when individual liner companies try to undercut the agreement. This is usually dealt with in the conference by the setting up of more complex agreements between members, permitting the central organisation to monitor the activities of individual lines, to ensure that cargo lifting and capacity agreements are honoured.

Appendix 1 shows how the incentive to undercut is created.

7.7   PRICE DISCRIMINATION IN THE LINER TRADES

The discussion about the competitive pressures on the liner trades, generated by air freight and tramp operations, suggests that different commodities being carried by the liner trades have different freight rate elasticities of demand. Very high value commodities with low weight can use air freight as a substitute. The commodities in the middle, too heavy to be moved by air but too complex and valuable to be moved easily in bulk, are the commodities with the lowest own price elasticities of derived demand. Tramp competition for bulk cargoes again raises the price elasticity, since they become good substitutes for liner services. The liner trades, and conferences, have taken advantage of this fact by setting discriminatory prices. Price discrimination exists when the conference sets different rates to move different cargoes whose cost is the same; thus different rates for cargoes even when the marginal cost of these cargoes is identical. Shippers are not in themselves interested in the rates charged by the conferences for goods which are quite distinct from their own. This allows the conference members to practice price discrimination.

One might expect to observe a demand curve that looks like the one drawn in Figure 7.6. At high rates per tonne, demand is more elastic or flatter than in the midrange, which is where there is the least external competition. Low value commodities also face increased competition, generating a rather odd shaped demand or average revenue curve.

The principles of price discrimination are laid out in Appendix 2.

Essentially, profit maximising behaviour by a conference, or indeed, any oligopoly supplier such as one facing an inelastic demand curve, suggests that the market should be segmented and, if possible, different prices set in each segment. This always leads to the generation of greater total revenues and hence greater profit for a given level of total costs.

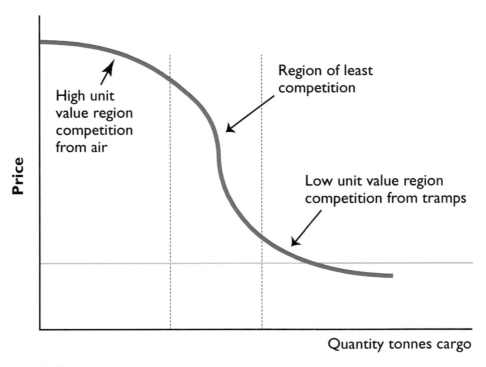

Fig 7.4 Elasticity of Demand

7.8   THE CONFERENCE PARADOX

On the face of it, the conference system has all the classic features of a joint-profit maximising cartel. The lines band together to reduce capacity and raise rates thus raising profits. Entry is prevented by the closed conference. The threat of dishonest dealing between members may be dealt with by the use of trade share agreements.

If the conference system is a powerful monopoly, one would expect it to generate large and sustained profits. Yet the empirical evidence is precisely the opposite. The Rochdale Commission of Enquiry into British Shipping in 1970 and Deakin and Seward's study in 1973 provided evidence that, if anything, profits were lower than in other shipping sectors. On the other hand, the 2002 OECD study found that for 16 publicly quoted liner companies, the return on equity for the period 1990-2000 averaged 10.55%, compared with the return for road, rail and freight equities of 9.1614%. However, this comparison is difficult to make as many of the quoted companies are multi-activity operators and the returns are for the whole company, not the liner shipping element alone. Determining the profitability of just the liner segment is problematic.

The fact that the shipping conference cartel members seemed to make low profits has become known as the conference paradox. Economists have evolved a number of different explanations for this anomaly.

1. The Short-run Profit Maximisation Hypothesis, also known as the utilisation maximisation hypothesis;

2. the Contestable Markets thesis;

3. the Empty Core thesis.

7.8.1 The short-run profit maximisation hypothesis

Most textbook models assume that companies maximise profits. There are two types to be considered: short-run and long-run profits. In the conference system, it is argued that there is a strong incentive to maximise short-run rather than long-run profit. This will actually reduce long-run profit.

Since costs are very largely fixed, this is more or less identical to maximising revenues. If all costs were fixed it would be exactly the same because there are very low marginal costs in the short-run. Stopford, in *Maritime Economics Routledge. London, p.182*, provides an estimate that as only 15% of total costs are variable, and there is over-capacity, the best thing to do is to generate as much revenue as possible. This is achieved by taking every extra unit of business in which the extra revenue is greater than or equal to the extra cost. But since the extra cost is very low, this means that you take business whose average cost is greater than the extra revenue, although the extra revenue is larger than extra cost.

This implies that low value cargo will be taken, as long as the above condition is satisfied, at a price which is less than its long-run costs. Thus there will be some cross-subsidisation of high price, profitable cargo in long-run terms by low price, unprofitable cargo.

The diagram below illustrates the concept.

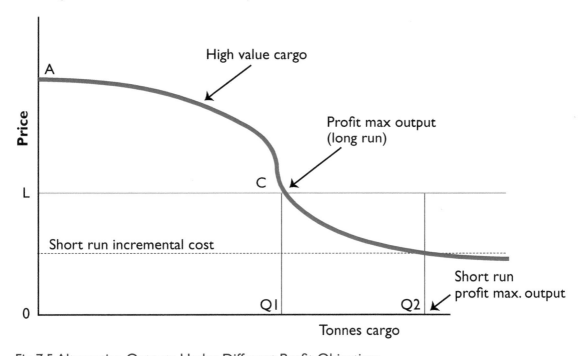

Fig 7.5 Alternative Outputs Under Different Profit Objectives

The implication of the existence of cross subsidisation is that profits are lower than they would otherwise be, hence this feature of the conference system generates lower long-run profits than might otherwise be expected.

The above figure implies that maximising long-run profits will lead to taking cargo quantities Q1 and accepting only high value cargo. But if short-run incremental costs are very low, and there is spare capacity, such as ships sailing half full, there is an incentive to forego long-run profits and take extra cargo, as long as the extra revenue derived from that cargo exceeds the associated additional costs. This generates an output level of Q2, which implies greater vessel utilisation. It also implies that some cargo is carried at unit prices which are lower than the long-run unit cost of providing the service. That is, they are being cross subsidised by the high value, profitable cargo.

Evidence

Figure 7.6 below, taken from J A Zerby and R M Conlon (1978), provides some support for the model.

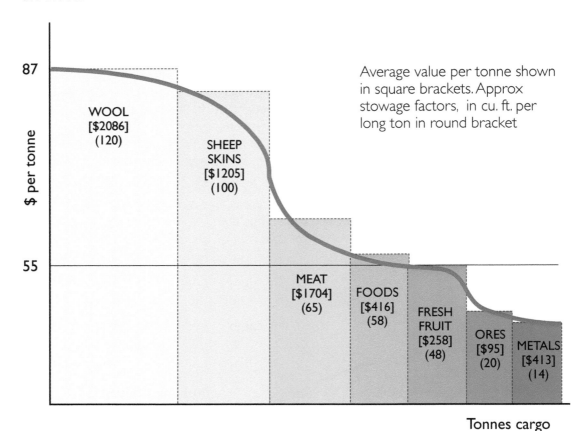

Fig 7.6 Behaviour of Average Rates on Australia-Europe Conference 1973

The bold curve reflects the estimated average revenue curve derived from data for the Australia-to-Europe conference for the years 1973-4. It shows very clearly the large difference in rates charged for the principal cargoes on that trade. The high value cargoes are carried at high freight rates. The rates taper off because of competition from air transport. The prices for metals and ores do not seem to cover average costs of $55 per tonne, but do cover the short-run incremental costs, which have been estimated at 20% of long-run average costs, as noted above. The estimated average incremental cost, in this case, is $11 a tonne.

The authors also estimate that the long-run costs were $55 per tonne and 36% of all Australian exports fell into categories which were charged close to that rate; cargoes such as meat, foods and fresh fruit.

The evidence quoted above does seem to provide tentative support for the persistence of the utilisation maximisation hypothesis and the average revenue schedule derived in Zerby and Conlon's study is very similar to that which can be hypothesised from the basic principle of price discrimination. It is a plausible explanation of the presence of cross subsidisation and low profits.

7.8.2 The contestable markets thesis

In 1981, the new President of the American Economics Association, William Baumol, gave his inaugural address. In it he summarised what has become known as the theory of Contestable Markets. It was meant to be an uprising in economic theory, as it claimed to develop techniques for modelling multi-product companies operating in several markets and developed new criteria for determining how competitive an industry or firm will be.

This new approach centred on the concept of potential competition. It was argued that even a single supplier of a product might be forced to behave in a very competitive way if conditions were right. The condition that ensured that a single supplier, a monopolist, would behave competitively, turned out to be the condition that new firms could enter and exit the market with no cost disadvantage to them.

This translates into the fact that a new entrant, if they chose to enter, would be able to offer the same quality of service as the present supplier, assuming it's a monopoly seller, at the same level of unit costs; it would therefore not be possible for the existing firm to drive the entrant out again by the simple device of cutting prices.

On the other hand, the new entrant, once in, would have no difficulty in leaving. It could find another company willing to purchase the assets needed to enter the market at the same price it paid for them.

Under these rather special conditions, it can be shown that the monopoly seller must behave exactly like a competitive firm. The firm may appear to have monopoly power, but potential competition is sufficient to prevent it from exploiting that power. If it were to raise prices above the competitive norm, potential entrants would become real entrants and the incumbent firm would be forced to reduce prices again.

This is the essence of contestable markets. It points to the fact that industries that appear to be monopolies or oligopolies may in fact be forced to act very competitively, provided the special conditions outlined above are satisfied.

Some economists have argued that the low profits of conference members can be explained in this way. They point to the fact that in many cases, non-conference lines can compete for business. They can also enter and leave trade routes quickly and easily, at little or no extra cost compared to the incumbent lines. For these reasons, they argue that liner conferences make only normal profit because they are forced to be competitive.

Other authors have not accepted this position. It has been argued that there are substantial exit costs in the liner trades. If a liner company goes bankrupt, the sale of its ships seldom realises the book value that they were recorded at. Entry involves a risk of substantial loss, if it is not successful.

7.8.3 The empty core thesis

The final alternative to be put forward is a recent and novel argument. It argues that the conference system was developed in order to create the very market in which it evolved. In essence, the market for regular scheduled sailings between fixed ports is only sustainable if the conference system acts to regulate competition for this type of business. In other words, the market would fail without the institutional structure given to it by the conference system itself.

The argument put forward to justify this position is a technical one, but its essence can be outlined. The cost structure of companies operating in the liner trades is such that the bulk of their costs are fixed. If companies have a high proportion of fixed costs, then ruinous price wars are more likely, because short-run variable costs, the costs determining the floor for prices, will be very low. There is good reason to expect that there will be marked price instability. But as liner companies are being driven out of the market at low prices, it is argued that there will be insufficient supply. In other words, the market will never converge to a stable market equilibrium.

The definition of a liner service is the provision of regular guaranteed services and this will not be possible under the above conditions. It follows that the conference structure provides the necessary stability as a replacement for the chaos that would occur if the market were left to its own devices.

7.9 DEVELOPMENTS IN THE LINER TRADES

7.9.1 The rise of global alliances

In the last thirty years, liner companies have got bigger, operating larger fleets and using larger capacity vessels. The capital needed to support such expansion has led to the emergence of container consortia providing such services jointly. One notable feature of the trade is the fact that these consortia can be found both inside and outside the conference system. There appears to be an increasing level of fluidity, as large individual companies switch in and out of conference membership and in and out of strategic alliances with other liner operators. The European Commission, prompted by complaints from large European shippers, has investigated a number of practices employed in these trades. In addition, the US Government has examined some of the capacity management agreements that have evolved on trades into and out of its ports.

7.9.2 Strategic alliances

The liner trades have continually evolved new routes and new services as a means of competing with each other and to meet evolving shipper needs. One innovation started in the mid 1980s was the introduction of two-way-round–the-world (RTW) services, a concept pioneered by Evergreen, the Taiwanese based container operator. A number of other companies followed suit, such as American President Lines, but it ran into difficulties and abandoned the service. In 2002, Evergreen also had to discontinue this kind of service. To offer such a service, the owners had to use Panamax vessels of about 5,000-teu. As much larger vessels were introduced that provided economies of scale, the competition became untenable.

Other lines have combined to run highly competitive services in strategic alliances, offering shippers fast, regular and reliable sailings. An example of joint services can be found in Table 7.1.

It has been argued by Midoro, R & Pitto A, in *A critical evaluation of strategic alliances in liner shipping, Maritime Policy & Management 2000, Vol. 27, No.1* that:

'The advent of such agreements, dubbed as global strategic alliances, can be considered as a substantial breakthrough in the industry's co-operative practice since, unlike previous partnerships, they are not limited to a single trade lane, but aim to cover every major route as well as a number of relevant north-south trades and regional/feeder links. At the same time, these strategic alliances extend their area of influence well beyond vessel operations towards the shared use of terminals, joint equipment management, inland transport and logistics, joint purchasing and procurement.'

The article goes on to suggest that: '"firms can achieve a satisfactory level of stability and efficiency by focusing on one or more of the three following measures, reduction in the number of partners, differentiation in their roles and contributions and co-ordination of sales and marketing activities'.

Existing links between alliance members were modified by the merger of P&O Containers and NedLloyd in 1996 as these companies had been in rival alliances in the past. The industry has claimed that such alliances are essential if the operators are to provide the necessary frequency of service at competitive rates. The pooling of resources permits the lowering of overhead, increased utilisation and better sailing schedules.

It should be pointed out that many of these arrangements exist outside the conference system. The market share of conferences on some routes has declined to 50% or 60% in recent years and in some, conferences are illegal. This does not mean that conferences are ineffective.

In trades where conference shares have declined, a relatively new phenomenon, Capacity Management Agreements, have arrived to take their place. On trans-Pacific routes, a Tonnage Stabilisation Agreement was introduced in 1989. In 1996, it covered 90% of the companies offering liner services on this route, although conference membership covered only 55% of the trade.

7.10 THE EUROPEAN COMMISSION AND THE LINER TRADES

The treaty of Rome prohibits anti-competitive agreements which significantly affect trade between the member states. It also prohibits abuse of dominant market positions. However, the Director General for Competition has power to grant block exemptions. The block exemption must be applied for, and companies participating in such agreements have to notify the DG Competition of the agreement.

The agreement will be approved if it contributes to improving the production or distribution of goods or economic progress, while allowing consumers a fair share of the resulting benefit, and which does not:

- Impose on the undertakings concerned restrictions which are not indispensable to the attainment of these objectives;

- Afford such undertakings the possibility of eliminating competition in respect of a substantial part of the products in question.

In 1986 the Council of the Commission approved Regulation 4056/86, which granted block exemption to liner conference agreements '*provided that they have as their objective the fixing of rates and conditions of carriage*'. It also permitted the other principal functions, namely the co-ordination of timetables, frequency of sailings and regulation of cargo capacity. The exemption is subject to the proviso that equivalently placed shippers will not be discriminated against without objective justification and that certain obligations are observed, such as the maintenance of price transparency through publicly available tariffs.

In 1994, the EC prohibited the Transatlantic Trade Agreement (TAA) and in January 1995, it took proceedings against the similar Europe-Australia Trade Agreement (EATA), which are capacity management agreements for these trades. The European Commission objected to such agreements and regarded them as a restraint of trade, which inevitably leads to higher prices.

The EC has also taken action over multi modal pricing, as liner conference tariffs have been extended to cover the land based legs of door-to-door shipment. The result was that some European shippers have accused Liner Conferences of extending their market power, enabling them to discriminate between shippers who use their door-to-door services and those that just use the sea-leg part. The argument is that land-based carriers are subject to the EU's anti-trust rules, but the conference players are not, as they have been exempted from the block exemption for Liner Conferences.

The European Commission found in favour of the shippers and in effect outlawed multi-modal tariffing by conferences. It pointed to the fact that independent Asian lines appeared to be able to operate in complete independence of the conference system and concluded that a conference is no more than a simple profit maximising cartel.

The Far East Freight Conference was in litigation with the EC for several years over this issue. It argued that multi-modal pricing was the norm. The EC did not accept this position.

Similar action occurred in the US, with the Federal Maritime Commission acting to ensure that the Transpacific Stabilisation Agreement (TSA), first put in place in 1989, became ineffective in limiting capacity. In general, the EC accepted that strategic alliances and co-operative arrangements were within the law, because they did not involve price setting or exchanging information on prices.

In 2004, the EU published a White paper in response to the OECD led inquiry into competitive practices in various industries, including international maritime transport. The OECD report, published in 2002 stated that

...it is recommended that Member countries, when reviewing the application of competition policy in the liner shipping sector, should seriously consider removing anti-trust exemptions for price fixing and rate discussions..."

The European Commission published its own White Paper, reviewing the block exemption and the application of competition rules to maritime transport, in particular, to review the block exemption granted to liner shipping conferences under that regulation. After taking evidence from shippers' councils, the liner companies and the conference organisations, together with submissions from academics, the Commission proposed that provisions of the regulation be repealed and to consider what kind of legal instrument would be needed to replace the regulation.

One of the principal groups affected by the repeal of the block exemption is, of course, the shipping lines, represented by the European Liner Affairs Association (ELAA). It responded by submitting a proposal that the new regulatory instrument should exempt the following elements of an information exchange system among carriers:

- Exchange and discussion between lines of aggregated capacity utilisation and market size data by trade and on a region/zone to region/zone basis (with a month delay)

- Exchange, discussion and evaluation of commodity development by trade (aggregated, with a month delay)

- Discussion and evaluation of aggregate supply and demand data by trade/commodity; demand forecasts would be published

- Lines will obtain own market share data by trade, region and by port (aggregated with a month delay)

- Price index differentiated by type of equipment (e.g. reefer, dry) and/or trade (data aggregated with a quarterly delay): this information would be made publicly available

- Surcharges and ancillary charges based on publicly available and transparent formulae, the details of which would be discussed with shippers.

This proposal was analysed and the Commission concluded that information exchange systems can have both pro and anti-competitive effects. On the one hand, sharing information on current and future prices and quantities improves the chances of collusion, whereas providing more informed knowledge of market share and output of incumbents might encourage entry. Given the extensive list of information that would be exchanged under the ELAA proposals, the issue of whether the net effect is anti-competitive is an open one.

In September 2006 the Council of the European Union repealed block exemption to anti-trust immunity for liner services. The regulation was phased out in October 2008.

It is worth quoting the four main arguments given by the European Council in support of its decision:

1. The existing restrictive agreement on price fixing and supply regulation cannot be shown to generate improvements in the production or distribution of goods or promote technical or economic progress

2. Consumers do not appear to be compensated for the negative effects arising from restricting competition. '*Transport users or the companies using the liner service, consider that conferences operate for the benefit of the least efficient members.*'

3. Price fixing and capacity regulation are not indispensable for the provision of liner services. Global alliances do the same job with no price control.

4. Liner conferences are subject to external competition. While there may be some price competition on the ocean freight rate, there is hardly any competition with respect to the surcharges and ancillary charges. The fact that conference members are permitted to exchange price information in the conference and then exchange information to conference members, who are in the same alliance or co-operation agreement, means the determination of the degree of external and internal competition is now so complex it can only be analysed on a case by case basis.

The ramifications of the new legal position in Europe have also impacted on dry cargo and tankers, in that pooling operations which are found quite frequently in these sectors, have to be very carefully set up in order to avoid breaching the competition regulations of the EU.

7.11 CONCLUSION

This chapter has tried to cover a very large amount of material. The liner trades have been transformed over the past 35 years, as the containerisation revolution disseminated throughout the globe. Despite this transformation, certain key features still exist, namely the application of price discrimination and the conference system. Economic models of the conference system were explored, in an attempt to explain what has become known as the Conference Paradox. Lastly, the development of global alliances and the relationship between the European Community and shipping conferences was discussed.

APPENDIX 1

The determination of market equilibrium in a two liner conference

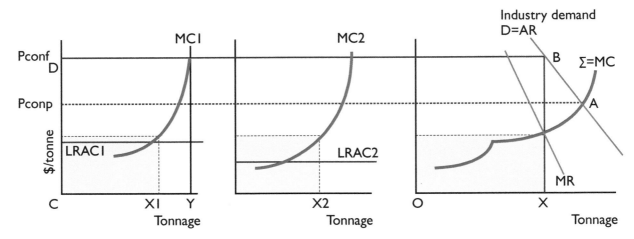

Fig A1 Benefits derived from a reduction in competition

If two liner companies collude in the transportation of a particular commodity between two named ports, they are able to raise both prices and profits, according to the standard model of cartel behaviour. Figure A1 above illustrates the idea. Figure A1a shows the short-run marginal cost of moving extra cargo tonnage faced by liner company one (MC1). Its long-run costs are given by LRAC1, which is drawn as a horizontal line to reflect the assumption that there are constant returns to scale in the industry. A similar set of curves are drawn to represent the cost structure of liner company two (MC2). Note that by assumption, this company has lower average costs than company one.

In order to construct the industry supply curve, the two marginal cost curves are added up in a special way. The result is shown in Figure A1c. The kink arises because at very low prices, only liner company two can still set marginal cost equal to price; company one has left the market. The combined MC curve must have a flatter slope than any single MC curve, because when output is expanded by one unit from, say, company two , company one's output and therefore MC is unchanged. When the next increment in output is being considered, company two's MC has increased, but MC1 has not. Successive additions made in this way imply that the overall MC rises more slowly than any individual MC, in other words, it is flatter.

Competitive equilibrium

If the market were competitive, price would be determined at the point where supply equals demand, at point A in Figure A1c. Each firm would be profit maximising and in the model above, both companies would be profitable.

Conference equilibrium

If the companies organise themselves into a closed conference, they behave as a single monopoly supplier. A monopoly supplier maximises profits by setting its marginal costs to its marginal revenue schedule, in this case the MR derived from industry demand shown in Figure A1c.

As can be seen, the new position involves setting a higher common price, and restricting output. Both companies limit supply; each produces X1 and X2 respectively, with the combined output equalling X in Figure A1c.

Cheating

The diagram can clearly show the reasons for conferences to regulate tonnes as well as prices. From company one's point of view, the regulated market price is now D, but its output is only X1. If it took the market price as given, behaving as if it was a in perfectly competitive environment, its own profit maximising output level would be Y, where its MC = Pconf. But this involves cheating on the conference, by offering shippers secret rates just below D in order to attract extra business. Conference organisations can limit this process by setting tonnage share limits for each of the conference members. This would be defined in terms of the tonnes of cargo or market share of the trade that the company is permitted to carry. These days, slots on container vessels are used to measure capacity; a new entrant to a conference is often described as taking up the slot capacity of a line which it has replaced.

APPENDIX 2

The principles of price discrimination

In many sectors of the economy, companies use price discrimination to increase the total revenues they generate from the sale of their goods or services. It is important to realise that discrimination does not necessarily require that a monopoly exists.

A good example to illustrate this point is the Film and Video industry. When a new film is released in a country, it is first shown in the cinema. Hopefully, all the development costs of the film will be recovered during this phase, but it is not always the case. When the film's popularity declines the rights to show it are sold. When these markets are exhausted, the film is released on video, on a rental basis. Even here, video companies charge a premium rate for products that are recently released in the format.

The company is using price discrimination over time to maximise the revenue potential of its product. Each film can be said to be unique, but it faces strong competition from the hundreds of other films available, newly released or on video. By limiting its release to each segment over different time periods and charging different prices, the company maximises its revenues and, hence, profits.

The ability to carry out this kind of discrimination depends on these factors.

 1. There must be different market segments with differing own price elasticities of demand;

 2. the company must be able to prevent resale. That is to prevent one client from reselling the product or service to another client.

Different elasticities have to exist to make price discrimination worthwhile. If each sector had the same elasticity, they would respond in the same way to a price change and, from the economic point of view, can then be treated as the same sector.

If the company cannot prevent customers trading with each other, it is clear that if customer A is charged £30 and B £10. A could persuade B to buy two units at £10 and then resell one on, say at £12. A saves £18 and B gains £2. The loser is the company.

Pure price discrimination

Suppose that the product supplied by a company could be sold, unit by unit, at a market. An auction would be a good example. The supplier would offer the first unit at the auction and receive the highest bid for it, then the second, the third, and so on. The first item would sell at the highest price, as it would be unique. The second would fetch slightly less. This situation is shown in Figure A2.1 below.

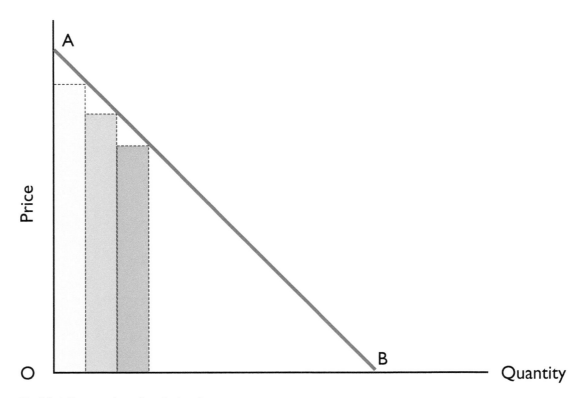

Fig A2.1 Pure price discrimination

If one calculates the Total Revenue generated by selling every possible unit in this way, it will equal the area OAB. Furthermore, the extra revenue generated from the sale of one more unit must be equal to the price that the unit sells at, since it is being sold by auction. It follows that under these special circumstances, price or average revenue, is identical to marginal revenue.

Price discrimination and profit maximisation

The traditional rule for maximising profits is to set marginal revenue equal to marginal cost. In the traditional model, this leads to a single price charged for all units sold, as shown in Figure A2.2 below. In contrast, Figure A2.3 shows the effect of applying pure price discrimination to the market. It is clear that output, total revenues and, by implication, profits are higher than in the usual case.

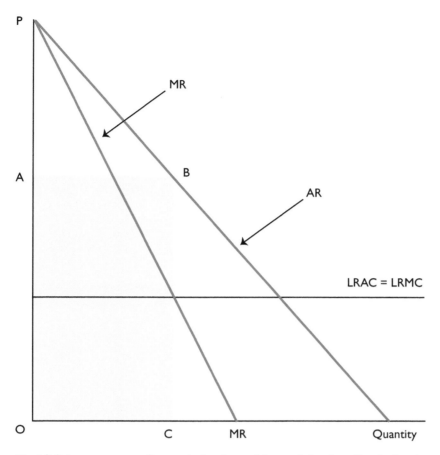

Fig A2.2 Long-run profit maximisation with partial price discrimination

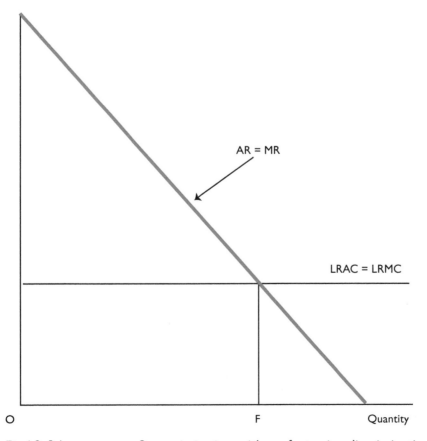

Fig A2. 3 Long-run profit maximisation with perfect price discrimination

Figure A2.2 shows the long-run profit maximising equilibrium for a seller with some ability to differentiate their service from rivals. Output will be set at C units and a standard price of A is set. The shaded area represents total profits.

In comparison, the profit maximising firm would do better if they could sell each unit at a specific price, because then the Average and Marginal Revenue curves are the same and profit maximising output is F in Figure A2.3. There is no such thing as an average price here, because each unit is sold at the maximum it could fetch on the market. Total Revenue is then area ODEF, much larger than OABC, assuming identical demand conditions. It is clear that profits are larger in the second case, as Total Costs would be given by the height of the average cost curve multiplied by the number of units sold.

Cross subsidisation and price discrimination

In the particular conditions of the liner trades it was noted that average incremental cost or short-run marginal cost was very low, much lower than long-run average cost. Figure A2.4 shows the short-run profit maximising equilibrium achieved under these conditions. Note that certain units are being sold at less than their long-run average and marginal cost of production, even if they still cover their short-run attributable or direct costs. This is called cross subsidisation, as it implies that certain services (units Q1Q2) are being sold to the market at less than the long-run opportunity cost of production. This is regarded as inefficient, since it implies a misallocation of resources; those resources would generate better returns if they were applied elsewhere in the economy.

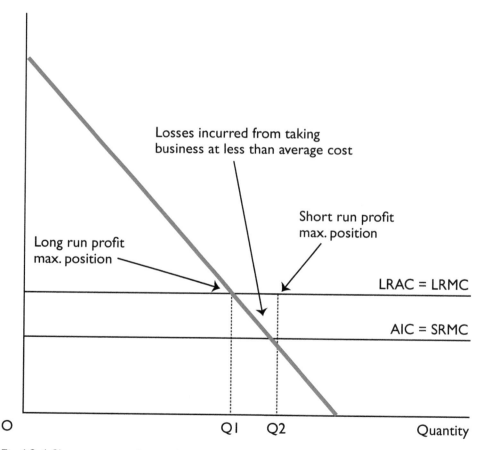

Fig A2.4 Short-run profit maximisation and cross subsidisation

Chapter 8

. . . .

PORTS, SEA CANALS AND WATERWAYS

The world's worst inflation was in Hungary in June 1946, when the 1931 gold pengo was valued at 130 million trillion paper pengos.

8   INTRODUCTION

Unlike other modes of transport, ocean and coastal shipping have no need for an infrastructure of tracks, signalling, bridges and roads. But ships do need elaborate and usually extremely expensive terminal facilities in the shape of harbours and ports. This is probably one of the most difficult tasks of maritime economics, the allocation of resources in an optimum way to create an economically efficient port. The problem is highlighted in two ways; first where a massive and very expensive port investment has been undertaken to construct a port that few vessels visit. Second, where a port lacks necessary investment, long and costly delays are imposed on vessels awaiting a berth. Some of the basic elements of the problem will be examined in this chapter. Ideally ports and the facilities they provide should be designed as part of an integrated transport system. Account should be taken of the ships that will use them, the port facilities at the other end of the major routes, the role of ship canals and waterways where applicable as well as the interaction with land transport.

Port ownership structures are now quite complex, ranging from public ownership and operation through to private ownership and operation. There is now a wide variation in the arrangements between port owners and ship operators, ranging from complete integration where the same company owns the landside and waterside assets to complete separation where the ownership of the ship and the ownership of the port assets are independent of each other.

8.1   DEFINITION OF PORTS AND HARBOURS

The following definitions apply:

A harbour is a haven for the protection of ships; a place where vessels can shelter from inclement weather and if required, undergo repairs or re-victualling and undertake their normal business. Harbours are of two distinct types, either natural or artificial. Natural harbours are those sufficiently protected by their situation not to require any artificial add-ons. They are physically protected or enclosed by the coastline. Prime examples of this type are Sydney Harbour, the bay at Rio de Janeiro and Milford Haven.

Artificial harbours are those which require the natural configuration of the coast to be supplemented to a greater or lesser extent by breakwaters and the like. A harbour is formed by the natural structure but requires man-made breakwaters, piers or jetties to complete the task.

Prime examples of this are Dover Harbour in the United Kingdom, which is almost purely artificial, possessing a length of breakwater of over 3km, and Tema in Ghana.

The majority of harbours are a combination of the two types. The latter, artificial harbour, is the most important from an economic cost point of view as it will generally be the most expensive, using a large amount of factors of production particularly capital in its construction and maintenance.

A port is sometimes referred to as a commercial harbour since ports are primarily designed and organised for commercial use. They are often called gateways between land and sea or water as ports can refer to seaports, river ports or ports on canals or waterways.

The central function of a port is to be a point of transfer of commodities and people from land to water and vice versa. It is a place where land and water transport modes come into contact and the services are provided for the purpose of the interchange of cargoes and passengers as an essential feature of the whole national and international transport network.

8.2   THE FUNCTION OF PORTS

There are four general categories of a port's functions. These functions are:

a.   Traditional functions;

b.   Transport or transit functions;

c.   Industrial functions;

d.   Network functions.

It is necessary in any analysis to make clear the close inter-relationship between these functions.

a) Traditional functions of ports These can be looked at from a broad perspective. Firstly, the seaport performs an important link in the total chain of transport. Secondly, seaports usually provide areas or facilities for the storage of goods until transported to their destination. The storage function can range from a simple parking area for road haulage vehicles to massive tanks holding millions of barrels of crude oil. Thirdly, seaports are often alternative locations for industry, particularly heavy industry and those associated with shipping.

b) Transport functions of ports Not only do ports provide the essential link in the transport network, a further distinction has to be made in the area of trans-shipment of goods. Trans-shipments can be from seagoing vessel to barges using canals and waterways, railway trucks, road haulage, aircraft or any other modes of transport. Increasingly it is between seagoing vessel and another seagoing vessel. The transport function is characterised essentially by the transport mode used, which in turn is a function of the type of goods carried and the length of journey to be made as well as the geographic and other conditions. The storage function of a seaport is directly related to its transport function. Seagoing vessels are several times larger than units of inland transport, so for transport overland the total cargo carried in one trip by a seagoing vessel has to be split up into smaller consignments. These are consignments which are going to be conveyed along a route determined by factors other than those that influence the need to dispose of a ship's total cargo as quickly as possible. The provision of storage space provides an obvious answer for perishable and non-perishable goods which do not depend on onward shipping by sea transport.

c) The industrial function of a port This is the logical offspring of the two previous functions. The consideration that trans-shipment always involves handling costs as well as onward shipping in smaller, generally more expensive, transport has induced many industries, notably those of processing raw materials to locate in seaports. For a port to fulfill these various functions facilities are needed for ships, waterways, harbour bases, berths for inland transport, canals, roads, railways and storage and industrial land and buildings as well as the services they require. All these facilities call for a large investment with a very long life-span which will impact upon the physical and economic environment of the region.

d) Network functions: hub and spoke ports or the load centre concept The increased use of containerisation methods in shipping has led to a change in the way that ports are viewed. Because of the need to exploit scale economies, which require large cargo volumes, ports serving the liner trades have become increasingly specialised into one of two types: hub ports and feeder ports.

A hub port, or load centre, as it is sometimes called, acts as an important focus of container trading activities. It is served by many ships calling to load and discharge cargo on many different routes. It has become a centre of cargo distribution which is often of great regional geographic importance, rather than merely a national or local one. Singapore and Hong Kong both serve this function in the Far East. Rotterdam does the same in Europe.

A feeder port, as its name implies, is of lesser significance, as cargo volumes are smaller. Economies of scale are not so easily exploited, so the routes it serves will be less busy, with smaller vessels engaged on them. A hub port will be at the centre of a local network of these smaller ports, a system which has been called hub and spoke operations, because of the fact that cargo is first moved to a hub port, and then radiated out along the spokes.

This arrangement is also to be observed in the world of air transport, where it is used for the same reason; to exploit scale economies by using large aircraft to serve the hubs and smaller ones on the feeder routes.

The development of the hub port concept means that ports in the future may not necessarily need to have large industrial hinterlands close to them. An example is the important container port of Algeciras, which has little or no industrial development close by, but it is ideally located to act as a transhipment terminal, where containers can be shifted from one vessel to another in order to minimise the liner companies' overall costs of providing shipping services. According to this viewpoint, port development will be closely tied in with its location, since this will determine its strategic importance to the liner companies' route networks.

e) Supply chain function The port is viewed as a crucial element in the operation of a modern logistical supply chain. The previous four functions have all tended to view the port as a discrete element, to be evaluated independently of its relationship with the rest of the economy, although industrial function and network functions do imply some external links. In modern cargo transport, great weight has been placed on the concept of the logistics supply chain. With increased trade liberalisation and globalisation, the supply chain can now extend from Chinese factories to New York retail shops, from Australian coal and iron ore mines to Chinese steel mills and from Japanese car plants to European garages.

Seeing the functions of a modern port in the context of supply chain analysis may help to explain competition between ports, which can be seen as competition between different supply chains, of which ports are a part.

8.3   PORT COSTS AND SHIPS' TIME

8.3.1   Port infrastructure and investment

One of the basic elements of which all students of transport or shipping economics must be aware is the functional difference between mobile plant and fixed plant from an economic point of view because it has a major impact on the industry. The economic characteristics of mobile plant or equipment, for example, motor vehicles, planes or ships, are that they are cheap relative to the investment expenditure involved in setting up a large infrastructure item, such as a port or an airport. Aircraft or ships also have a short economic life relative to ports and airports. Eurotunnel for instance has an assumed economic life of 50 years.

Economists have pointed out that fixed plant or infrastructure has four important characteristics:

- The extremely high cost of investment;
- once constructed it is exceptionally long-lasting; ancient ports and roads are still in commercial use;
- little or no alternative uses, as they are unwanted in any other function than the original use;
- often possess considerable potential for economies of scale.

To summarise, transport infrastructure, like ports, canals and waterways, is typically expensive, single purpose and offers economies of scale if it can be designed and built from the start for a high volume of traffic or cargo.

178   Institute of Chartered Shipbrokers

Criteria for investment appraisal

A number of methods have been developed to enable the systematic evaluation of investment in large capital items, such as port facilities. They can be split into two broad categories: Those that do not involve discounted cash flow techniques and those that do. A brief outline of these techniques is given here:

a) Non-discounting methods

The simplest form of this is the payback method. Essentially, an investment project is evaluated by estimating the cash outflows associated with the project over the initial period of its construction, the expected cash outflows generated by operating the facility once it is in use, and the cash inflows arising from the charges levied on users of the facility. This is to be done for every year of the asset's economic life, which may be a considerable period, lasting many years, in the case of port investments. Finally, estimates are made of any inflow arising from the sale of the asset at the end of its life or additional costs involved with its disposal.

This method builds up a cashflow profile of revenues and costs associated with the asset. In fact, all systematic appraisal techniques use this as the basis.

The payback method simply finds the answer to the following questions:

1. How much has been expended on setting up the asset. In other words, what is the value of the investment?

2. How many years will it take before the surplus from revenues less the operating costs of the asset accumulates to a sum equal to the value of the investment?

The answer to question two is the payback period. Companies repeat this exercise for all projects they are evaluating, and then rank them by the payback period. They then select a criteria. For instance, Shell UK may require all investments to have a payback of three years. If the proposed project meets this criterion, it will be approved for funding. If the funds are available, the project can be undertaken.

The United Nations UNCTAD Secretariat in its handbook entitled **Port Development** examines a number of evaluations of the nature and magnitude of port investment. In particular it looks at the payback period method which is illustrated in the following figure.

The payback method must be taken literally: it means that there is a considerable time gap, a period of years, required to recover or pay back the initial investment. Section one is the installation period; the time it takes to construct the facility. During this period there are only costs and no revenue or income. Income begins in section two when the facilities are beginning to operate and therefore gaining revenue from tariffs. Section three shows a period where income is in excess of operating costs. The payback period in this example is clearly a long time, as the accumulation of capital from section one and the losses incurred in the start-up period in section two, will have to be recouped from the surpluses of revenue over operating costs expected in section three.

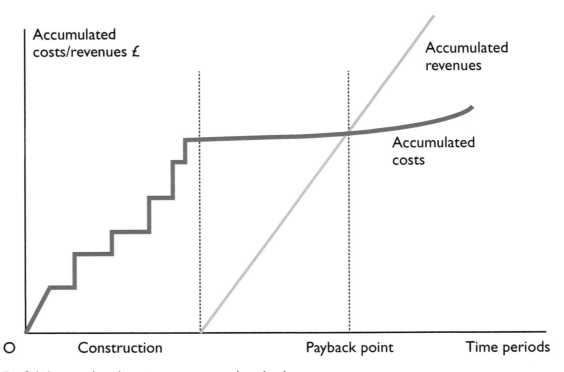

Fig 8.1 Accumulated costs, revenues and payback

The payback period has many advantages. It is simple to understand and is easy to apply, once the cash flow projections have been made. Unfortunately, it is logically wrong and deeply flawed as a technique.

One reason for its logical failure is simple to see. In the introductory section, it was suggested that certain projects might require expense at the end of their lives. For example, Shell ran into great difficulty over the disposal of an old oil rig, which it planned to sink at sea. This would cost it very little. But public pressure forced them to abandon the idea after Greenpeace occupied it. They had to spend millions of pounds on the safe disposal of the rig. This additional expenditure appears at the end of the asset's life, and is not included in a Payback calculation.

A second and more fundamental flaw is somewhat more difficult to convey. The fact is that cash earned by a company in one year is not perhaps worth the same as cash generated in the following year, which itself is not worth the same as cash in two year's time, and so on. In fact, the further forward one goes, the less is the current or present value of that cash. The implication of this is simple. Without adjustment, one cannot simply add up this year's and next year's cash, because they do not have the same value.

b) Discounted cash flow methods

Discounted cash flow analysis has been developed to deal with this problem. There are two principal investment appraisal techniques which use discounted cash flow analysis. They are known as Net Present Value and Internal Rate of Return.

Net Present Value (NPV)

The computation of the net present value of a project would start in the same fashion as the payback procedure. The first step would be to set out the cash flow profile that the project is expected to generate. The second step is to multiply net cash inflows or outflows by the appropriate discount factor for the year of the project. The third step is to add up the discounted cash flows, taking due account of the sign of the cash flow itself; positive for inflow, negative for outflow. Finally, the net present value rule is applied. This states that it is worthwhile for a company to invest in any capital project at the assumed discount rate, if the net present value is positive. In other words, if the result of adding up the discounted negative and positive cash flows, over the entire life of the project, yields a number greater than zero.

This approach is clearly much more complicated than payback, but it has the merit that it incorporates all the cash flow information into the final result and correctly adjusts for differences in the value of money over time.

Internal Rate of Return (IRR)

This technique is very similar to that of the NPV. Indeed, it can be shown to rely on the same basic equation linking the value of the investment to the cash flows it generates. However, it asks a slightly different question, which is:

What rate of interest, or yield, generates a net present value of zero for the cash flow projections of a given project?

In other words, what rate of interest makes the present value of the capital investment going into the project exactly match the present value of the excess of revenues over operating costs which are generated by the project? Since these are negative and positive respectively, their sum will equal zero when this condition is met.

The rate of interest which achieves this is called the internal rate of return, or IRR.

The IRR rule stated simply, is: Invest in any project in which the IRR exceeds the opportunity cost of capital to the firm. The latter may be measured by the borrowing rate, if the firm finances the project by 100% loans or the firm's own required rate of return.

NPV and IRR are general investment techniques and can be applied equally well to ships as to port investment. Indeed, NPV and IRR are standard procedures in marine banks, when evaluating any proposal for a loan for ship finance.

A more detailed explanation of these techniques is beyond the scope of this text.

8.3.2 Ships and port time

Turning to the consumer, or customer of ports, it must be emphasised that the size of the ship in terms of deadweight tonnes will be very closely related to the time it spends in a particular port. The following rules hold in virtually all cases. The less time the ship stays or lies in a port the larger will be the size of the vessel employed.

Staying in port means that the ship is not earning income; it has an opportunity cost in terms of income foregone. Large ships forego more lost income than small ships, hence decreasing port time means that larger ships can be employed, as the higher foregone income per day is offset by the fewer days spent in port.

If port time or port turn-round in certain trades is slow, then the smaller the size of the ship will be. If the cargo a ship will carry in a certain trade is difficult and time consuming to handle in port (for example loose dressed timber) the optimum size of the ship will be less than for carrying other easily handled cargoes. If on the other hand the cargo is easily loaded or unloaded (for example oil or ore), the vessel's size will be considerably greater.

Obviously steaming distance will be of importance. Short sea or coastal vessels will be in port very often therefore port time must be seen in its wider sense. Thus the preferred vessel size tends to be inversely related to the proportion of time that it has to spend in port.

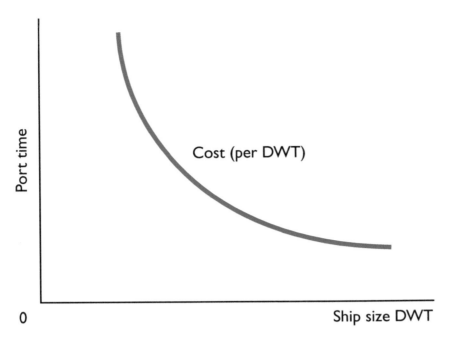

Fig 8.2 The correlation between port time and ship size

All other things being equal, one sees that as port time increases, ship size dimension in economic terms decreases. As port time reduces, ships size increases. Therefore larger vessels become more economic as illustrated in Table 8.1.

	Passenger	Cargo	Deep Sea	Container	Tankers
Percentage time at sea	63	40	57	72	81
Percentage time in port	37	60	43	28	19

Table 8.1 Average % of Ship Time at Sea and in Port (early 1980s) (Source: Drewrys Shipping Statistics and Economics)

This table illustrates the fact that vessel size will relate very closely to port time. Tankers and bulk carriers not included in the table have become massive in size for a number of reasons. One factor which encourages the growth in size has been the fact that load and discharge times have not been increased, thus reducing the proportion of time spent in port. On the other hand general cargo ships spend 60% of their time in port. One of the principal gains arising from containerisation has been a dramatic reduction in the proportion of time spent in port by container vessels compared to general cargo ships. This has permitted them to become significantly larger.

Anecdotal evidence suggests that the proportion of time that a modern container ship spends at sea has increased to 80 per cent, a reflection of their increased size and the greater opportunity cost of their port time. Indeed, the very largest container ships, operated on the long haul routes, could have sea time levels higher than this.

8.3.3 Port efficiency or inefficiency with regard to ship turn round time

Port time is time required for any ship to carry out the essential functions in port and can be divided for the purposes of analysis into three parts:

1. Time spent at anchor. This is perhaps the greatest variable due largely to congestion. It is the first point about which managers must be particularly concerned as it can be the time consuming proportion which is subject to the greatest variable and hence the greatest opportunity for reduction in port time. A vital consideration in shippers', freighters' and ship's costs is the aim to remove congestion.

2. Time spent in internal manoeuvres. Some of the time spent in motion in the channel waiting for tugs and pilots, shipping towards berths and time lost before and after cargo handling can be subject to improvement only within strict limits. For example, moving a ship too quickly within a port might cause damage or accident.

3. Cargo handling time. The truly productive time at a berth is from the commencement of cargo handling until its completion. This encompasses a large number of sub-systems, each of which will have different handling times which may, of course, include periods of storage.

8.4   PORT COST STRUCTURE

The purpose of a port is as previously defined, to make a smooth transfer of freight between sea and land transport. This is a productive process for port and other management. The following sub-sections provide an analysis of the production and particularly the all important cost functions.

8.4.1   Port costs:

The port costs (strictly the shore costs) are made up of two parts:

a) The fixed cost component (FC) that is independent of the tonnage throughput, which involves the capital costs of quays, sheds, cranes and so forth. As the tonnage handled at the berth increases, such fixed costs or fixed components, expressed as costs per tonne, decrease. Curve A shows the average fixed cost declining with traffic volume, as the same total fixed cost is divided by larger and larger units.

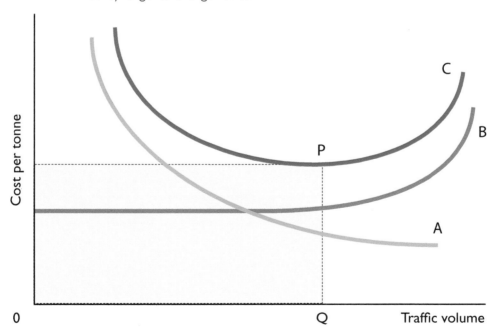

Fig 8.3 Average port costs and traffic volume

b) The variable component or variable cost which depends on throughput, includes labour, staff costs, fuel, container costs and suchlike. This variable cost when expressed as an average cost per tonne will remain fairly stable until the port berth comes under pressure to achieve higher tonnage throughput. The average variable cost per tonne will tend to rise at this point, owing to the need to use more costly methods of handling cargo (curve B). The model illustrates the relationship between port costs per tonne and throughput or traffic volume. The average total cost curve (C) is the sum of the average fixed (A) and variable cost (B) components, reaching a minimum at point P. Traffic volume at this point is Q. This is the most efficient level of traffic volume, because average total costs which are incurred by the port are now minimised. In other words, the lowest cost per tonne possible is achieved with a cargo throughput of Q. It would therefore be in the port management's interest to try to ensure that cargoes actually handled were close to this target figure.

8.4.2   Ships' costs

The above model would be appropriate from a purely commercial or private perspective. The port authorities would be primarily concerned with their own costs and their own revenues. But economists sometimes take a broader view, examining the total resource costs involved in the operation of a large entity like a port, which is often publicly owned and controlled. The efficient working of a port affects the way that ships can be used, so the value of their time can also be included as a port-related cost from this broad perspective. If both shipowner and port are from the same country, the analysis is being conducted in terms of the social costs and benefits that efficient port operation may bring, rather than focusing on the ports own direct commercial interests.

A ship's time spent in port is made up of two parts. Firstly the time the ship spends at the berth, that is berth utilisation, when the ships are actually loading or unloading. Secondly, the time the ship spends waiting for a berth to become vacant. As traffic increases the time spent waiting to get alongside or onto a berth increases at high berth occupation.

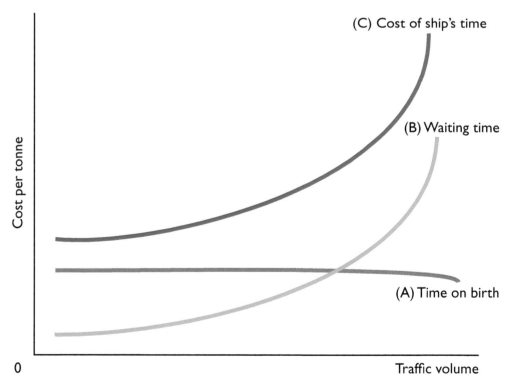

Fig 8.4 Ship's time costs in port and traffic volume

In the above model, curve A represents the time on berth, while curve B shows the extent to which the costs will increase quite rapidly with waiting time. This rapid increase occurs when the port is operating close to full capacity. The World Bank report of 1996 has highlighted the growing threat to further economic development in the Far East created by a failure to expand port capacities and related transport infrastructure in line with recent strong economic growth. The result is that many ports in the region are operating inefficiently, imposing congestion costs on ship operators in the region.

The cost of a ship's time in port is shown as curve C, a summation of curve A, (ship's time) and curve B, (berth and waiting time). Note that all of these curves are measured on an average cost or per tonne basis.

8.4.3 Total port costs

The average total costs incurred by both ships when in port and the port operations themselves, are found by adding together actual port costs and the costs of the ship, i.e. figure 8.3 and figure 8.4 will equal figure 8.5.

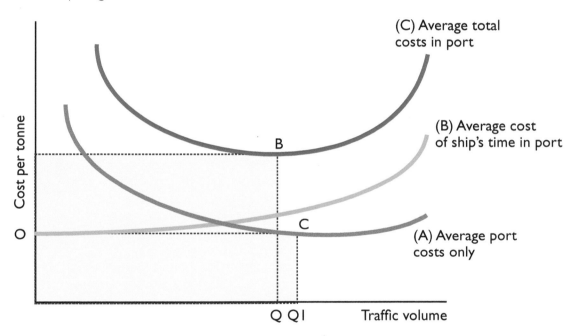

Fig 8.5 Combined average costs of port operations and ship's time

The average total cost per tonne curve is at minimum point at point B. This means that from the broader point of view (i.e. taking into account both ships time and port operating costs) the lowest level of average total cost occurs at Traffic Volume Q.

It is important to note that this is not the volume that minimises the average total cost of the port itself. Minimising of the average total cost of the port (CQ1) occurs at traffic volume Q1, which is greater than Q. In other words, port managers have a cost incentive to run a port at a greater traffic volume level than might be deemed efficient from a broader viewpoint. Indeed, the consumer may well be very concerned, as minimising port costs on their own will generally result in an unsatisfactory level of service for the consumer (in this case the shipowner or ship operator) whose costs of ship time in port increase rapidly beyond BQ. This can lead to conflict and is commercially and economically unacceptable.

Indeed, this model may well explain why so many large ship operators either lease or build their own dedicated terminal facilities. Large oil companies build private terminals linked directly to their refineries; ferry companies own or lease facilities to speed up their own ferry turnaround times; liner companies lease or jointly own large container terminals as part of an investment in through transport. In every case, the shipowner has vertically integrated the ship operation and port operation sides of the business in order to minimize the overall costs of delivering the product. By this means, they are in effect including the cost of ships time as well as the costs of ports themselves.

An example illustrates the potential conflict that can arise between users and operators. In 1983 the Ports Corporation of Queensland, Australia, a state owned corporation, built the Dalrymple Bay Coal Terminal as a common user facility. In 2001 the asset was privatized under a long lease. The facility was still owned by the Queensland government, but leased to Babcock and Brown Infrastructure (BBI). The behaviour of the operator of the terminal was monitored by the Queensland Competition Authority, a body created to regulate such companies given that they had potential monopoly power over their customers. The QCA had to declare that the terminal was a natural monopoly and that declaration meant that obligations and responsibilities were imposed on both users and owners of the terminal.

The terminal had originally been designed with an annual capacity of 15 million tonnes. By 2003 that capacity had been increased to 44 million and to 54 million in 2005. Further expansion plans were designed to eliminate the congestion that occurred in 2005, following the boom in demand from China and elsewhere. In April and May 2005, ship queues and demurrage cost were estimated at $2m per day. The Australian Competition and Consumer Commission (ACCC) had given interim authorisation to the terminal operator to implement a queue management system to reduce ship congestion. New user rates were to be negotiated and the terminal operator proposed increasing the loading charge from $2.08/tonne to $2.77/tonne. Terminal users offered $1.00 per tonne. This can be cited as evidence of the implicit cost of congestion, as users were only willing to offer $1.00/tonne because of the other costs they had suffered.

This particular dispute was resolved by the QCA arbitrating and determining that the rate should be $1.56/tonne. This draft value was met with the terminal operator stating that further expansion plans would not go ahead, as the rate set was too low to make their plans viable. The queue management system was in fact, a stop gap designed to improve the use of existing facilities, given that the expansion programme had been halted. Ultimately, a revised rate of $1.72/tonne was agreed and the expansion plan was restarted. This case illustrates the potential for conflict when the terminal operator and terminal users have differing objectives. It also illustrates issues of regulatory efficiency when monopoly assets are operated privately.

8.5 THE AIMS OR PRINCIPLES OF PORT TARIFFS

Port tariffs will be the main instrument by which port authorities cover their costs or earn some surplus or profit. But such tariffs for port services are not merely instruments to ensure the accounts are balanced. The port tariffs have an important effect in encouraging or discouraging the use of port services. However, because of the importance of ports to national and particularly international trade and industry, it can be argued that general port policy is motivated by the desire to promote a country's interest. This concept has not been thoroughly worked out because it is often difficult to identify specifically national interests in the way particular port policies or tariffs are created. All ports will claim that one of their main concerns is to promote the national interest.

In order to understand the extent to which this idea underlies management pricing and investment in ports, it is necessary to examine the two main principles or doctrines on which port development generally tends to be based. These are known as:

i) Anglo Saxon or Peninsular doctrine;

ii) The European doctrine.

The Anglo Saxon doctrine states, notwithstanding the benefits to the hinterland, that the port should stand on its own feet, not incur losses and aim to make a reasonable profit. This is a principle on which many ports in the United Kingdom operate. This view has been sharpened by the privatisation of Associated British Ports (ABP), which runs many of the UK's ports and terminals. Now in the private sector, ports are driven by the profit motive and commercial considerations to a greater extent than they were before. ABP has since been purchased by a private equity capital venture, headed by Goldman-Sachs, but it still operates using the ABP name.

The European doctrine views the port as part of the social structure of the whole region. The value of the port should be assessed not solely on the accounts of the port but in terms of the progress of the industry, transport and trade of the port in the port region or hinterland. As the name suggests, this view lies behind the development of many European ports and is often the basis on which subsidies for port development are justified.

While implicit in both these principles is the requirement to cover costs and be efficient, the extent to which this will be the main aim will depend on the context within which pricing and investment decisions have to be made.

For management, therefore, the aim will either be:

a) to run an efficient port whose assets assist regional development, or;

b) have a policy for tariffs and investment geared to making money.

8.6 PORT PRIVATISATION: OWNERSHIP AND EFFICIENCY

Port management structures, like most other infrastructures, have been radically transformed in the last 25 years. For example, in the UK with the floating of the nationally owned trust ports and their privatisation. Associated British Ports (ABP) was first set up as a private company, running many of the UK's well known ports on a commercial basis. As mentioned earlier, it is now part of a venture capital operation led by Goldman-Sachs. Port privatisation is a policy that has spread to other countries where state ownership was previously the norm.

There are many conflicting arguments about the benefits and costs of such an approach. In the UK, privatisation has been accompanied by the abolition of the National Dockworkers scheme, making labour relations more flexible than they were. Ports can seek capital from private sources and have to operate in a commercial fashion. The privatisation and deregulation is sharply reinforced with these developments. UK ports have shed significant numbers in the labour force following these developments and, it is claimed, have become more efficient and more flexible.

The rising popularity of privatisation has led many observers to raise the question of the link between ownership and economic efficiency. There are those who argue that ports should be run as part of a nationally integrated plan and the best way of achieving this is through state ownership. There are others who argue that privately owned and run ports are more efficient, because they respond more flexibly to market needs.

The evidence on this question is mixed. It is best summed up by Professor Goss's analysis of the relative merits of the Ports of Singapore and Hong Kong. They are both regarded as being very efficient; but Singapore's is state owned, while Hong Kong's is private. Goss concluded that ownership was not the key issue; management competence, investment and cultural factors were of far greater significance.

There are now a wide variety of port operating arrangements. For example, the fully integrated terminal owned by shipping lines, for example AP Moller Ports, or Southampton Container Terminal, used by the container ship operators in the Grand Alliance, which included P&O NedLloyd at the time. It was jointly owned by Associated British Ports, ABP (51%) and P&O Ports (49%). Dubai Ports World (DPW) have bought out P&O Ports so the joint owners are ABP and DPW. The 51% share gives ABP the controlling interest.

The following table gives some idea of the possible combinations that now exist.

Port Authority Responsibilities			
Port Type	Infrastructure	Superstructure	Stevedoring
Landlord	Yes	No	No
Tool	Yes	Yes	No
Service	Yes	Yes	Yes

Table 8.1 Port Authority typologies (Source: Alderton, P. Port Management and Operations 2005, 2nd edn., p94)

Reading across the rows gives the different mixes of responsibility of the port authority. The landlord port just provides the quay, the deep water approaches, but nothing else; the tenant provides the rest. In the tool port the infrastructure and superstructure are both provided, such as cranes and cargo handling equipment, as well as the infrastructure. Where the authority provides all services, it is called, not surprisingly, a service port.

8.7 PORT COMPETITION

Ports are often in an uneasy relationship with one another. If they share the same hinterland, they may try to compete by offering better facilities for cargo handling, storage and distribution or through simple price competition. For example, there is considerable rivalry between Antwerp and Rotterdam. Both of these ports are subsidised by their respective local and national governments, as both believe that they have a major impact on their domestic economies. By contrast, the well known decline of London as a major port was not accompanied by any subsidies from the UK Government.

From an economic viewpoint, it can be argued that competitive subsidies offered by Antwerp and Rotterdam are inefficient. Both ports serve the larger European market. Both should therefore compete on equal terms. The fact that many ports are still in national hands will always create a risk that political considerations will lead to interference in the way the port sets its tariffs and runs its affairs.

8.8 PORTS IN THE LOGISTICS SUPPLY CHAIN

The analysis of ports presented so far has implicitly taken them to be an independent entity. The issue of conflicting interest between user and provider has been touched upon, but it still has an individualistic element in the analysis. The supply chain approach alters that perspective because it treats the entire process of producing, distributing and delivering the consumer product as part of a continuous supply chain. Clearly, if the supply chain can be shortened in some way, the stock levels held by producers will fall, lowering operating costs. If other aspects of product quality can be improved as well (such as the reduction of stock losses, increased accuracy of information flows and so on), everyone wins.

Ports are indeed becoming more integrated into supply processes. The electronic transmission of cargo documents means trucks can enter the container terminal to deliver or pick up boxes with a minimum of delay. A ship's loading plans can be transmitted to the port authority to ensure container boxes are stacked in the correct areas for faster cargo loading. These are some of the ways that the chain can be shortened. Another way is to integrate the services. NYK Lines has started its own land based logistics service. While the capital requirements for entering the container shipping business are large, the capital requirements for setting up a trucking operation are not. Greater integration can also occur within the port itself.

Robinson has suggested the following diagram captures the changes taking place in the port value chains. In his view, ports will compete with other ports as part of an embedded supply chain; i.e. competition is not between ports *per se* but between competing supply chains. In his view, the role of the port would be *'defined by its function as an element in the value driven chain system'*

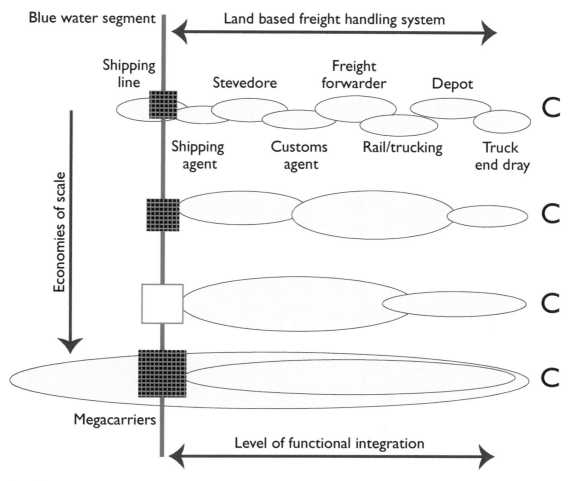

Fig 8.6 Port oriented value-driven chain systems (Source: Robinson, 2002, p249)

8.9   SEA CANALS AND INLAND WATERWAYS

The economic importance and effect of sea canals and waterways can be summarised as reducing nautical distance, due charges, economics of ship size and hinterland and port development.

There are a number of reasons for constructing major waterways; economic, political, strategic or military. There are two important categories of waterways. Firstly sea canals like Suez, Panama, Kiel and the Corinth which join two seas or oceans. Secondly, those providing internal access, for example the St. Lawrence Seaway.

At its simplest, these waterways reduce nautical mileage as the following table illustrates:

From the Port of Rotterdam to	Via Suez	Via Cape of Good Hope	Via Panama
Kuwait	6,500	11,300	-
Auckland	12,670	13,480	11,380
Melbourne	11,060	11,900	12,950
Yokohama	11,150	14,470	12,520

Table 8.2 Different nautical distances

Such shortening of distance appears to present shipowners or operators with extremely simple choices, but these choices are far more complicated than at first sight. This is best seen by constructing a number of simple voyage estimates. Although the rate data is very out of date, the principles are unchanged to this day.

The model assumes:

i) A cargo of grain conveyed from Sydney Australia to Liverpool;

ii) there are three routes which can be used;

iii) the decisive factor will be in the choice of bunker and canal costs;

iv) daily revenue or earnings are given as $700;

v) the vessel is able to find employment all the time. Extra days taken to make the same journey therefore create an opportunity cost, of foregone earnings, which in this case is taken to be $700 per day.

Nautical Distances are:

Routes	Nautical Miles	Knots	Days
Sydney to Liverpool			
Via the Cape of Good Hope	12,300	11	46
Via the Suez Canal	11,500	11	43
Via the Panama Canal	12,500	11	47

Approximate calculation would be:

1. Via The Cape of Good Hope:	$
Operating Cost 46 Days average $350	16,100
Oil: 46 Days average 12 tons average 14$	7,728
Total	**23,828**

2. Via The Suez Canal:	$
Operating Cost 43 Days average $350	15,050
Oil: 43 Days average 12 tons average $14	7,224
Canal Charges	6,300
Total	**28,574**

3. Via The Panama Canal:	$
Operating Cost 47 Days average $350	16,450
Oil: 47 Days average 12 tons average $14	7,896
Canal Charges	2,800
Total	**27,146**

To these figures must be added the opportunity cost of lost earnings if the journey time is longer than the minimum (43 days).

Loss of Earnings: ($700 a day)
Via Cape Debit Three Days   2,100
Via Panama Canal Debit Four Days   2,800

The total costs (direct expenses plus opportunity cost) would be:

	$
Via Cape	25,928
Suez	28,524
Panama	29,996

Other factors could also be added to the analysis, for example:

1. Bunkers were cheaper at Panama.

2. Via Suez the ship can carry an additional 200 tons of cargo.

3. Via Cape in winter, bad weather causes delays of up to 5 days.

In all this discussion the level of freights will be of major importance, for example high freight rates will make time saving important.

Another model, on a slightly different basis is presented below. Here the voyage is between Newcastle, Australia and Rotterdam with a cargo of coal.

Nautical Distance Via	Miles	Knots	Distance per Day
Cape of Good Hope	12,765	14	336
Suez	11,464	14	336
Distance Saved	1,301		

Suez Route Nautical Miles Saved:

1,301 miles 336 Distance per day = 3.87 Days

Cost Per Day	$
Running	4,500
Bunkers $100 tonne average 40 tons	4,000
Total	**8,500**

Reduction in Expenses if Suez Canal used $

3.87 Days x 8,500 Daily cost	32,887
Cost of using Suez Canal Dues	120,000

Cost of using Suez rather than Cape of Good Hope = Cost of Canal dues minus the saving that the shorter journey makes to expenses when compared to the Cape

Canal dues minus cost saving = $120,000 - $32,887 = ($87,113)

It follows from the model that under normal conditions the Suez routes would be the more expensive, adding $87,000 to costs. Such a simple model does not take into consideration a number of factors, the most obvious being the weather condition for rounding the Cape of Good Hope and the level of freight rates which could make time saving an important criteria.

It should also be pointed out that both the Panama and Suez Canal operating companies bear the costs of alternative routes in mind when setting their toll charges. In this case, a toll of only $30,000 would have reversed the conclusion of the example. Canal authorities will monitor rates and bunker costs when setting their charges; they will not be determined just by costs.

It has been argued here that the basic aim of any canal system is to cut distance, increase speed of transit and lower costs. While the models used examples of sea canals, they served to highlight that these basic aims, for example of shortening nautical distance, do not in all circumstances satisfy the economic efficiency criteria of minimising costs.

8.10 CONCLUSION

The aim of this chapter has been to analyse port sea canals and waterways and their interaction with the shipping industry. These combine to make up what is referred to as the maritime industry or maritime transport. The chapter defined ports by their central function, ports as an essential link in the transport network and sea canals and waterways as shorteners of the transport gap. Much of the discussion was around their importance in relation to ships' costs and the problems this creates. Emphasis was also given to the relationship between the mobile transport unit (the ship) which is relatively inexpensive and its infrastructure. This infrastructure it was pointed out, was exceedingly expensive, had a very long economic life and was built to perform a single function which meant it had no alternative use, factors which are of vital importance in any operational or economic analysis.

In the ICS examination a student may well be required to apply this theoretical analysis to examples of different ports throughout the world. It is important, therefore, that as part of your understanding of this chapter you can assess the extent to which it applies to ports and trade routes with which you are familiar as well as the major ports in the world.

Chapter 9
. . . .
SHIPPING AND INTERNATIONAL TRADE

Half the population of the world earns only 5% of the world's total wealth.

9 INTRODUCTION

This chapter discusses the relationship between international trading activity and shipping demand. It then presents the principal explanations of those trade flows used by economists as an aid to understanding their development. The arguments for and against free trade are briefly discussed, as is the role and significance of transport costs as a barrier to trade. The chapter concludes with brief outline of the role the World Trade Organisation.

9.1 THE GROWTH AND PATTERN OF WORLD TRADE

World trade has increased dramatically over the past half century. Figure 9.1 shows that real GDP has grown nearly thirty-one fold over the period 1970 – 2005, but export in value grew even faster, by fifty fold. This growth has generated a corresponding growth of demand for transportation services, both in shipping and elsewhere. Some parts of the world have grown much more rapidly than others over this period. Western Europe and the USA dominated in the 1950s and 1960s, Japan and the Far East in the 1970s and 1980s and the Asian Tigers in the period 1990-1997. Since China's preparation for entry into the WTO, stimulation to world trade has come from its 10% per year economic growth since 1995, as well as from India's switch from protectionist to liberalised trading policies. Together with the recovery of Japanese economic growth, world trade has maintained a good momentum in the past few years, leading to buoyant market conditions in many shipping markets. Since 2008 the growth of world trade has slowed down due to the economic crisis gripping the US and Europe. The continued overall growth is carried by the emerging economies of China, India and Brazil.

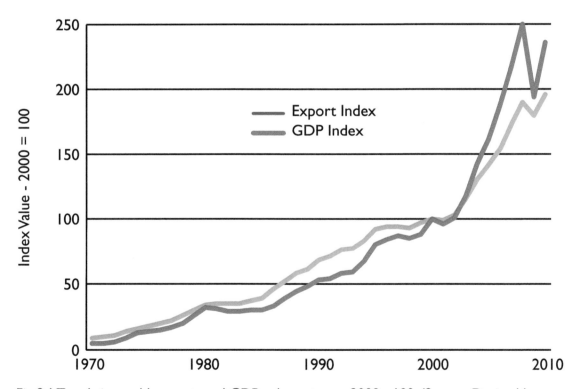

Fig 9.1 Trends in world exports and GDP, volume terms, 2000 =100. (Source: Derived by author from WTO data)

Further inspection of Figure 9.1 also shows that export growth has not been constant over the period. By comparing the slopes of the two series, it is clear that export volume growth has exceeded growth in world real GDP since 2003, but has been slower than income growth in other periods, particularly the late 1970s and early 1980s.

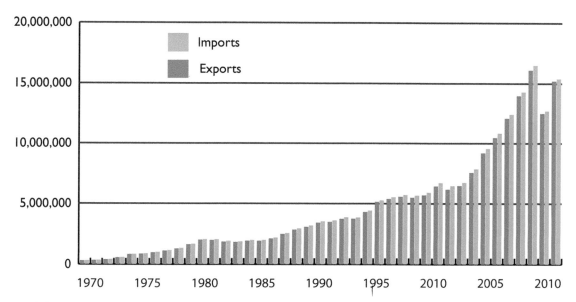

Fig 9.2 Growth in world merchandise trade by value, 1995–2005 (Source: Derived from WTO Trade Statistics Database, at www.wto.org)

Figure 9.2 shows that World Merchandise Trade or the trade in goods, in dollar terms, tripled between 1995 and 2006, reaching an estimated $15.23 trillion, increasing from $5.16 trillion. Trade in commercial services or invisibles also rose from $1.17 trillion to $3.69 trillion. It is important to note that these are value figures and are affected by changes in the prices of the traded goods and services. For example, fluctuations in the price of crude oil will affect the value of trade in oil and especially affect the export earnings of countries that are dependent on oil as their primary export. The period 2002 to 2005 saw sharp increases in commodity prices, such as in oil, coal and iron ore, and the increases have raised the value of trade faster than the volume of trade.

How is this trade shared between countries? There are a number of ways of considering the data. One is to split countries by level of development or industrialisation. Table 9.3 presents data which shows that over the period 2000–2005, industrialised economies accounted for 65% of trade by value and developing countries the rest.

The first two rows of the table show different estimates of world trade values, but the differences are mostly quite small. The next three rows present estimates of the amount of trade generated by the European Union, the oil exporting countries and the non-oil developing countries. The latter two terms recognise the critical role that oil has played in some countries exports. As such putting all developing economies together may give a misleading impression. These figures are in billions of US Dollars. The final part of the table gives estimates in percentage share terms that the industrial and developing economies account for in world trade.

The EU has become a major player, especially with the increase to 25 countries and a further increase to 27 in 2007. Some of the increase between 2000 and 2005 is due to the widening of its membership. By 2005 it accounted for 35% of world imports and 39% of the world s exports. In 2005, oil exporting countries accounted for 3.4% of the world's exports, up from 2.6% in 2000. This increase is partly driven by higher crude oil prices. A more detailed analysis of shares is shown in the lower part of the table, which splits developing countries into their geographic location.

World Trade Shares and Values, 2000 and 2005 ($bn)				
	Exports		Imports	
Year	2000	2005	2000	2005
IFS data	6,380.6	10,355.3	6,573.3	10,602.4
DoT data	6,386.4	10,334.7	5,591.1	10,718.6
Share ($bn)				
European Union	2,436.7	4,000.6	2,317.2	3,796.9
Oil Exporting countries	166.9	354.0	364.4	690.8
Non-Oil developing countries	1,915.9	3,470.3	2,084.3	3,966.8
Share (Percentage)				
Industrial countries	66.4	61.8	61.9	55.1
Developing countries	32.6	37.0	37.2	43.5
Africa	1.7	2.0	2.1	2.6
Asia	17.5	19.5	20.1	22.9
Europe	5.1	7.3	5.0	7.1
Middle east	2.7	3.4	4.1	5.0
Western Hemisphere	5.7	4.8	5.8	5.9
Other n.i.e.	1.0	1.2	0.9	1.4

Table 9.1 Developments in shares of world trade, 2000–2005 (Source: IMF Direction of Trade Statistics Yearbook 2006, Table 001, p.4.)

The developing economies exports rose from $2.1 trillion in 2000 to $3.8 trillion in 2005. Asian economies did well, with their share rising from 17.5 % to 19.5% or about $2bn for exports, and 20.1% to 22.9% or $2.45bn for imports. The African developing countries increased their share of both exports and imports but this is primarily due to changes in commodity prices.

Figure 9.4 provides a list of the major exporters and importers in 2005. There are a lot of useful points to be made from the information in this table. First, the rise of China is dramatically indicated through its rise to first place in export and second place in import ranking. This is an understatement of the position, because if Hong Kong s trade is considered, a large part of its trade is re-export, at $386bn. A large part of Hong Kong s re-exports originate from China. Second, you will note that four countries are from outside Europe and North America in the top 15, namely China, Japan, Singapore and Korea. (We are not considering Hong Kong as a separate country.) Trade in both merchandise and services is still dominated by Western Europe and North America. China's rapid growth has largely corrected that imbalance, but there are no African countries in the list and none from South America. In 2010, the Russian Federation ranks 13th, Canada 14th and Mexico 15th. The highest ranked African exporter is Nigeria, ranking 37th in 2010. The first South American country is Brazil, ranking 22nd.

Rank	Exporters	Value	Share	Rank	Importers	Value	Share
1	Germany	969.9	9.3	1	United States	1732.4	16.1
2	United States	904.4	8.7	2	Germany	773.8	7.2
3	China	762.0	7.3	3	China	660.0	6.1
4	Japan	594.9	5.7	4	Japan	514.9	4.8
5	France	460.2	4.4	5	United Kingdom	510.2	4.7
6	Netherlands	402.4	3.9	6	France	497.9	4.6
7	United Kingdom	382.8	3.7	7	Italy	379.8	3.5
8	Italy	367.2	3.5	8	Netherlands	359.1	3.3
9	Canada	359.4	3.4	9	Canada	319.7	3.0
10	Belgium	334.3	3.2	10	Belgium	318.7	3.0
11	Hong Kong, China	292.1	2.8	11	Hong Kong, China	300.2	2.8
	domestic exports	20.1	0.2		retained imports	28.1	0.3
	re-exports	272.1	2.6				
	World	**10431.0**	**100.0**		**World**	**10783.0**	**100.0**

Table 9.2 Leading Merchandise Traders, 2005 (Source: Table 1.5, International Trade Statistics 2006, WTO. Available at http://www.wto.org/english/res_e/statis_e/)

Note: World Trade total includes re-exports and re-imports

The third point to note is the dominant position still played by just one economy, the United States. It was responsible for 16.1% of the world's imports, and 8.7% of the world's exports. It has lost its number one position in exports partly because the dollar has fallen in value against other major currencies in the past few years and this increases the value of other countries exports in dollar terms. Some of the changes that occur on a year-to-year basis are due to exchange rate volatility, rather than changes in volume.

Finally, it should be pointed out that the rankings in Figure 9.4 are very different if the European Union is taken as a single trading entity. Since six of the countries listed in the top 15 are in the EU, countries such as India, Brazil and Australia would appear. The interested reader is encouraged to explore the information available at the WTO web site, which is excellent.

Another important aspect to consider are the trade patterns. The commonly held view of trade is a rich, developed country with a large industrial base exporting finished and semi-finished goods and services to less developed countries which provide a market for the finished goods and supply the developed country with raw materials for the production process. Whilst this may be partially correct, its accuracy is very limited. The view implies that trade predominantly takes place between developed and developing countries.

Modern trade is much more complex and sophisticated than implied by the above crude model. Modern multinational car companies regularly generate trade flows that do not fit the above stereotype. For example, Ford's engine plant in Bridgend, South Wales, regularly exports large numbers of car engines to other Ford car assembly plants in Belgium, Spain, and Germany. The engines become parts of new Fiestas in Spain or Mondeos in Belgium and Germany. The newly assembled cars are then exported to the UK. What was exported by the UK (the engines) becomes part of an imported finished product and note that this trade is between developed market economies under the UN definition.

These facts must be borne in mind when discussing economic explanations of trade flows, as some of the early and most widely known theories are not designed to explain examples such as that given above. The point is reinforced by examination of the information provided in Table 9.5, which shows the pattern of inter-regional merchandise exports in 2010.

Take North America as a trading region (i.e. USA, Canada and Mexico). In 2010, 48.68% of its trade was with itself, i.e. within region. For Europe the figure is 65.30%, for Asia, 52.58%. In terms of world trade, the regional trade in North America, Europe and Asia adds up to 45.69% of total world exports in 2010. This point can be made at a country level as well.

The UK's trade with the European Union accounted for 56% of its exports and 53% of its imports in 1995. By 2010, these figures had changed to 53.6% of exports, 51.5% of imports, hardly a significant change. In contrast, only 21% of its exports went to developing countries and only 29% was imported from such countries in 2005. In the same year, 76% of the UK's exports went to industrial countries and 68% of its imports came from industrial countries.

These kinds of proportions are not new. A 1991 study showed that the main trading partners of developed economies were other developed economies and, perhaps surprisingly, it also showed that around 60% of developing countries trade was with other developing countries. It appears that levels of economic development determine your trading partners and that the most likely trading partner is another country with a similar level of economic development.

From	Destination						
	North America	**South & Central America**	**Middle East**	**European Union**	**Asia**	**Africa**	**World**
North America	956,452	165,256	52,713	287,124	413,118	32,477	1,964,618
South & Central America	137,966	147,911	14,937	94,903	133,974	14,982	577,013
Middle East	78,972	7,281	89,142	89,162	470,603	29,014	894,928
European Union	377,788	90,112	137,733	3,365,148	472,969	162,155	5,153,225
Asia	800,928	148,391	197,897	745,047	2,464,187	128,421	4,686,139
Africa	85,272	13,604	18,738	165,511	122,532	62,476	508,045
World	2,508,397	586,635	560,542	5,308,622	4,216,415	452,763	14,850,565
Share of Inter-regional trade flows in each region's total merchandise exports							
North America	48.68	8.41	2.68	14.61	21.03	1.65	100.00
South & Central America	23.91	25.63	2.59	16.45	23.22	2.60	100.00
Middle East	8.82	0.81	9.96	9.96	52.59	3.24	100.00
European Union	7.33	1.75	2.67	65.30	9.18	3.15	100.00
Asia	17.09	3.17	4.22	15.90	52.58	2.74	100.00
Africa	16.78	2.68	3.69	32.58	24.12	12.30	100.00
World	16.89	3.95	3.77	35.75	28.39	3.05	100.00
Share of regional trade flows in world merchandise exports							
North America	6.44	1.11	0.35	1.93	2.78	0.22	13.23
South & Central America	0.93	1.00	0.10	0.64	0.90	0.10	3.89
Middle East	0.53	0.05	0.60	0.60	3.17	0.20	6.03
European Union	2.54	0.61	0.93	22.66	3.18	1.09	34.70
Asia	5.39	1.00	1.33	5.02	16.59	0.86	31.56
Africa	0.57	0.09	0.13	1.11	0.83	0.42	3.42
World	16.89	3.95	3.77	35.75	28.39	3.05	100.00

Table 9.3 Intra – and Inter-Regional Merchandise Trade, 2005 (Source: International Trade Statistics 2006, World Trade Organisation).

9.2 TRADE AND ECONOMIC GROWTH

The above section has highlighted the growth of world trade and noted the broad pattern of trade that has evolved in the past 15 years or so. The link between world GDP and trade was illustrated in Figure 9.1. Figure 9.6 presents more detailed information of the differing pace of growth over the period.

		Exports		
Year	World gdp	Value	Volume index	Volume
1960	1,358,387,167,557.41	130,000,000,000.00		
1961	1,410,608,233,685.96	136,000,000,000.00		
1962	1,513,404,695,377.64	143,000,000,000.00		
1963	1,628,388,004,738.53	157,000,000,000.00		
1964	1,784,360,982,526.69	176,000,000,000.00		
1965	1,942,254,025,641.97	190,000,000,000.00		
1966	2,107,207,965,227.99	208,000,000,000.00		
1967	2,241,542,227,890.60	218,000,000,000.00		
1968	2,416,450,291,754.34	242,000,000,000.00		
1969	2,659,110,000,252.50	277,000,000,000.00		
1970	2,891,362,474,231.58	317,000,000,000.00		
1971	3,194,568,442,049.53	354,000,000,000.00		
1972	3,689,964,015,142.10	419,000,000,000.00		
1973	4,506,166,017,259.41	580,000,000,000.00		
1974	5,200,206,052,521.42	840,000,000,000.00		
1975	5,801,135,254,578.26	877,000,000,000.00		
1976	6,316,371,676,484.16	992,000,000,000.00		
1977	7,149,062,801,386.29	1,128,000,000,000.00		
1978	8,415,669,042,995.36	1,307,000,000,000.00		
1979	9,774,093,034,233.56	1,659,000,000,000.00		
1980	10,999,665,872,673.80	2,034,000,000,000.00	100.00	0.00
1981	11,283,752,102,526.80	2,010,000,000,000.00	98.80	-1.20
1982	11,174,973,288,455.30	1,883,000,000,000.00	93.60	-6.40
1983	11,416,604,244,429.60	1,846,000,000,000.00	98.00	-2.00
1984	11,850,927,683,167.60	1,956,000,000,000.00	105.90	5.90
1985	12,445,405,016,965.60	1,954,000,000,000.00	99.70	-0.30
1986	14,720,588,914,103.90	2,138,000,000,000.00	109.40	9.40
1987	16,718,094,850,408.20	2,516,000,000,000.00	117.50	17.50
1988	18,698,481,211,395.10	2,869,000,000,000.00	113.70	13.70
1989	19,624,364,867,905.00	3,098,000,000,000.00	107.80	7.80

1990	21,920,792,256,960.00	3,449,000,000,000.00	112.90	12.90
1991	22,995,566,641,243.60	3,515,000,000,000.00	101.50	1.50
1992	24,546,395,695,297.80	3,766,000,000,000.00	106.70	6.70
1993	24,915,078,827,178.50	3,782,000,000,000.00	99.80	-0.20
1994	26,752,109,865,946.30	4,326,000,000,000.00	113.60	13.60
1995	29,692,894,750,906.30	5,164,000,000,000.00	119.30	19.30
1996	30,303,289,996,658.90	5,403,000,000,000.00	104.60	4.60
1997	30,222,356,622,951.40	5,591,000,000,000.00	103.40	3.40
1998	30,115,107,530,226.90	5,501,000,000,000.00	98.70	-1.30
1999	31,231,321,824,407.90	5,712,000,000,000.00	103.90	3.90
2000	32,240,383,199,090.10	6,456,000,000,000.00	112.90	12.90
2001	32,046,348,810,620.30	6,191,000,000,000.00	95.90	-4.10
2002	33,304,640,616,151.20	6,492,000,000,000.00	104.80	4.80
2003	37,465,967,921,629.80	7,586,000,000,000.00	116.90	16.90
2004	42,228,984,476,590.60	9,218,000,000,000.00	121.60	21.60
2005	45,658,316,886,272.40	10,489,000,000,000.00	113.90	13.90
2006	49,506,293,314,880.40	12,113,000,000,000.00	115.60	15.60
2007	55,848,896,227,304.20	14,003,000,000,000.00	115.70	15.70
2008	61,304,541,579,435.60	16,120,000,000,000.00	115.30	15.30
2009	58,088,277,293,607.50	12,516,000,000,000.00	77.40	-22.60
2010	63,123,887,517,709.30	15,237,000,000,000.00	121.70	21.70

Table 9.4 Growth rates of world GDP, exports and production, 1950 -2005 (source: Derived from Appendix Table A.1, International Trade Statistics 2006, WTO)

The table is of interest because it reveals that the highest rates of trade growth (in value terms) were experienced in the 25 year period after the end of World War II. Trade growth slowed down after 1973 and then recovered, for reasons you should be aware of from Chapter 6. The period 1990-1999 saw a higher level of growth in export value than the period in the 1980s, but a slower growth in GDP growth. However, recent rates of growth in value terms are much higher than those experienced in the 1980s and 1990s because commodity prices fell in the 1980s but have risen since 2000. It is also worth noting that there was only one period in which world trade volume growth was lower than the rate of growth of GDP in the period, namely, 1980-1989. In every other period, trade has grown faster than world economic activity, implying that economies have become more integrated, more open than they were before.

The World Bank has researched the link between trading performance and economic growth over many years and in many countries and has concluded that two key features appear to be vital ingredients for an efficient, dynamic economy.

The two major features are:

a) the development of increasingly open economies, and

b) the liberalisation of markets.

An 'open' economy is defined by the degree of openness, the extent to which the national economy is affected by trade growth. One way of measuring this is to measure the value of a country's exports and express it as a percentage of the Gross Domestic Product of the country, the GDP. Since exports are a part of the total output generated within the economy, the higher this figure, the larger the degree of dependence of that economy on world trade growth and the more competitive that economy has to be in world markets. Alternatively, the ratio of imports to GDP can be measured. A third way is to add up the value of exports and imports and express this as a ratio of national GDP. These ratios can be calculated for merchandise goods and commercial services. Figure 9.7 presents information on export and import ratios for a number of countries for 2010 and also presents the average of the two export and import ratios. In all of these cases, the denominator is GDP at current prices for 2010, measured in US Dollars.

Rank	Country	Exports	Imports	GDP	Export Ratio	Import Ratio	Average Ratio
1	Hong Kong, China	787,216,130,471	558,182,105,841	224,457,859,239	350.72	248.68	299.70
2	Singapore	521,008,171,207	310,791,083,000	208,765,019,308	249.57	148.87	199.22
3	Belgium	412,222,796,369	390,443,203,325	469,374,172,185	87.82	83.18	85.50
9	Netherlands	573,359,637,006	516,926,795,177	779,356,291,391	73.57	66.33	69.95
38	Korea, Republic of	466,383,756,000	425,212,161,000	1,014,483,158,314	45.97	41.91	43.94
64	Germany	1,268,873,596,651	1,066,839,292,906	3,280,529,801,325	38.68	32.52	35.60
77	Nigeria	82,000,000,000	44,235,269,000	193,668,738,107	42.34	22.84	32.59
112	Albania	1,550,100,000	4,600,736,000	11,786,099,138	13.15	39.04	26.10
122	China	1,577,824,000,000	1,395,099,000,000	5,926,612,009,750	26.62	23.54	25.08
123	Canada	388,018,594,640	402,280,000,000	1,577,040,082,218	24.60	25.51	25.06
132	Italy	447,534,815,222	483,813,714,422	2,051,412,153,370	21.82	23.58	22.70
135	France	520,661,368,131	605,705,959,753	2,560,002,000,000	20.34	23.66	22.00
136	Russian Federation	400,132,000,000	248,738,000,000	1,479,819,314,058	27.04	16.81	21.93
138	United Kingdom	405,666,275,471	560,096,757,220	2,248,831,038,714	18.04	24.91	21.48
168	Japan	769,838,947,000	694,051,724,384	5,458,836,663,871	14.10	12.71	13.41
171	United States	1,278,263,200,000	1,969,183,900,000	14,586,736,313,339	8.76	13.50	11.13
172	Brazil	201,915,000,000	191,491,100,000	2,087,889,553,822	9.67	9.17	9.42

Table 9.5 The openness of selected economies, 2005 (Source: Derived from Country Trade Profiles at www.wto.org)

The first point to notice is that two of the largest economies in the world in absolute terms, USA and Japan, are ranked at the bottom of the table in terms of openness .The USA imports 12.79% of the world's merchandise imports (See Figure 9.4) and yet its import ratio is only 13.50%. Its domestic economy is so large that imports account for, roughly 1 dollar in 7 in the US national income. Its exports only account for 1 dollar in 12. It is important to realise that this implies the USA can affect the world trading environment without its own economy being as affected. It is still relatively isolated from world trade. Albania has been included to emphasise this point. This very poor country still manages a higher trade ratio than either the USA or Japan. On the other hand, Hong Kong, part of China, has an export ratio of more than 100%. This is possible because most of its trade is re-exports and most of the re-exports are sourced from China itself. The same situation explains the position of Belgium, as the Port of Antwerp and Zeebrugge are big exporting ports. The same can be said for the Netherlands and Rotterdam. The Dutch and Belgian trade figures are distorted by this fact. Another very good example is the position of Singapore.

9.3   TYPES OF TRADE FLOWS: INTRA-INDUSTRY TRADE AND INTER-INDUSTRY TRADE

Here are a few facts about trade flows for 2005. Albania's exports were 81% manufactured and its imports were 71% manufactured. The UK exports were 78% manufactured, 12% fuel, and imports are 71% manufactured. 58% of the UK's exports go to EU members. The USA exports 81% manufactured, 9% agricultural goods, and imports 72% manufactured, 20% fuels/mining. 92% of China's exports are manufactured and 75% of its imports are manufactured.

These statistics tell us that the dominant element in trade by value is the manufacturing sector. But they also tell us that trade does not fit with the common-sense view mentioned above. Many countries trade large volumes of similar products with each other.

An important distinction is now made between inter-industry and intra-industry trade. When Saudi Arabia exports crude oil to Japan and in exchange imports manufactured goods such as cars, electrical equipment or ships, the trade so generated is known as inter-industry trade. It fits in with the conception of trade discussed earlier. But nowadays, only 50% or so of world trade is of this type. The other 50% is what is known as intra-industry trade. When Rolls-Royce and Jaguar, both British-based companies, export luxury cars to Germany and BMW and Mercedes, both German-based companies, export luxury cars to the UK, it is not clear why such trade takes place, as both countries are capable of producing luxury cars and only one country can have a cost advantage over another, not both at the same time.

When IBM export computers to Japan and Japan exports computers to the USA, who has the cost advantage?

When Ford exports Focuses from Dagenham UK to Germany, and Mondeos from Germany to the UK, who has the cost advantage in car manufacturing?

It is clear that this type of trade flow has to be explained in a different way from the oil/cars trade between Saudi Arabia and Japan.

One important factor underlying some of the trade flows mentioned above involves the rise of multinational corporations as important players in world trade. It has been estimated that one third of world trade is between two subsidiaries of the same multinational corporation (MNC).

Such trade flows may be dictated by factors that have little to do with relative costs in the countries concerned but reflect transfer pricing and differential tax regimes. Transfer pricing is the device used by large multinational corporations to maximise the value added processing of its subsidiaries in the countries of low taxation. For example, a subsidiary in a high tax country can sell its product at a low price to a country with a low tax regime, so that the greater mark up is made in the country with the lowest tax. Since the MNC owns both subsidiaries, where the accounting profit is made is largely immaterial. Tax minimisation becomes a factor in determining the value of trade flows since export prices are affected by these considerations.

The above points highlight the fact that in today's global markets it is no longer possible to explain all trade flows with just one economic model or theory of trade.

9.4 TRADE GROWTH AND THE DEMAND FOR SHIPPING SERVICES

The spectacular growth in world trade has generated a corresponding growth in the demand for transportation services, particularly shipping. The volume of cargoes moved, both in tonne/miles and tonnes of cargo generated per year, has grown in line with the growth in world trade volumes. It is a good idea to review the data provided in chapter 2, which demonstrated the growth in volume of cargo moved, there being a strong link between the growth in world trade, industrial production and seaborne trade.

This point is worth re-emphasising. All industry analyses of the shipping markets begin with an analysis of the key elements generating the demand for those services, which are to be found in the volume and pattern of world trade. The changing demand for oil tankers is linked to changes in trade patterns for crude oil. The growth of the containerised liner trades is most marked in the Far East, which is the region with the highest rates of economic growth and industrialisation in recent years. No self-respecting shipping analyst examines the demand for any shipping sector without first examining and analysing trends in the markets that generate the demand, namely the flows of current and expected world trade.

9.5 ECONOMIC MODELS OF TRADE FLOWS

There are two traditional explanations of trade flows, both concentrating on the supply side of the economy. They essentially argue that trade flows are driven by relative costs only. The models try to explain why one country exports certain commodities and imports other, different commodities in exchange. It implies that one country has a cost advantage relative to the other country for one industry. Thus Saudi Arabia is abundant in oil, which can be extracted cheaply because its fields are on land and can be moved to the coast for export. It has a cost advantage in oil production. On the other hand, Japan has a cost advantage in car production, so both can trade. Note that this is inter-industry trade, not intra-industry trade.

9.5.1 Absolute advantage

The first economist to develop the theory of absolute advantage was Adam Smith. The theory basically argues that a country will export those commodities which it produces more cheaply than any other country, and in exchange import those products which it produces less cheaply than elsewhere. The obvious examples of absolute advantage would be a country's natural endowment of raw materials and natural resources. In Saudi Arabia's case, as mentioned above, an absolute advantage exists in oil production, as it does in other Middle Eastern economies which are similarly blessed. Brazil and Australia are endowed with iron ore, while Japan has none. A natural trade is for Japan to import these essential manufacturing raw materials as it has no such materials itself.

However, one question arises with this theory. Suppose economy A was absolutely more efficient in production in all goods, compared to another economy, B. If the doctrine is correct, it would appear that economy A should never trade with B, since it is capable of producing both products more cheaply than B. Since, in real life, it is often argued that Japan or the US is capable of producing all goods more cheaply than the UK, then why should these two economies trade?

It turns out that Smith's theory is flawed. It has been pointed out that absolute advantage is not required to generate trading opportunities. The major traditional theory of international trade is known as the theory of comparative advantage as developed by David Ricardo.

9.5.2 Comparative advantage

The doctrine of comparative advantage is the most widely known theory of trade flows. The idea is best understood with the aid of an example. Suppose that you are a computer whiz and also good at decorating and painting. In fact, you are better at these two activities than your neighbour, Fred. Fred is not too good at computing, but very good at decorating and painting, though not as good as you.

Initially, both you and Fred spend equal amounts of time in both activities. But if you trade, both can gain. This is because Fred is comparatively good at painting and decorating; if he concentrates on that activity, while you concentrate on computing. You can trade the service to each other and both would be better off. This gain arises from the fact that resources have been reallocated towards their most efficient uses. As a result, more total output of computer services and paint/decorating is produced, to be reallocated between the two people. In reality, comparative advantage is nothing more than the extension of Adam Smith's principle of the division of labour to trade between countries. Each country will tend to specialise in producing those products which it is relatively good at producing and trade some of the increased output from the expanded sector for imports which replace the output lost from the shrinking, less productive sector.

9.5.3 Formal models of comparative advantage

A formal model of the principle of comparative advantage is presented below:

Model 1 - Assumptions

1. There are two countries, country Home (HC) and Foreign (FC);

2. Both have one factor of production, labour, which is used in producing the outputs;

3. Labour productivity, average and marginal, is constant in all sectors;

4. Total person hours available are 12,000 per year in both HC and FC. This implies that both economies are of a similar size;

5. Technology is identical in both countries;

6. There are two products, cars and rice, produced in both countries;

7. There is no trade between the two countries to begin with;

8. Initially, each country allocates 50% of its resources to each product. This implies demand conditions are identical in each country;

9. Labour is always fully employed in both countries;

10. Competitive conditions prevail, leading to prices equalling opportunity costs.

Table 9.8 shows the labour input requirements in each country per unit of output.

Labour input requirements per unit of output (person hours)		
	Home Country (HC)	**Foreign Country (FC)**
Cars	20	60
Rice	60	20

Table 9.6

Given the information in the assumptions above, Table 9.9 shows the maximum output achievable if all the available labour is employed in that sector.

Maximum output achievable in the two countries (assuming resources allocated to only one industry)		
	HC	**FC**
Cars	600	200
Rice	200	600

Table 9.7

If country HC puts all its resources into car production, it can produce 12,000/20 = 600 cars per period. FC, on the other hand, can produce 200 (12,000/60). They are less efficient in car production than HC. Country FC can produce 12,000/20 = 600 units of rice per period if labour is solely devoted to rice production, whilst HC can produce a maximum of 200 (12,000/60). Given the assumption that resources are split 50:50 between cars and rice in the pre trade situation, or autarky as it is called in economics texts, the actual output and self-sufficient consumption is given in Table 9.10.

Initial Production and Consumption in the two non-trading economies			
	HC	**FC**	**World**
Cars	300	100	400
Rice	100	300	400

Table 9.8

It is very important that you note the assumption being made in this model that labour productivity is constant, no matter how many units of labour are being employed in car or rice production. This assumption means that the trade-off between the two outputs is always the same. If one less car is produced in country HC, it follows that 20 labour hours are released. If moved into rice production, the 20 extra hours will generate 1/3 of a unit of rice, since one unit of rice requires 60 hours. In country FC, the loss of one unit of car production frees up 60 labour hours, by assumption, but rice production requires only 20 hours per unit. So the shift in resources would generate three extra units of rice. These trade-offs are assumed to be the same, whether we are talking about the loss of the 600th unit of car production in country HC such as the very last unit or the very first unit. This assumption implies that the opportunity cost of output is a constant in both countries, although the value of that constant differs between them.

Opportunity Cost

How do these two countries gain from trade? Recall the earlier example. If one country is better at making one good relative to the other country, then an opportunity for trade may exist. In order to measure relative efficiencies, economists use the concept of Opportunity Cost. Opportunity Cost is defined as the output foregone as a consequence of producing one more unit of output. In country HC, one extra unit of car costs 1/3rd of a unit of rice, since producing one more car takes up 20 hours. So for releasing 1/3rd of a unit of rice, the equation is 1/3*(60) = 20 hours. Alternatively, the production of one more unit of rice requires 60 extra person hours in HC, or three cars foregone.

The opportunity costs for the two countries are shown in Table 9.11.

Opportunity Costs of Extra Output		
	HC	**FC**
1 Extra Car	1/3 Rice	3 Rice
1 Extra Rice	3 Cars	1/3 Car

Table 9.9

It is clear that the two countries have differences in the pre-trade opportunity cost ratios. Country HC can produce cars at the least opportunity cost (1/3 < 3), while country FC can produce rice at the least opportunity cost (1/3< 3). It is clear that there is a potential for a global increase in production and consumption, if specialisation and trade are introduced.

In the pre-trade position, both countries are limited to consuming exactly what they produce. Table 9.10 above therefore can be read as a table of consumption levels in both countries as well as production. But once trade is permitted, consumption and production can differ by the amount of exports and imports generated. An assumption has to be made about the rate at which the two commodities exchange with each other.

The Opportunity Cost ratios which exist in the pre-trade position provide limits on the Opportunity Cost ratio that will be agreed. Assumption 10 stated that Opportunity Cost ratios can be viewed as price ratios. The equilibrium trade ratio must therefore lie between the two ratios that already exist.

Opportunity Cost cars;   1/3 Rice (HC) < x < 3 Rice (FC)   (1)

Opportunity Cost rice;   3 Cars (HC) > y > 1/3 Cars (FC)   (2)

Note that the relationships above are closely related; the second relationship is simply the same as the first, but inverted. Once one is satisfied, the other must be.

In order to determine the final position, an agreed rate of exchange must be determined. The rate of 1R = 1C has been selected, but note that it falls between the extremes given in one and two. At this rate it is more profitable for country HC to specialise in car production and import rice from FC. Each extra unit of car costs it 1/3rd of a unit of rice domestically speaking, but exchanges for one unit of rice when traded with FC. Thus by switching more resources to car production and trading with FC, an extra 2/3rds of a unit of rice is created. The creation occurs because labour is moved to the sector in which it is relatively most efficient, in both countries.

If FC reduces car production by one unit, resource capable of producing 3 extra units of rice is released. So, rice production goes up by three in FC. If we want to keep the world car production equal HC has to increase production by one. This is at the cost of 1/3 rice. By this reallocation of resources, two and 2/3rds extra units of rice have been generated, which can be split between the two countries. As world car production was unchanged, it follows that world consumption and production is greater than in the no trade situation. Free trade has created larger output and greater consumption.

As there is no change in the relative opportunity costs described in the above paragraph, the incentive to raise production of cars in HC and production of rice in FC exists all the time. The process must stop only when it no longer becomes possible for resources to be switched into the expanding sector, which only occurs in this example, when all of HC's labour resources are employed in car production. At this point, the production figures are shown in Table 9.12. Based on the assumption of equal-sized economies, in this example both economies will end up specialising completely in the sector in which they have a comparative advantage. Where economies are unequal in size, specialisation would be incomplete as the benefits of further trade are limited when the smaller economy becomes fully specialised in its export sector.

Final Production levels with free trade			
	HC	**FC**	**World**
Cars	600	0	600
Rice	0	600	600

Table 9.10

Comparing Table 9.12 with Table 9.9, it is clear that trade has increased production. In this example, both car and rice production are increased. (Other examples can be constructed where only one commodity is increased in the process.) From a global viewpoint, it is clear that both countries can be materially better off, since there are more cars and more rice to go round.

The example can now be completed by assuming final consumption points for HC and FC. The model developed above does not explain the final consumption points and models that do are beyond the scope of this text. The consumption points chosen are therefore somewhat arbitrary, but they illustrate the point that both countries can gain from trade. It will be assumed that country HC exchanges 300 units of cars for 300 units of rice, which is the agreed rate of exchange for trade. Using HC's domestic Opportunity Cost ratio, HC's gain of one car unit costs it 1/3 of a rice unit in lost production. But if FC were to increase its rice production by 1/3 of a rice unit, it would cost 1/9th (1/3 × 1/3) of a unit of a car. This reallocation of resources, exploiting the greater productivities in each the efficient sectors of each economy, creates the gains from trade. Table 9.5 provides one possible equilibrium position for both countries and the implied trade flows.

Final consumption Assuming 50:50 in both countries			
	HC	**FC**	**World**
Cars	300	300	600
Rice	300	300	600

Final trade position				
	HC		**FC**	
Cars	300	Exports	300	Exports
Rice	300	Imports	300	Imports

Table 9.11

Note that the rate of exchange of rice to cars is 1:1 and both HC and FC completely specialise. HC specialises in cars, FC in rice. Trade is balanced in the sense that at the going rate of exchange, each country's value of imports equals the value of their exports. In the world of comparative advantage there are never any crises generated by trade imbalances.

Both countries consumption levels are higher than they were in the pre-trade position. Country HC has 200 more units of rice and the same level of consumption of cars; country FC has 200 more units of cars and the same level of consumption of rice. Both countries are better off from obtaining higher levels of consumption from the same given set of resources through free trade.

Gains from trade and the terms of trade

The example above generated gains to both parties. This arose because the agreed rate of exchange or the terms of trade differed from the pre-trade price ratios that existed in both countries. When a large country trades with a small one, it is likely that the price ratio in the large country will not be affected by the trade volume itself. In this case, all the gains from trade would accrue to the small country, since the difference between the pre-trade price ratio and the agreed terms of trade determines the degree to which a country can reach a consumption point which was not previously open to that country. For example, if the relative price of computers and apples is unchanged in the USA following its opening up of trade with New Zealand, but New Zealanders find that the relative price of apples to computers has increased, New Zealand will benefit from increased apple production and trade with the USA at these higher prices. The gains will go to New Zealand, since the resource reallocation that occurs in the USA is at exactly the same rate as would have occurred in the absence of trade.

The distribution of trading advantages can be affected by movements in the relative prices of imported and exported goods. When in 1973 world oil prices increased by 400%, the terms of trade for oil exporters moved sharply in their favour, whilst oil importers experienced the opposite effect. An improvement in the terms of trade for oil exporters means that for a given volume of oil sold abroad, a larger physical quantity of imports can be financed. The oil exporting countries found themselves much better off and the oil importing countries much worse off as a result of this change. The decline in oil prices between 1980 and the mid-1990s had the opposite effect, which was noted in earlier sections, when the decline of OPEC's share of world trade was highlighted.

Model 2 Comparative Advantage with Variable Opportunity Cost

The above model, although complicated, is not complex enough for a complete analysis of comparative advantage. Two key assumptions have to be modified to improve the analysis. Firstly, the assumption of constant Opportunity Cost has to be dropped. Secondly, production is undertaken with several factors of production (such as land, labour and capital) which are combined to produce either cars or rice. If the assumption is made that rice requires a relatively large amount of land and car production requires a relatively large amount of capital, it no longer becomes possible to assume that the Opportunity Cost of cars or rice remain constant as resources are reallocated.

The reason for this is not too difficult to understand. Suppose that HC has a relatively large amount of capital and FC a large amount of land. Now suppose all HC's resources are concentrated on car production. Then it moves some of those resources into rice production. Efficient reallocation would mean moving the factors which are most productive in generating rice (such as the wettest lands) and the most suitable labour are diverted from car production to rice production. This process is repeated. But each time it is repeated, the land that is shifted and the labour that is moved is slightly less appropriate for rice production and more appropriate for car production. This means that in terms of opportunity costs, early movements of resources do not reduce the production of cars by much but they increase the output of rice a great deal. In economic jargon, the marginal product of factors employed in car production is low, since all resources have been pushed that way. The extra rice produced, from an initial value of zero, will be very large and the marginal product of factor inputs in rice production will be high. This relative situation will alter as resources shift into rice production. The marginal product of the last land was used for rice long ago, so that expensive methods of irrigating dry land need to be employed. The resources being switched are in fact much better used in car production and are less efficient in terms of output when employed in the rice sector.

The Production Possibility Frontier

In order to understand how the variation in Opportunity Cost can be modelled, the concept of the Production Possibility Frontier (PPF) has to be defined. Figures 9.8 and 9.9 show two such frontiers for countries HC and FC respectively.

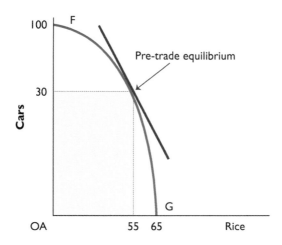

Figure 9.3 Country HC s Production Possibility Frontier

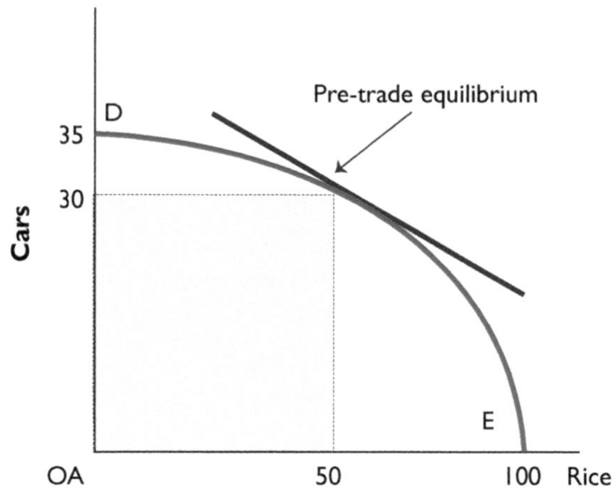

Figure 9.4 Country FC s Production Possibility Frontier

NB. Figures are not drawn to scale.

The PPF for HC shows that if all its resources are fully employed in car production, 100 cars per year will be produced. If all of HC's resources are employed in rice production, only 65 units of rice will be produced. This is consistent with the idea that HC's resources are best suited to car production because it has more capital and less suitable land than FC. The curve FG shows all the possible combinations of cars and rice that can be produced with the full employment of resources in country HC. Consider the process of moving from point G to point F. When there is a large level of rice output, no cars are being produced; releasing capital and labour from rice production will reduce rice output and increase car output.

Under the model's assumptions, there will be a large increase in car output at the cost of a small reduction in rice production. The reason for this is that the resources being released at this stage are the ones most suited to car production and least suited to rice production. The marginal product of factors employed in cars will be large at this stage, but the marginal product of the inputs in rice will be low. So, in terms of foregone rice production, extra car production does not cost much. By the time resources have been shifted to point F, this is no longer true. The resources being released from rice production will now be the most productive ones, the best lands and the best farmers. They will help increase car production, but not by much. At point F, the marginal product of those few factors remaining in rice production has become very high. The opportunity cost of one extra car now becomes very much greater and much larger losses of rice production occur.

These changes are the reason for the changing slope of the line FG. In fact, the slope of FG measures the opportunity cost, the price paid for an extra unit of cars as measured by the lost output of rice. This opportunity cost is very high when car production is high and low when rice production is high. It varies as the relative mix of cars and rice is varied.

The same arguments apply to country FC. Figure 9.9 is drawn to reflect FC's greater facility in producing rice relative to cars. Initial production is assumed to be as shown in the Figures. World production of cars is 30 in HC, 30 in FC, totalling 60. Rice production is 100, 50 in HC, and 50 in FC.

Trade Equilibrium

Figures 9.3 and 9.4 show that the Opportunity Cost ratios are quite different in countries HC and FC. The slope of the straight line drawn tangent at HC's pre-trade equilibrium is flatter or greater than the equivalent line for FC. This means that the Opportunity Cost of rice relative to cars in HC is greater than the opportunity cost of rice relative to cars in FC. Under the assumption of competitive conditions in all sectors, this also implies that the relative price of rice relative to cars is greater in HC than in FC. Rice is therefore relatively expensive in HC, relatively cheap in FC.

If trade is permitted and there are no transport costs, these two relative prices must converge to a common, equilibrium one. But this means that the relative price of rice will fall in country HC and rise in country FC while the relative price of cars will fall in country FC. The differences in the pre-trade relative prices and the common post-trade prices will create incentives for producers in both countries. In country HC, car producers will find it attractive to make more cars and sell them to country FC. Production of cars will expand and rice production will contract. This is seen more clearly in Figure 9.5. A similar process will occur in country FC, but in this case the expanding sector will be the rice sector. The changes are shown in Figures 9.5 and 9.6 respectively.

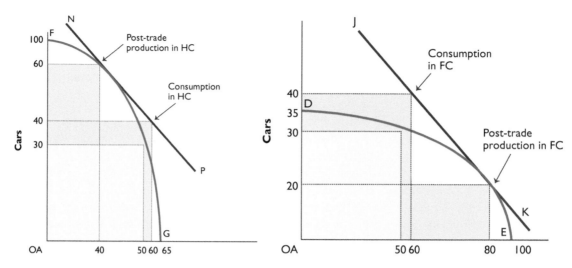

Fig 9.5 Post Trade Equilibrium in HC   Fig 9.6 Post Trade Equilibrium in FC

Country HC will end up producing 60 cars and 40 rice units, whilst country FC produces 20 cars and 80 rice units. Both countries have shifted resources into the sector in which they have a comparative advantage, but note that neither completely specialises in that sector. This is because of the fact that the relative prices alter as resources are shifted between the sectors. A second point to note is that both countries end up at consumption points which would not be possible in the absence of trade; both have gained. Country HC now consumes 40 cars and 60 rice units while pre-trade it was 30C, 50R. And country FC consumes 40 cars and 60 rice units when pre-trade it was 30C, 50R. Country HC exports 20 cars and imports 20 units of rice; country FC exports 20 units of rice and imports 20 cars. The implied post-trade rate of exchange is one car = one unit of rice, that is the relative price ratio and equals unity.

It is important to note that the lines NP and JK have the same slope of unity. This must be the case, because the slopes of these lines measure the agreed common rate of exchange between cars and rice for the two trading partners. One can also see how production has shifted towards the good in which each country has the comparative advantage.

World production and consumption has increased as a result of trade. World production, before trade was 60C and 100R. After trade, it changes to 80C and 120R. The gain of 20C and 20R, has been evenly distributed in this example, with country HC gaining 10C and 10R in terms of consumption. It was 30C, 50R, but now is 40C, 60R.

Similar numbers are found for country FC when the relevant figures are examined. The numerical example has been simplified, but the principle that at least one party gains in overall consumption is a result which is not conditioned on the precise examples used.

It is quite a difficult model to grasp because of the number of assumptions used and the hidden nature of the economics on which it draws. The following paragraphs provide a succinct summary of the basic conclusions derivable from the analysis of this model.

1. HC country is endowed with a number of resources, some of which are more abundant than others. Saudi Arabia has an abundance of oil, Australia an abundance of minerals and the USA an abundance of capital. In each case, abundance is defined in relative terms, i.e. oil relative to capital, minerals relative to capital and so on.

2. If competitive conditions prevail in every sector and if technology is the same in these countries, each country will produce certain goods relatively more cheaply than other countries. The goods that they can produce cheaply will be those that use large amounts of the abundant factor. Thus the USA will export goods which involve large amounts of capital relative to labour, because these will be the goods it can make relatively cheaply. India has a large amount

of labour relative to capital. Therefore, it should export labour-intensive products such as textiles and garments. Natural resource-abundant countries, such as Saudi Arabia and Brazil, should export natural resources according to this theory.

Implications and limitations of the theories of Comparative Advantage

A very important implication that arises from the model discussed above is that trade will be one directional. If Saudi Arabia has a comparative advantage in oil, it exports oil. It will import cars, luxury goods and so on in exchange. If the USA has a comparative advantage in computer equipment, it will export such equipment and import labour intensive goods such as textiles. This type of trade has been defined as inter-industry trade. But a significant proportion of the world's trade is now intra-industry trade. The theory of comparative advantage does not explain this type of trade flow at all. For example, if the USA imports computers and exports computers at the same time, say from Japan or Singapore, which country has then the comparative advantage? The model does not allow for both countries to have the comparative advantage. Economists have developed additional theories to help analyse this type of trade.

The predictions of the comparative advantage models were also based upon a number of crucial assumptions, the most important of which are listed below:

1) Full employment of resources exists in both economies;

2) Model only explains balanced trade, value of exports = value of imports;

3) The model is of a barter economy where money does not exist;

4) The model is static - there is no explanation of growth;

5) Economies of scale are not allowed for;

6) Each sector is competitive with no allowance for monopolies.

These assumptions should make it clear that the model is not terribly realistic. Yet it has provided the basis for the liberal intellectual argument in support of free trade, because of the gains that have been demonstrated in the models discussed above.

9.5.4 Multinational corporation trade: the international product life cycle

One key statistic noted is that multinational corporations are now responsible for a significant proportion of trade flows. There are three points worth noting here:

- That the trade between subsidiaries of the same MNC may help to explain the observed trade in computers, say, between the USA and Japan. Nippon IBM and IBM (US) may well be trading with each other, each specialising in a certain computer type and then trading. Such processes may help to explain intra-industry trade.

- That Multinational Corporations can shift the profits that they earn to the country with the lowest rate of corporation tax by the use of transfer pricing. Since all subsidiaries are usually wholly owned by the parent multinational, the prices charged by one subsidiary to another are largely immaterial. It does not really matter if accounting profits are struck in Brazil or in the USA. But if tax rates are lower in Brazil, it would be better to ensure that the trading profit which arises is located, as far as possible, in the Brazilian subsidiary. This may sometimes be done by charging the US subsidiary artificially high rates for services provided, thus shifting profits to Brazil. Transfer pricing is difficult to prove since many of these transactions are internal to the MNC and are never made public. MNCs can therefore locate production in the cheapest place and serve global markets.

A good example is to follow the history of the trade in pocket calculators. First designed and launched in the USA by Texas Instruments in the mid-1960s, they were priced at around $500 and replaced mechanical adding machines that were then still widely used. The production facilities were located in the USA, with North America the first target market. After a few months, the same product was launched in Europe. This early market was met by exports from the USA. As the market expanded in Europe it became feasible to source the market from European factories, as the production costs fell enough to make EC tariff barriers and the transport cost from the USA a more expensive option. Rapid technical change and increased competition drove down calculator prices. TI s response was to relocate production to Malaysia and Singapore, taking advantage of the global mobility of capital and low transport costs. Now the product is imported into both the USA and Europe from this source.

Note that this example generates three different trade flows. First, calculators are exported from the USA, as technology leading products. Second, they are made in Europe and other markets, so that US exports decline. Finally, the same product is exported from the Far East (by TI) back into the USA and into Europe. Such trade flows cannot be explained by comparative advantage.

9.5.5 Economies of scale and product differentiation as sources of trade advantage

The newer economic theories of trade shift attention from cost differences and allow for the fact that products are often generated by companies, not by industries. BMW cars are regarded as being superior to Ford cars by many consumers in Europe; Coca-Cola is different from Pepsi-Cola and so on. The traditional comparative advantage model assumes that every company within an industry is identical, thus ignoring these differences. New theories of trade have shown how trade in similar goods can flow in both directions at once, if consumers show preferences for particular types of products and if economies of scale exist. Under standard competitive assumptions, a trade equilibrium can be found which explains why the UK sells luxury cars to Germany and Germany sells luxury cars to the UK. The explanation is simple. The individual markets in Germany and the UK are not sufficiently large to create efficient production levels for this type of car and there are not enough consumers to create sufficient demand. In order to exploit economies of scale, each company has to sell abroad as well. If consumers view BMW cars as slightly different from Rolls-Royces or Mercedes, this means that both BMW and Roll-Royce can sell in each other's home market and not take too much business away from each other. Consumers view the product as being differentiated. Under this assumption about demand, it is possible to arrive at an equilibrium position in which the combined UK and German market for luxury cars is served by several luxury car manufacturers. Each manufacturer will sell some of its products in its home market and some abroad. This gives rise to the trade in luxury cars going in both directions at once because no one country has a comparative advantage. The advantage is better understood in terms of each company creating a niche for itself in both its home and export markets by producing a similar, yet slightly different product.

9.6 THE BENEFITS AND COSTS OF FREE TRADE

The above models of trade have also been used to provide the basis for the debate over the benefits and costs of moving towards freer trade. The theory of comparative advantage illustrated that, in principle, everyone in society would be on balance be better off than without trade. This conclusion is arrived at by assuming that every person in society has the same economic weight and importance as everyone else. The loss to one member of society such as a producer who has to cut output because of import penetration is regarded as being offset by the gains to consumers, who pay lower prices because of the extra competition. It can be shown that under certain special assumptions the net gains to consumers more than offsets the losses to domestic producers. The principal gains arise because consumers pay lower prices and because domestic resources are redeployed to more efficient and productive uses, thus generating production efficiency gains.

Therefore, it should appear that free trade is an unalloyed blessing. But in reality many countries have deliberately created barriers to trade, to protect their domestic economy from external competition. Why the difference between theory and practice?

There are a number of reasons for this:

1. The model of free trade assumes that resources displaced by the opening up of markets are redeployed in other sectors. In the real world, import penetration often leads to job losses and unemployment, so there are economic and political pressures generated by those who stand to lose in this process.

2. One very significant group who stand to lose from free trade are the producers who currently survive behind relatively high domestic prices for their goods or services. Unlike the model, if they are few in number and large employers, they may well be able to exert significant political pressure on the government to resist free trade pressures.

3. The major beneficiaries of free trade are domestic consumers. But there are many millions of them and each will perhaps gain only a very small individual amount from lower prices. Thus consumers tend to have less political influence on the decision-making process.

4. There are some economically justified arguments which can be put forward by a country in support of a policy of limiting free trade, such as a policy of protecting the domestic economy from import pressures.

9.7 FREE TRADE VERSUS PROTECTIONISM

There are five main economic arguments which can be employed in the support of government regulation of free trade. They are:

9.7.1 The infant industry argument

The infant industry argument is very simple. It basically states that a country may protect a young, growing industry from the full rigours of global competition in order to permit the industry to develop in both size and technical knowledge. When mature, the industry would be capable of competing against foreign companies with no government support, either via subsidy, by tariff barrier or by quota. The argument rests on the implicit assumption that small industries are unable to exploit scale economies open to large firms in other countries and therefore operate at a competitive disadvantage. The playing field is therefore being levelled by government support.

The objection to this argument is simple. When does an infant industry become a teenage industry? At what point, precisely, should a subsidy or a quota be withdrawn? Once created, the industry may come to rely on the subsidy rather than become more efficient and competitive.

9.7.2 Smoothing the reallocation of resources argument

A second argument, less popular now that many countries have industrialised is that protection is required in certain sectors of the economy so that the transition of resources may be more smoothly carried out. The argument has been applied in support of protecting the agricultural sectors of many countries. In the past, because of its low productivity, rural farming supported many workers. Governments feared that opening up their markets to open competition would generate large levels of rural unemployment and would exacerbate population drift to the towns. This argument has less force for countries which have industrialised as the proportion of their work force engaged in agriculture declines steadily. But it is still employed as a justification for support. The European Union has a social fund which subsidises certain activities in the poorer parts of the community for just this reason.

9.7.3 The strategically important industry argument

The third argument employed in support of protecting an industry is that it is strategically vital for domestic production capability to be maintained. The obvious reason for this is to provide that capability for wartime conditions, when reliance on imported goods becomes a weakness. Many countries have justified support for domestic agriculture for this reason. Some also support their domestic shipbuilders for the same reason. It used to be hard to imagine the UK, Germany or the USA ever allowing their domestic ship repair and shipbuilding facilities to disappear, no matter how efficient the world's competitors become.

9.7.4 To counter dumping behaviour by foreign governments or companies

The fourth argument put forward for protecting the economy from foreign competition is based on the observation that sometimes companies may sell products in overseas markets at a price that is less than the real costs of making and transporting it. This undercuts even the efficient home producer and can occur if the exporter deliberately cross-subsidises the exported goods from excess profits made in their protected home market. The fear is that once the imported goods have captured the home market, the producer can use their monopoly position to drive prices up afterwards. The US government has accused Japanese manufacturers of memory chips of doing just this to its domestic market. It threatened to retaliate by imposing a 100% tariff on the offending products. The problem was resolved by the appreciation of the Yen, which increased the dollar price (in dollar) of the chips concerned. The US also accused British Steel of dumping steel on the US market in the early 1990s. Such disputes can be potentially damaging to all parties if retaliation actually takes place.

9.7.5 To correct a temporary balance of payments disequilibrium

Protection for this reason is only justified if the disequilibrium is temporary, since a permanent disequilibrium represents a more deep-seated problem in the economy itself. The increasing openness of world trade together with the formation of regional trading blocs such as the EU (which prohibits its members from using such tactics against other members) has meant that adopting protectionist measures to cure a temporary problem is less and less common. In the 1960s, the UK government imposed a 15% import surcharge on goods but at the time it was only a member of the European Free Trade Association, EFTA. Such an action would be illegal under EU rules if levied on other EU member countries' exports to the UK. A number of other arguments are often put forward in support of protection, but they do not carry much economic justification.

a) Retaliation

A government may be tempted to retaliate if a trading partner imposes a restriction on its exports. The threat of retaliation may be employed as a means of persuading the trading partner to lift the proposed restriction. When the other EU countries announced a ban on all UK exports of beef, following the discovery that BSE (Bovine Spongiform Encephalopathy or mad-cow disease) can be transmitted to calves, the UK government tried to find non-retaliatory solutions to the problem. It argued that British health standards had been improved enough to ensure that the disease would not be transmitted to Europe via the export of cattle. It was only in 2006 that France finally lifted the ban on UK beef imports.

Retaliation was widespread in the 1930s, when world trade volumes collapsed. Retaliation leaves both countries worse off than they were before. The World Trade Organisation now has a forum designed to allow the resolution of trade disputes before they reach this stage. It should be noted that the USA has often used the threat in negotiations to reduce the huge trade deficit it has with Japan. As noted earlier, the USA would be less affected by such disputes than European countries, which have a higher proportion of trade to national income than has the USA.

b) The cheap foreign labour argument

Often national businessmen complain about unfair competition from companies located in low-cost labour economies. There is an important distinction to be made between low wages and low labour costs. A low-wage economy can in fact be a high labour-cost economy, if labour productivity is also very low. Unit labour costs are determined by the unit cost of labour, divided by the unit productivity of labour. Low labour productivity and low wages often offset each other. If low labour unit costs do exist in one country rather than another, this may well reflect on the relative abundance of the factors of production.

It is interesting to note that Japan's labour force earns higher real wages than the UK's. This has been achieved after 30 years of fantastic growth, both in economic output and in labour productivity. Japanese firms may well still have lower unit labour costs than a rival UK firm, if the growth in labour productivity has outpaced the growth in their wages. The argument that once was applied to Japan is now being applied to China's development, with many citing low wages as the reason for its rapid growth over the period 1995-2005. Economists expect that rising real incomes in China will lead to rising real wages and a convergence of growth, although this process may take many years given the size and level of development of China's economy even in 2011.

Of course we cannot forget that industries and companies will often lobby with governments for protection. Very different arguments can be used from time to time, pointing out differences in regulation between countries. For example, a company can also point out its strategic importance for the country, such as the financial sector in the City of London.

The above arguments notwithstanding, many economists are convinced that freer trade is a more desirable goal for the world community to aim for than regulated or restricted trade. The principal reason for this has already been highlighted in that free trade encourages innovation and competition, rewards the efficient and involves less government intervention. The invisible hand of the market directs resources.

9.8 METHODS OF PROTECTION

There are six main ways of creating barriers to trade;

- tariffs;
- quotas;
- voluntary export restraints;
- exchange controls;
- production subsidies.

All have effects which can be observed in the market place, via their effects on price. In addition, governments can influence trading patterns via a number of more subtle ways. These include public procurement policies, product quality standards and health and hygiene regulations. Economists put these into two categories: tariff and non-tariff barriers to trade.

9.8.1 Tariffs

A tariff is a tax imposed on a commodity import. It may be levied in two basic ways: on an ad valorem basis or as a specific duty. More complex schemes exist, combining these two, but the basic blocks are *ad valorem* or specific duty.

Ad valorem

This is a tariff which is levied as a percentage of the import price. For example, if computers from the USA are imported into the UK, an EU common external tariff of 5% might be levied. A £1,000 computer costs the importer £1,050, plus carriage, insurance and freight. If the price were to rise to £2,000, the duty to be levied would rise to £100. The UK price thus varies in proportion with the world price if an *ad valorem* tariff is used.

Specific duty

The amount of the tax to be paid is always fixed no matter what the price of the imported commodity. It might be 10p per kilo of tomatoes. If the world price of tomatoes was 20p a kilo, the price in the UK would become 30p. If the world price doubled to 40p, the UK price rises to 50p, which is less than double. This is because the tariff is fixed in absolute terms, rather than being determined as a proportion of the import price.

Tariffs as a source of revenue

It should be noted that tariffs can generate significant revenues to the government that levies them. This assumes of course that any tariff that is imposed is not set at such a high level that imports are completely eliminated. It would be pointless from the revenue point of view to set a tariff so high that the domestic market was served only by domestic suppliers. This would mean no imports and no imports means no tariff revenues.

The effect of a tariff

The simple model of demand and supply can be used to illustrate the economic effects of a tariff. By imposing what is in effect an import tax, the government raises the domestic price level of a product, stimulates domestic production, reduces or eliminates imports and raises revenues for the exchequer. All of these effects are measured relative to the free trade position. The model is drawn under the following assumptions in Figure 9.12:

• Competition exists in the domestic market for the product

• The world supply of the product is perfectly elastic. This means that the domestic economy can obtain as much or as little as it likes of the product at the prevailing world price, which is constant. Variations in demand from the home economy have no effect on that price as it is too small an economy in the world market to have any impact.

• Under these assumptions, the world supply curve is given by WS, the domestic supply curve ST, and the domestic demand curve DD. In the absence of any government interference, and in the presence of free trade, the domestic market price must be the same as the world price, OW.

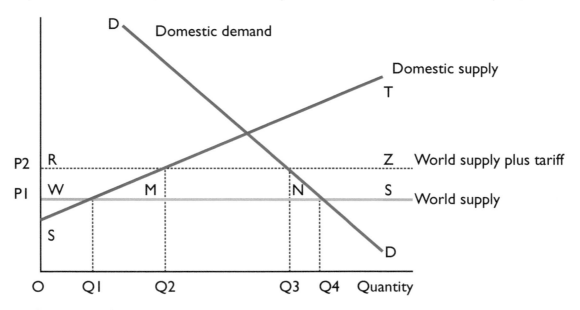

Fig 9.7 Free trade versus protection

Given the market price is W, market demand at that price is Q4. This is met by producing Q1 from domestic companies, as ST shows the amounts that domestic firms are willing to supply at any market price. The quantity Q1Q4 will be supplied by imports, as the world supply schedule implies that overseas companies can supply any amount at that price. Note the small domestic sector. Now a tariff is imposed. It is reflected in the vertical difference between the line WS and the line RZ, which represents the new price of imported goods after the tariff has been levied. This raises market price, which generates three principal effects. First, market demand declines slightly, so total sales fall from Q4 to Q3. The precise size of this fall will depend on the slope of the demand curve or the own price elasticity of demand. The second effect is that domestic supply is increased, as domestic producers are willing to supply more at a higher market price. Thirdly, the importers suffer a decline in business, as import volumes fall to Q2Q3.

This does not mean that the economy would be better off being protected. Two principal effects can be observed in the diagram. Firstly, consumers are worse off than they were in the free trade position. They have to pay higher prices and, as a consequence, they buy less of the product which is being protected. They are clearly worse off. Their precise loss is in fact measured by the triangle N, which measures their loss of consumer surplus. To see this, note that at the old price consumers bought Q3. They also bought Q3 when the price rose to P2 from P1. In a sense, they were willing to pay P2 even when the price was at P1. This willingness to pay is measured by the vertical distance between the price actually paid and the demand curve for each unit of output. The output range Q3Q4 generates the area shown by the triangle N as a result.

It appears that producers are better off as they have expanded. In a sense they are, but this is a false impression. Remember that the comparative advantage model assumes full employment. This means that the resources that have been redeployed in the protected sector have been moved from elsewhere. It follows that output in another part of the economy must have fallen as a result. These two effects can be shown to lead to the economy being worse off overall. Look carefully at the triangle marked M. This shows the difference between what it cost the economy to import the quantity Q1Q2, and what it now costs to produce the same amount in the domestic economy (e.g. the Q2th unit used to cost P1 as it was imported but now after the tariff is imposed, it costs P2, a difference of P1P2). Repeating the same process for all units between Q1 and Q2 generates a total resource cost of M.

Overall, there is a loss to consumers and also an efficiency loss on the production side, as resources are redeployed in an inefficient manner. These two aspects lead to the argument that free trade is superior to protected trade.

9.8.2   Quotas

These are quantity limits imposed on the amount of imports that can be landed in the country in a particular time period, usually a year. They operate by the simple device of the issuing of licenses which are needed by any importer to bring their goods through customs. The most common form of quota is to determine the number of units to be permitted to enter the economy under license although the quota limit might be set in value terms as an alternative. This second type might be used if the primary objective is to save a given quantity of foreign exchange, since the amount is predetermined.

The USA has quotas limiting the amount of sugar imported into the country. In Europe, the EU has sugar quotas for sugar produced by the West Indian economies, primarily to protect its own internal sugar beet industry, but these are set to expire in 2015.

The economic effect of a quota is identical to those generated by tariffs. Domestic market price and production are increased. Instead of raising revenue from tariffs, the government can generate it from the sale of import licenses. Since the domestic market has been restricted, the higher price means that importers are willing to pay a premium to obtain the licence. If the licenses are given away for nothing, the beneficiaries will be the importers who receive the entire excess profit because they pay the world price and receive the full domestic price.

It is easy to see how corruption can creep in when governments determine who should receive the licenses.

Quotas are in some sense easier to monitor than a tariff as they can be easily measured. The effect of a tariff on market price depends on demand conditions, which may be less easy to determine. On the other hand, quotas may lead to severe shortages if the product cannot be easily supplied by the home market. It may also be difficult to adjust the required quota amount to changes in demand conditions. What is appropriate this year may be inadequate next year if demand grows rapidly.

9.8.3 Voluntary export restraints

In the 1980s, the growing openness of the world economy meant that individual countries found it increasingly difficult to use tariffs and quotas to protect their own economies as these were regulated by the various trading rounds of General Agreements on Tariff and Trade (GATT). What emerged in this period was the growth of what has become known as Voluntary Export Restraints (VERs) as a substitute. In the UK for example, the practice was first introduced in 1975, as a means of limiting the share that Japanese car manufacturers were taking of the domestic car market. The UK Government and the Japanese car makers association entered an agreement whereby Japanese car manufacturers agreed to limit their exports to the UK to be no more than 15% of the total car market in any one year. This practice spread. The EC found that Italy had a limit of 11%, France 10% on the same product. The arrangement, being voluntary, was not illegal under the existing GATT rules, which explains its rise. The USA negotiated a similar agreement with Japanese car manufacturers when its domestic market suffered the same fate. In 2006, a VER was agreed between the EU and China over China's exports of textiles. This arrangement is compatible with the WTO rules, because China agreed to be subject to such restraints during the transition phase to full WTO membership in 2010. After that date, such restraints will be incompatible with the WTO trade rules.

9.8.4 Exchange control

Exchange control refers to measures implemented by the Government to ensure that there is a limited supply of the domestic currency onto the foreign exchange markets. By limiting the amount available to be exchanged for foreign currencies, its value in terms of those currencies is also controlled. Many countries used to limit the amount of their domestic currency that could be taken abroad by tourists.

This device is increasingly uncommon, as the trend towards greater liberalisation of the world's economies continues. For example, the UK Government abolished all limitations on currency movements in 1981. Any UK citizen can enter any UK bank and open an account denominated in any currency they wish. This would not have been possible before 1981. The EC insists that any new member country abolishes its exchange controls vis-à-vis other members over a period of time to permit the free movement of capital. For example, Greece liberalised its currency controls in 1996. Even Japan is moving in this direction. Many developing countries have found that support from the World Bank has been conditional on a similar liberalising of their exchange controls.

9.8.5 Embargoes

Embargoes or trade sanctions prevent the export of all goods (or a range of selected goods) to a particular economy. It is normally the result of political events rather than economic ones and can be very effective. For example no country permits the import of cocaine or other hard drugs. They are illegal substances, so unless they are required for medical purposes, they are not legally available. More spectacular cases have arisen in which trade with a particular economy is prohibited by one or more countries. The USA has embargoed all trade with Cuba since Castro's takeover of that country. As many of you will be aware, the Cuban economy is now in some disarray, especially following the loss of trade with Soviet Bloc economies who had ignored the American sanctions. Trade with South Africa was embargoed by the UN. Nelson Mandela actively encouraged the boycott of South African exports prior to the ending of the apartheid regime. Since January 2012 the EU has imposed an embargo on the import of Iranian oil.

9.8.6 Subsidies

A subsidy is a payment by the government agency to the domestic producers of goods which permits them to charge lower prices for their products. There are two types of subsidy: an export subsidy and a general subsidy.

As its name implies, an export subsidy is received by producers selling products into overseas markets. A very good example is the use of cheap finance which was offered by Japanese shipbuilders to overseas shipowners who decided to place an order for a new ship in a Japanese yard. Before the OECD standard terms were agreed which outlawed such practices each shipyard would offer more and more attractive finance deals to overseas owners, as a means of competing. The Japanese Government met the cost difference between the loan terms offered to the owner and the cost of the finance to the shipyard, in effect, a subsidy. Under OECD rules, all such finance is now offered under standard terms.

Subsidies can also be offered in the form of location grants, tax relief on profits and subsidised raw materials. All these devices have the effect of lowering production costs and prices.

A general subsidy is any support which is granted to domestic producers irrespective of their export performance. Such subsidies drive down the domestic price of the products, therefore limiting the market share taken by imports. The subsidy is funded by higher general taxation, so the consumer finds lower prices but higher taxes.

9.8.7 Criticisms of the free trade argument

Many economists have pointed out the limitations of the arguments underlying Free Trade.

The main ones are listed below.

1. The strong gain: there is a general failure to analyse the way that gains from trade are distributed between the trading partners. Some have argued that only strong economies have gained, with weak ones losing out. The rise of the Asian Tigers may perhaps be seen as a counter to this position. These economies have demonstrated an ability to exploit trading opportunities to a greater extent than Europe or North America has in the past 15 years.

2. Infant industries: it is argued that certain industries will always need to be protected or supported before they can become large enough to become competitive on a global basis. A good example is the rise of Airbus Industrie, a European consortium which by 1996 had obtained a 50% share of the world's large commercial aircraft market, formerly dominated by Boeing. It has achieved this with the aid of subsidies from the EC. Boeing and Airbus have accused each other for a number of years of both receiving subsidies. The WTO ruled in August 2010 and May 2011 that Airbus Industrie had received improper government subsidies from several EU countries in the form of loans with below market interest rates. In February 2011, in a separate ruling, WTO found that Boeing had received local and federal subsidies in violation of the WTO rules.

3. Unemployed Resources: the basic model of comparative advantage assumes that resources are fully employed. No economic model has been developed to ascertain the net effect if increased trade leads to permanently higher unemployment. But it should be noted that while the historically high levels of unemployment observed in the 1930s in Europe (and the rest of the world) were associated with falling trade volumes, the general consensus is that trade stimulates jobs rather than destroying them.

4. Monopoly Elements: it used to be argued that the free trade argument was flawed because the comparative advantage model is based on the assumption that all sectors of the economy are competitive. It is well known that many sectors of real economies contain monopoly or oligopoly elements. Their existence was used to argue that for free trade was weaker as a result. But some of the modern theories of trade are based explicitly on the presence of oligopoly and economies of scale. These theories have still demonstrated that more trade is better than less trade .

9.9 TRANSPORT COSTS AND INTERNATIONAL TRADE

The discussion of the benefits from trade has so far been conducted on the assumption that goods can be moved without cost. What happens to the model if transport costs are introduced? The answer is that the presence of transport costs means that there is another potential barrier to trade, the size of the transport cost element itself. If transport costs are high, they act just as if the price of the import has been increased. After all, the consumer has to pay both the import price and the costs of delivery. If transport costs can be reduced, then it follows that trade can be stimulated. The size of and trends in transport costs can thus influence the way the market develops.

Transport costs are defined here as any costs which are incurred in the act of transferring the commodity from its origin in one country to its final destination in another. This clearly includes seaborne transport costs, port loading and discharge costs, transfer costs and land transport costs as well as insurance premiums and interest costs arising from inventory or bank credit.

The presence of such costs explains why some goods are not traded in significant amounts.

A good example is brewing. There is very little exporting of beer, relative to domestic production and market size. The reason is simple: 95% of the product is water. Beer is a bulky and heavy product, which generates very high transport costs for road distribution. It is cheaper to build breweries near major consumption centres and serve markets this way than it is to develop a large international trade in beer. When major brewing companies achieve export success, they license a domestic brewer to make the product. Many successful European lagers are actually made by UK brewers to meet UK consumption rather than being exported.

Figure 9.13 opposite shows the effect that the incorporation of a constant transport unit cost has on prices and output. Transport costs have the effect of raising the price of the imported goods from W to R, an increase in price of WR per unit. The inclusion of transport costs thus has exactly the same affect as a tariff: it raises the domestic price and helps protect domestic suppliers. It follows that falling transport costs actually help to stimulate world trade, as they make it easier for imported goods to compete with domestically produced ones. Shipping has played a role in this process over the past thirty years with the use of larger ships and the spread of containerisation. These two technical changes have helped to lower transport costs and thus assist the development of world trade.

Another model of the affect of transport costs on trade is shown in Figure 9.14. This shows the affect in a slightly different way. It focuses on the market for imported goods. The demand curve, DD1 in the Figure, shows the demand for the imported goods only, in contrast to the demand curve in the previous figure. If there were zero transport costs, equilibrium imports would be given by Q, at price Pw. The addition of transport costs raises the domestic price of the import and demand falls. Sales now run at Q1. In this model the supply curve is upward sloping, so that a fall in price discourages suppliers. The new equilibrium price is Pw+t, but suppliers only receive P. The difference, PPw+t, represents the transport cost element. The model shows that this is divided between suppliers and consumers, as suppliers previously received Pw per unit, so they have lost PPw per unit to transport.

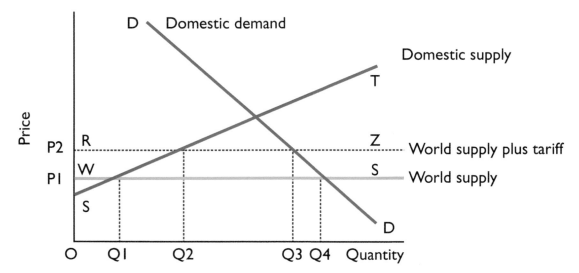

Fig 9.8 The Effect of transport costs on trade

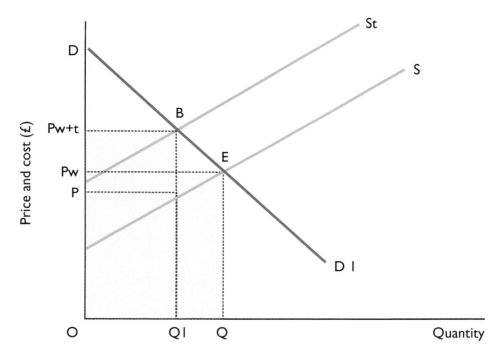

Fig 9.9 The effect of transport costs on the market for imported goods

Similarly, consumers now pay the extra amount PwPw+t compared to the no transport case. The distribution of the burden of transport costs depends on the relative slopes of demand and supply. If you were to imagine that the demand curve was almost vertical (technically-speaking, perfectly price inelastic), there would be little or no change in the output sold and the full amount of the transport cost element is passed on to consumers. If the demand curve was horizontal or perfectly elastic, the market price would not change and suppliers would have to absorb the transport cost element. This would entail the suppliers reducing output sufficiently and lowering production costs to create the necessary margin to fund the transport element.

If shipping companies are able to reduce the size of transport costs relative to market demand, the effect is to stimulate output and lower prices.

9.10 DEVELOPING FREE INTERNATIONAL TRADE: THE ROLE OF THE WORLD TRADE ORGANISATION

The World Trade Organisation (WTO) came into being in 1995, replacing the General Agreement on Tariffs and Trade (GATT), which had been set up after the Second World War with the express purpose of reducing the size and extent of barriers to trade which had existed in 1939. It did this by meeting every few years to conduct a round of negotiations between member countries, the aim of which was the lowering of external tariff barriers. The famous Kennedy round made a significant contribution towards the lowering of tariffs on manufactured goods, which averaged 40% in 1947. By 1995, the Uruguay round had seen this figure drop to less than 5%. As manufacturing tariffs dropped, tariffs in the agricultural sectors and barriers to trade in services became the centre of attention.

The WTO policy objectives, in both the short and long run, have been seriously questioned by demonstrations and protests in the example of Seattle and Genoa. Those serve to cast a shadow over its activities, particularly in areas like the environment and the developing countries trading potential. Based in Geneva, the WTO has as its own objective the further liberalising of trade and its focus has shifted towards the resolution of such problems as the non-recognition of American and European copyright and patent rights in some Far East countries and the reduction of import restrictions imposed on textile manufacturers by the Multi-Fibre Agreement. In addition, trade conflicts, the determination of internationally accepted standards in, for example, food hygiene, are all current issues on the WTO's agenda.

Since 1995, WTO membership has grown with hardly any country outside its orbit. Some 150 countries are full members and most others have observer status, which usually ends with accession. Becoming a member implies responsibilities as well as rights of access to world markets at agreed rates.

The present multilateral round at the WTO, the Doha round, started in 2001 and is not yet agreed. As membership has grown, the need for unanimous consent means reaching agreement has become more difficult. This is reinforced by the fact that manufacturing tariffs are now at a very low level and the main potential for further trade liberalisation lies in agriculture. The Doha round is still stalled because the EU and the USA cannot agree on cutting the large subsidies they both provide to their agricultural sectors. If they manage to reduce the subsidy, present distortions in world agricultural prices and greater trade flows in these goods can be expected.

The future growth of shipping markets will be shaped by the success of this organisation in further stimulating trade.

9.11 CONCLUSION

This chapter has provided information about the growth and pattern of world trade, which of course is the key driving force for shipping demand. Types of trade flows have been examined and economic theories of trade have been briefly outlined. The arguments for and against free trade policies were reviewed, as well as discussing the main forms of protection. The concepts employed in this chapter have been introduced in earlier chapters so if you have had difficulty with them, please refer back to:

chapter 1 for the production possibility frontier;

chapter 2 for demand and elasticity of demand and

chapter 3 for supply concepts.

Chapter 10
· ·

THE BALANCE OF PAYMENTS AND EXCHANGE RATES

As a cheque is only an instruction to a bank, it can be written on anything. In the past people have written cheques on such things as stone slabs, bananas and cows.

10 INTRODUCTION

This Chapter is concerned with certain aspects of international trade; the balance of payments, exchange rates and the way that shipping activities are recorded in international transactions.

Balance of payment accounting is complex because of the numerous and different items that appear in international trade. There is one simple principle underlying the accounts: that all transactions that involve resources, such as the export of iron ore, oil, coal etc., involves a credit to the exporting country. Most transactions that appear in the balance of payments accounts also involve a corresponding financial adjustment, which is entered in a separate part of those accounts. This procedure is called double-entry book-keeping, and explains why the overall balance of payments account is expected to sum to zero. The reason is that the financial entry is entered with an opposite sign from the resource entry, so if all transactions were perfectly matched, they would sum to zero.

A simple example is given below, to make this fundamental point clear.

Suppose there was only one trade between the UK and Germany in the year. The UK exports £1m worth of cars to Germany and Germany exports nothing to the UK. Two transactions would appear in the balance of payments accounts. The flows that relate to resources would appear on the current account and are shown in Table 10.1 below.

In the case being considered at present, the payment for the cars would create a need for the German importer to buy sterling to settle the account. The UK has, by selling goods abroad, created an increase in the UK's holdings of overseas assets. There will be a demand for sterling from Germany in order to settle this debt, which will be funded by a supply of Germany's currency, the Euro, onto the foreign exchange market. Every resource transaction creates a matching change in the assets and liabilities position of the economy and these changes are recorded in the second part of the balance of payments accounts, now called the Capital and Financial accounts of the UK Balance of Payments.

Note that changes that increase a country's assets are, by convention, awarded a negative sign; those that increase a country's external liabilities are given a positive sign. This is very important to remember when studying the accounts.

Current Account (measuring resource flows)	£millions	
Exports of Goods	1	
Imports of Goods	0	
Current Account Balance	+1	(1)
Transactions in UK Assets and Liabilities		
UK's Overseas Assets	-1	(2)
Balancing Item	0	(3)
Balance (1) + (2) + (3) 0	0	

Table 10.1 Hypothetical example of UK Balance of Payments Account

The simple example in Table 10.1 highlights another important point. Credit items on the current account create a demand for a country's currency, while debit items create a supply of the country's currency seeking to purchase other currencies. Hence a deficit in the balance of payments means a country is losing reserve assets and a surplus means they are increasing these assets. There is a link between the balance of payments position and movements in the exchange rate, with countries that experience weak growth and persistent deficits finding that their currencies depreciate over time. It should be noted that a deficit in the current account need not create, for a number of reasons, an immediate change in the value of the currency. One significant factor is the growth in the volume and values of financial transactions that are not related to the trading of physical goods. In many countries, such as the UK, these flows are several times larger than the flows of capital that would be required to finance trade. This means that trade imbalances are no longer the sole determinant of currency movements and other explanations for the behaviour of currency values has to be sought. Capital mobility and the liberalisation of international capital movements is often a key part of IMF reforms when considering giving support to developing economies. Shipping can play an important factor in the balance of payments calculations at a number of levels which will be discussed below.

10.1 DEFINITION OF THE BALANCE OF PAYMENTS

International trade will give rise to indebtedness between countries. Such indebtedness is the central element of the balance of payments. It may be defined as a systematic record of all economic transactions between the residents of the reporting country and the residents of all foreign countries over a given period of time. The term resident covers both individuals being permanently in a country and corporate bodies located therein, but not their overseas branches and subsidiaries. It also includes government agencies and military forces located abroad. The term economic transactions includes exchange of currency for goods and services, but also the transferring of currencies and valuable assets abroad and exchange of goods for other goods involved. Care also must be taken of the word 'balance'. It is to be understood in the sense of a relationship rather than as an exact equality, since it is unlikely that goods and services bought by residents of a country from abroad will be exactly balanced by those sales and services to foreign countries.

To define the balance of payments from a slightly different point of view, rather than simply stating what it is, look at what it is for. From an economic point of view its object is to identify and record transactions between residents of the domestic economy and all other economies. It uses a method that is suitable for analysing the economic relationships between the domestic economy and the rest of the world. Such transactions may involve the movement of real resources, goods, services or property incomes, between the domestic economy and foreign economies, as well as the change in the domestic economy's foreign assets, liabilities or transfer payments.

It is usual to set out the economic transactions of the domestic economy with all other foreign economies as a series of credit and debits. These transactions are divided into three broad areas. They are:

1. Accounts relating to the flows of goods and services currently being produced by the domestic economy or owned by residents of the domestic economy. All these transactions appear in the current account.

2. Accounts relating to changes in the stock of assets or liabilities of permanent residents of that country. This part of the account records changes in the net wealth of the country and is recorded in the capital and financial accounts.

3. An account of the total holdings by residents of assets abroad and of holdings by overseas residents of assets in the country is called the international investment position.

10.2 THE STRUCTURE OF THE BALANCE OF PAYMENTS

The account headings listed above can be examined in greater detail:

i) Current Account: covers transactions of trade in goods, the visibles, trade in services, investment incomes and transfers, the invisibles.

ii) Capital and Financial accounts cover several important sections of the balance of payments accounts. It records changes in the flows of direct investment, changes in the flows of portfolio investment, transactions by banks and the general government account. The latter records changes in official reserves, borrowing and lending of currencies and the take up or repayment of loans from the International Monetary Fund (IMF).

iii) Net errors and omissions represent the net total of errors and omissions arising throughout the account. These arise mainly through timing errors in recording transactions and on recording capital flows. As in the hypothetical example in Table 10.1, the sum of all flows in i) and ii) above should equal zero. The net errors and omissions item ensures that this convention is met.

iv) International investment covers the levels of identified external assets and liabilities.

Note that the fourth item mentioned above is not shown in these accounts. The overall international investment position is shown elsewhere.

1.	**Current Account**				
1.1	**Trade in Goods** Exports	(+)		Imports	(-)
	Net Position		=	Visible Trade Balance	
1.2	**Trade in Services Services** Exports	(+)		Services Imports	(-)
	Net Position		=	Services Trade Balance	
1.3	**Investment Income** Interest Payments Profits Dividends	(+) (+) (+)		Interest Payments Profits Dividends	(-) (-) (-)
	Net Position		=	Investment Income Balance	
1.4	**Transfers** Govt receipts from abroad	(+)		Govt payments abroad	(-)
	Private receipts from abroad	(+)		Private payments abroad	(-)
	Net Position		=	Transfers Balance	
Current Account Balance = sum of balances from 1.1, 1.2, 1.3, and 1.4. Note: Services and Investment Income Trades are sometimes called Invisible Trades.					
2.	**Capital Account**				
2.1	**Capital Account** Capital Transfers Acquisition/disposal of non-produced, non financial assets				
3.	**Financial Account**				
3.1	**Direct Investment** UK companies investing abroad	(-)		Foreign companies investing in UK	(+)
	Net position				
3.2	**Portfolio Investment** UK residents purchase of UK stocks and shares	(-)		Foreign residents purchase of overseas stocks and shares	(+)
	Net position				
3.3	**Financial Derivatives**				
3.4	**Other Investment**				
3.5	**Reserve Assets**				
4.	**Net errors and omissions**				
Balance on Current Account = Balance on Capital Account + Net errors and omissions					

Table 10.2 Outline of the Balance of Payments

Figure 10.1 is derived from the basic structure of the UK balance of payments accounts as presented by the Office for National Statistics (ONS) in the Pink Book for 2006. There has been a number of changes in nomenclature and individual items of the years, but the basic structure remains unchanged. Details may vary from country to country, but in each case, it should be possible to identify the current account, some kind of capital account recording private sector transactions and government capital transactions, a balancing item and a record of the present stocks of a country's overseas assets and liabilities.

It is worth outlining the conventions in a little more detail. Table 10.1 provides a detailed outline of how certain entries are recorded in the balance of payments accounts. Comparison of the outline with Table 10.2 should help in your understanding of the basic structure of the accounts.

For example, Table 10.2 shows that the UK has run a persistent trade deficit in its visible trade balance. It is negative in all the years shown. Put simply, UK residents import a larger value of traded goods than they export. Whilst a deficit of £98 thousand million might appear to be large, the UK's GDP for 2010 was £1,206,818 billion, which means the visible trade deficit was 6.74% of GDP. The overall current account trade deficit was 2.73% of GDP, well within the targets set for good management of a modern economy.

The UK has run a consistent surplus on the trade balance in services. This reached £1,453,620 million in 2010, representing a difference in exports of £112 billion and imports of £58 billion. The performance of the City of London as a major financial centre and with a still significant role as a global centre for maritime services such as marine banking, insurance, legal services and arbitration, helps generate this surplus.

There is also a large deficit on the transfers account. One significant item here is the flows of payments to and from the European Union, as well as government expenditures on activities abroad, ranging from support of embassies to financing wars.

The net balance of current account trading will generate counterparts on the capital account, as has been shown above. But there are extremely large flows that enter the capital and financial accounts independently of the trade in goods and services. For example, in 2010 overseas residents purchased £162 billion worth of direct investment, creating additional liabilities for the UK, so treated in the capital account as a credit. On the other hand, UK residents purchased £139 billion of overseas direct investment, creating additional potential assets for UK residents. This is entered as a debit on the financial account, with the net position on this one item being $162,366 million − £138938 million = £23039 million net credit. In other words, in 2010 more investment came into the UK in this category than went out.

The size of the flows of the financial account is very large, larger than the current account flows. In 2010, the value of exported goods was $266 billion, with a further flow of £171 billion of service exports. Imported goods ran at £364 billion, imported services, £112 billion. The value of direct investment in the UK was £692.9 billion, that of portfolio investment in the UK £2523.1 billion and other investment such as loans and currency deposits, £4047.6 billion. The corresponding debit flows such as purchases by UK residents abroad, in the financial accounts for the UK in 2010 were £1078.5 billion direct investment, £2076.1 billion portfolio investment and £3794.3 billion of other investment. Some of these flows are larger than those created by trade and help to emphasise that understanding modern currency movements is as much about understanding the determinants of financial flows as it is about understanding the link between trade deficits and currency values.

Table 10.2 provides summary data for the UK's Accounts on this basis.

	2000	2005	2006	2007	2008	2009	2010
Current Account							
Trade in Goods	-33,030	-68,784	-76,569	-90,605	-94,181	-82,852	-98,462
Trade in Services	15,013	26,080	35,838	47,956	55,057	57,215	58,778
Investment Income	1,813	22,496	10,470	22,103	33,851	20,656	23,428
Transfers Balance	-9,775	-11,849	-11,876	-13,546	-13,765	-15,076	-20,081
Current Balance	-25,829	-32,667	-43,095	-34,826	-19,753	-20,316	-36,726
Capital and Financial Account Balance							
Capital Account	1,703	1,503	975	2,566	3,241	3,637	3,708
Financial Account	23,133	35,235	33,976	24,982	25,985	24,765	41,517
Net Errors and Omissions	993	-4,071	8,144	7,278	-9,473	-8,086	-8,499

Table 10.3 Summary Account of the UK's Balance of Payments 2000-2005 (Source: Table 1.1, Summary of Balance of Payments, UK Balance of Payments 2006, Office of National Statistics London)

* Increases in assets are shown with a negative sign. © Crown Copyright

To recap on the basic structure of the balance of payments

Whatever the exact form the figures take in any particular country, they will include payments arising from:

- visible trade, that is the sale and purchase of goods;
- invisible trade, that is payments for interest, profits and dividends and services of which shipping would be an example,
- the transfer of capital from one country to another.

In addition there will be a category known as net errors and omissions which covers mistakes made and items omitted or items undeclared, which ensures that the double entry balance of payments always does balance overall.

In this chapter, in order to highlight the factors influencing the balance of payments, the experience of the UK is used as a general example. The points made will all, to a lesser or greater degree, apply to the balance of payments of other countries.

Throughout the chapter the reader should attempt to evaluate the extent to which the factors discussed apply to their own country. The basic headings of the UK balance of payments are:

1. Current account;

2. Capital and financial accounts;

3. Net errors and omissions;

4. The international asset position;.

Table 10.1 presented the net position for these flows, except for item 4.

10.2.1 The current account

Trade in visible goods

The current account is the account of which the general public is usually made most aware, since it is concerned in part with actual goods exported and imported by a country. This includes raw materials, fuel, foodstuffs, semi-processed and finished manufactures. All items are important to the industrial base of a country and its standard of living. The official definition is transactions in goods which are freighted into and out of a country. This section of the balance of payments, the visibles in the current account is known as the balance of trade or trade figures and often features in the national news. When figures are prepared for the balance of payments they are based on the overseas trade statistics compiled from H.M. Customs and Revenue records to which adjustments have been made. But it should be noted that trade flows inside the European Union cannot be collected this way, because with the creation of the single market in 1992, all internal customs monitoring of trade flows within the EU was stopped. The most important valuation adjustment made is the deduction of the freight and insurance elements from the CIF or cost, insurance, freight, valuation declared for imports to arrive at the required FOB or free on board valuation for the balance of payments. Freight and insurance are services and therefore included in the services section of the current account.

Tables 10.3 and 10.4 show an analysis of UK trade, by commodity and by geographical area.

Year	2000	2005	2006	2007	2008	2009	2010
EXPORTS							
Food, beverages and tobacco	9,908	10,647	10,945	11,754	13,776	14,572	16,103
Basic materials	2,603	3,981	4,892	5,517	6,631	5,194	7,346
Oil	15,598	19,866	23,223	22,455	31,975	24,656	31,298
Coal, gas and electricity	1,473	1,702	2,128	1,942	3,551	2,368	3,813
Semi-manufactured goods	47,515	59,630	64,414	68,305	76,433	71,702	80,190
Finished manufactured goods	109,043	114,554	136,654	109,213	117,827	107,472	124,177
Commodities and transactions not classified according to kind	1,686	1,118	1,308	1,161	1,784	2,162	2,787
Total	**187,826**	**211,498**	**243,564**	**220,347**	**251,977**	**228,126**	**265,714**
IMPORTS							
Food, beverages and tobacco	17,663	23,696	25,014	26,713	31,154	32,336	33,463
Basic materials	6,307	6,770	7,887	9,560	11,014	7,617	10,279
Oil	9,048	22,050	26,052	27,153	38,449	28,087	36,024
Coal, gas and electricity	968	3,932	4,921	5,160	10,602	7,444	8,875
Semi-manufactured goods	49,696	62,553	69,156	74,483	79,966	74,978	88,339
Finished manufactured goods	135,282	159,461	185,034	165,636	172,088	157,521	183,990
Commodities and transactions not classified according to kind	1,892	1,820	2,069	2,247	2,885	2,995	3,206
Total	**220,856**	**280,282**	**320,133**	**310,952**	**346,158**	**310,978**	**364,176**
BALANCES							
Food, beverages and tobacco	-7,755	-13,049	-14,069	-14,959	-17,378	-17,764	-17,360
Basic materials	-3,704	-2,789	-2,995	-4,043	-4,383	-2,423	-2,933
Oil	6,550	-2,184	-2,829	-4,698	-6,474	-3,431	-4,726
Coal, gas and electricity	505	-2,230	-2,793	-3,218	-7,051	-5,076	-5,062
Semi-manufactured goods	-2,181	-2,923	-4,742	-6,178	-3,533	-3,276	-8,149
Finished manufactured goods	-26,239	-44,907	-48,380	-56,423	-54,261	-50,049	-59,813
Commodities and transactions not classified according to kind	-206	-702	-761	-1,086	-1,101	-833	-419
Total	**-33,030**	**-68,784**	**-76,569**	**-90,605**	**-94,181**	**-82,852**	**-98,462**

Table 10.4 UK trade in goods in the balance of payments accounts by commodity group, 1985–2005 (selected years, £bn) (Source: United Kingdom Balance of Payments: The Pink Book 2006, Office of National Statistics, Table 2.1. © Crown Copyright)

Year	2000	2005	2006	2007	2008	2009	2010
EXPORTS							
European Union	140,621	170,216	206,197	190,174	211,516	192,908	210,148
Other Europe	20,103	24,892	26,793	29,516	34,464	31,009	35,135
Total Europe	160,724	195,108	232,990	219,690	245,980	223,917	245,283
North America	54,450	61,283	68,536	72,487	77,916	74,850	80,616
South America	5,095	6,783	7,455	8,354	10,274	10,012	11,389
Asia	36,695	52,026	52,868	55,116	65,264	63,750	72,843
Australasia and Oceania	5,023	6,263	6,317	6,858	8,217	8,139	9,543
Africa	7,676	9,544	10,883	11,480	15,163	14,881	17,081
Total	**269,663**	**331,007**	**379,049**	**373,985**	**422,814**	**395,549**	**436,755**
IMPORTS							
European Union	146,789	207,316	235,079	225,178	240,605	218,456	242,850
Other Europe	25,227	33,619	38,756	38,909	48,733	40,499	48,976
Total Europe	172,016	240,935	273,835	264,087	289,338	258,955	291,826
North America	47,643	44,385	49,158	51,756	54,069	50,210	54,869
South America	5,720	7,183	8,798	8,621	10,712	10,426	10,184
Asia	50,916	64,132	69,707	73,834	85,903	82,494	97,989
Australasia and Oceania	3,603	5,194	5,136	5,218	5,794	5,289	5,866
Africa	7,753	11,899	13,131	13,108	16,129	13,836	15,716
Total	**287,651**	**373,728**	**419,765**	**416,624**	**461,945**	**421,210**	**476,450**
BALANCES							
European Union	-6,168	-37,100	-28,882	-35,004	-29,089	-25,548	-32,702
Other Europe	-5,124	-8,727	-11,963	-9,393	-14,269	-9,490	-13,841
Total Europe	-11,292	-45,827	-40,845	-44,397	-43,358	-35,038	-46,543
North America	6,807	16,898	19,378	20,731	23,847	24,640	25,747
South America	-625	-400	-1,343	-267	-438	-414	1,205
Asia	-14,221	-12,106	-16,839	-18,718	-20,639	-18,744	-25,146
Australasia and Oceania	1,420	1,069	1,181	1,640	2,423	2,850	3,677
Africa	-77	-2,355	-2,248	-1,628	-966	1,045	1,365
Total	**-17,988**	**-42,721**	**-40,716**	**-42,639**	**-39,131**	**-25,661**	**-39,695**

Table 10.5 UK Trade in goods and services in the balance of payments accounts: geographical analysis, 1985 –2005 selected years, £bn (Source: United Kingdom Balance of Payments: The Pink Book 2006 , Table 9.3. © Crown Copyright)

Notes: 1. EU is defined as 15 countries for 2000
2. EU membership expanded to 25 in 2005, and to 27 in 2007
3. Mexico included in North America

Trade in services

The transactions that are concerned with the import and export of services are recorded in this section. These are, of course, a vital part of international trade and have played an important role in the UK balance of payments. Traditionally the UK has had a deficit on the visible trade part of its current account, that is it has imported more goods than it has exported, but this has often been compensated for by a surplus earned in services. This changed in the 1980s, as oil exports expanded, and the oil price peaked. The visible trade balance was in surplus between 1980 and 1982, after which it moved into deficit again. The traditional surplus on services, which reached £59 billion in 2010, has not proved large enough to prevent a persistent deficit on the overall trade in goods and services since 1985.

Some of the principal components of the trade in services account are:

a) transportation, including sea transport;

b) insurance services;

c) financial services.

Relevant components of these items are discussed below.

The sea transport account

This now forms part of the transportation account in the United Kingdom balance of payments Pink Book. It is important to note that it does not measure the total value of shipping to the balance of payments, for three main reasons.

The transactions are recorded on an expenditure basis, and not adjusted to measure the value added of each sector.

The transactions associated with shipping, and the provision of shipping services, such as marine insurance, cargo insurance and shipbroking services are recorded elsewhere in the accounts.

The figures do not allow for any knock on effects that the earnings might create for employment and additional domestic jobs related to the shipping industry. They must be regarded as very rough and ready measures of the role of shipping in the UK economy.

Appendix 10.1 reproduces part of the transportation account from the 2010 UK Balance of Payments, published by the Office for National Statistics (ONS). The figures available for sea transport are sub-divided into dry cargo, wet cargo and other which covers trade on coastal routes. Receipts include earnings from the country's merchant fleet, either owned by or chartered to residents of the home country, freight on UK exports, passenger revenue collected from abroad, time charter hire from abroad and payments of foreign ships in the ports of the home country. These are all credits to the home or recording country.

The payments on the debit side of the sea transport figures include home operators' payments abroad. The chartering of foreign vessels, freights and passenger payments to overseas operators and various disbursements such as canal dues, port charges and payments for tankers and other services to vessels. Only the net balances part of the Table is provided.

In the case of the UK, tankers owned by oil companies are considered to be UK operated. Table 10.5 shows that the UK's sea transport improved in the past few years, after running at a small net deficit for the late 1980s, 1990s and at the beginning of the 21st Century.

The shipping market boom has raised rates in the years 2005 and 2008, raising credits significantly and increasing the surplus. The introduction of the Tonnage Tax in 2002 has led to a recovery in the UK registered fleet, which also helps generate greater flows through the account. In 2010, some £9.6 billion of credit was generated and £6.3 billion paid out as debits. These flows are relatively small compared to those generated by the financial services sector, but nevertheless, they are still significant.

What were the reasons for the UK's long term relative decline and imbalances in its sea transport account over the last two decades?

It has been suggested that the following elements help understand the past decline:

1. The heavy commitment historically to sterling area trade and its cross trade which has grown at a slower rate than international trade.

2. The significant re-orientation of UK trade and movement away from the more distant markets towards the closer industrial regions, in particular Europe, has run counter to UK shipping which had traditionally concentrated on the long distance trades. 60% of UK merchandise trade is now with its European Union partners.

3. Shipping freights are usually related to cargo weight rather than value. British export tonnage has been declining since 1914 with a movement away from the heavy staple industries, developed in the 19th century exporting coal, iron, steel and textiles, towards more technologically sophisticated exports of high value and low weights.

4. The virtual disappearance of the re-export trade has been a depressive influence on the UK shipping's net contribution to the balance of payments, as most of this trade is now through Rotterdam or Antwerp.

Trade in financial services – the contribution of the City of London financial centre.

This category includes a wide range of financial and other services which generate foreign exchange earnings. This may be a very important item in the economies of certain countries, for example Hong Kong and Singapore and, of course, the UK. The financial sector includes receipts from and payments for insurance, banking, commodity trading, merchanting, brokerages, the earnings of investment trusts and pension funds. Some of these earnings are shown in Table 10.6. It is now not possible to identify both the Baltic Exchange and Lloyd's Register from the accounts. The insurance sections will incorporate the earnings of Lloyd's of London. The Lloyd's Annual Report for 2011, available at www.lloyds.com, reveals that marine insurance generated gross premiums of £16.3 billion in 2007, £17.9 billion in 2008, £21.9 billion in 2009, and £22.5 billion in 2010. Only 18% of Lloyd's total business was in the UK in 2010, so much of this insurance flow will be a credit, contributing to the net balances shown in Table 3 of The Pink Book 2011. The credits from marine and other types of insurance, which are also shipping related, are not separately recorded in these accounts.

In a study carried out by City Business Services in 2000, it was estimated that the UK maritime sector employed 13,800 people, largely in London and generated £1 billion in overseas earnings in addition to the contribution of British shipping. Gross premiums of marine insurance were estimated at £4 billion in 1998.

It should also be noted that the government account in the trade in services section is the location for debits arising from the maintenance of embassies and military establishments abroad. The UK Government has had a persistent net deficit on this account because of its expenditures on military bases overseas.

Year	2000	2005	2006	2007	2008	2009	2010
Credit	4,334	8,907	8,087	8,459	10,762	9,143	9,645
Debit	4,832	7,612	6,329	5,922	6,588	6,284	6,300
Balance	-498	1,295	1,758	2,537	4,174	2,859	3,345

Table 10.6 Shipping in UK Invisible Trade Balances contributions and expenditure annual average £millions 1985-2005 (Source: United Kingdom Balance of Payments: The Pink Book 2006, Table 3.2 Transportation, ONS. © Crown Copyright)

Years	2000	2005	2006	2007	2008	2009	2010
Freight Insurance	-680	-819	-936	-879	-975	-777	-1,337
Other direct Insurance	412	729	1,805	3,504	2,002	1,993	2,115
Reinsurance	-296	970	1,691	399	2,037	2,136	2,012
Baltic Exchange	336	777	744	802	999	724	779
Banks	3,847	8,839	11,166	14,631	16,059	16,578	14,182

Table 10.7 Earnings of selected financial and allied institutions (net balances) 1995 - 2005 - £millions (Source: The UK Balance of Payments: The Pink Book 2006, Tables 3.5 and 3.6, © Crown Copyright)

Investment income

The third component of the current account, items which are recorded here, have generated significant and growing surpluses in the past decade. The dramatic improvement in the UK's overall current account balance has been primarily due to a huge increase in the surplus on this account, rising from £21.9 billion in 2000 to £21 billion in 2005. By 2010 this balance had reached £23 billion, reflecting the UK's success in becoming one of the leading financial centres of the world, rivaling the USA in particular for leadership. The enormous growth in these figures reflects the increased globalisation of services that has occurred in the past decade. The principal items on this account are the earnings from profits, dividends and interest payments arising from the ownership of assets in the rest of the world and the payment of similar items to overseas residents who own assets in the UK.

Transfers

These items differ from all others on the current account because they do not correspond to an underlying resource transaction. They relate to the transfer of funds from one country to another. Government transfers, and include contributions and subscriptions to the EU and bilateral aid to developing countries. Private debits would include the repatriation of salaries by Indian workers in the UK to relatives in India. Transfers are not included in the calculation of either GDP or GNP.

Calculating the four net balances of the trade in visibles, trade in services, investment income, and transfers yields the current account balance.

10.2.2 The capital and financial accounts

The capital and financial accounts of the balance of payments contain the flows concerned with investment and other capital transactions and will include the accounts measuring changes in the government's reserves, which may be used from time to time if exchange rate movements become excessive, or if there is a run on the currency in the foreign exchange markets. In a freely global capital market, such direct intervention is very rare.

The two principal types of capital investments are recorded in this section of the accounts, direct investment and portfolio investment. Direct investment is the act of buying physical plant and equipment located in a different country. For example, the large investment by Nissan in setting up a car plant on Teesside in the UK would be direct inwards investment. GlaxoSmithKlein's setting up of a factory in Singapore to manufacture its drugs would be an outward direct investment. Portfolio investment refers to the purchase or sale of financial assets, such as stocks, bonds and shares. If a UK citizen decides to buy Microsoft shares, a capital outflow is created, as sterling is sold to pay for dollars to purchase the shares, but assets will increase. Other capital transactions cover the main borrowing and lending of banks and some other financial institutions in respect of non-residents.

An important distinction should be drawn between the current account and the investment sections of the capital account.

The current account refers to flows of expenditure which directly cause flows of goods and services and which are likely to be influenced by the level of income at home and abroad and by relative prices at home and abroad (imports, exports and home produced goods and services).

Transactions in the capital and financial accounts relate to changes in the national stock of assets and are likely to be influenced by relative rates of return and rates of interest in particular. For example, a UK company looking for development opportunities may choose to invest in factories abroad if the profits it is likely to earn (its rate of return) will be higher than could be earned in the UK. Increases in the rate of interest in the home country may result in foreigners investing in that country rather than in their own because they will earn more interest. This may have important implications for the rate of exchange which will be discussed below.

The recordings of movements in the capital account may give some difficulty to readers of this publication. It may seem strange, for example, that a capital outflow is recorded as a debit when it actually makes the country a creditor.

But it must be remembered that:

An **inflow** of capital, such as foreign direct or portfolio investment, is an immediate credit to the balance of payments. This would have the same effect as an inflow of funds paying for exports.

An **outflow** of capital, such as direct or portfolio investment overseas, is an immediate debit to the balance of payments. This would have the same effect as an outflow of funds paying for exports.

A net inflow of direct or portfolio investment might well be advantageous as it could result in a surplus on the balance of payments. However, it is important to remember this may only be a short-run advantage, for in the long-run the profits, interest etc. resulting from this investment will be a debit on the investment income section of the current account. This latter disadvantage would however also have to be weighed against the extent to which foreign investment significantly affects job opportunities for the home country's workers.

A net outflow of direct or portfolio investment may result in an initial deficit for the home country, but in the long run this will be compensated for by credits to the invisibles of the current market. This has historically been an important factor in the UK balance of payments. On the other hand, if the direct investment abroad takes jobs away from home country workers then it may have serious implications for the national economy.

Since the liberalisation of capital controls in 1981, the UK has steadily accumulated a large portfolio of overseas assets. In the early 1980s the outflow of funds was financed by the surpluses on the current account. At the same time overseas companies have built up ownership of UK factories or equity. For example, Maersk's takeover of P&O NedLloyd in 2006 is a form of purchase of UK equity, as was the recent sale of British Airports Authority to a Spanish company. The purchase by Vodafone of an Indian telecommunications company in 2007 would be an example of a flow in the opposite direction.

10.2.3 Accounting for government intervention in foreign exchange markets

An important section of the trading account in UK assets and liabilities measures the degree of intervention used by the domestic monetary authorities, such as Central Banks, in stabilising the exchange rate of their currency. In the case of the UK, the Bank of England monitors the par value of the pound and, from time to time, may intervene to try to stabilise it. The movements of funds required to finance these transactions recorded in several accounts, which will be discussed in more detail in the section on exchange rates. The principal means of intervention is the use of official reserves. The official Treasury definition of official reserves states that this item:

'consists of the sterling equivalent, at current rates of exchange, of drawings on and additions to, the gold, convertible currencies and Special Drawing Rights (SDR's) held in the Exchange Equalisation

Account and, from July 1972, changes in UK reserves in the IMF. From July 1979 it also included reserves of European Currency Units.'

It should be pointed out that one of Gordon Brown's first acts on becoming Chancellor of the Exchequer was to sell the last remaining stocks of gold – the UK no longer uses it as a reserve asset.

The Bank of England sells these reserves on the foreign exchange market when it wants to increase the demand for sterling and buys foreign currencies to add to its reserves when there is upward pressure on the pound. Intervention of this type is much less common than it used to be, because for most of the past 18 years, the pound's value has been driven by market forces. This is discussed in more detail below.

The absence of any persistent intervention, by the UK government, and its repayment of loans taken out in the 1970s from the IMF mean that many of the account entries are zero, as can be seen in Appendix 10.1. Transactions involving the Exchange Equalisation Account (EEA), allocations of SDR and IMF gold subscription account have all been non-existent. When the UK government has intervened, its intervention has shown up in borrowings from other European central banks and its use of official reserves. All of the action revolved around the UK's relationship with the exchange rate mechanism of the European Community, which became the single European Currency, the Euro, in 1999. The UK exercised its option to remain outside the Euro zone and retained sterling. This allows the UK currency to adjust to changes in world market conditions, rather than just using the single monetary instrument of the interest rate.

10.2.4 The International Monetary Fund (IMF)

The IMF was one outcome of the Bretton Woods Agreement which came into operation in 1947. The agreement was intended to encourage international co-operation in respect of the stabilisation of foreign exchange rates in the post war period. When a country becomes a member of the IMF, it is given a quota that is based on the member's national income, its stock of foreign exchange reserves and other signs of its economic importance. The quota is directly reflected in terms of the voting and drawing rights of that country. A subscription is paid by each member, 25% in gold and the remainder in the country's own currency. The IMF has a reserve of currencies from its members which it may later lend to countries with balance of payment deficits. A country may borrow up to 75% of its quota and any loan, plus service charges, has to be repaid usually within 3 to 5 years. Further drawings above the 75% may be made, but these normally result in the IMF imposing increasingly severe conditions on the country concerned in terms of the economic policies it should pursue. These additional drawings are not normally included in the balance of payments in terms of currency reserves because they are only lent under certain conditions.

Special Drawing Rights (SDRs)

These were agreed by the IMF in 1967 and came into operation in 1970. These are additional reserve assets, inconvertible paper money which is issued to members in proportion to their quota. Any member has free access to SDRs, but it must maintain 30% of its initial allocation over a five year period. Drawings may be used to purchase foreign exchange from other members.

SDRs are charged at a rate of 5% interest and since they are never repaid, they make a net addition to world reserves and so differ from ordinary drawing rights which have to be repaid.

10.3 EXCHANGE RATES AND THE BALANCE OF PAYMENTS

A glance at any of the financial press reveals that there are very wide fluctuations in currency values, a situation that has developed from the early 1970s. After discussing some different measures of exchange rates, this section gives a brief outline of the post war changes that have occurred in the way that the international monetary system has evolved since the Second World War. A simple model of exchange rate determination is then developed and its limitations discussed.

There is a number of different ways of defining the rate of exchange. The spot rate is the rate for immediate delivery of a currency, which is usually two or three days. The forward rate is the name given to a contract which promises to deliver a fixed amount of foreign exchange a certain period of time in advance, usually one or two months. Both of these rates are for specific currencies. Measuring the relative value of a currency against another is easily done with the spot rate, but countries trade with hundreds of partners. Economists now use a trade-weighted index to measure the overall performance of one currency against its trading partners, the weights being given by the relative shares of trade. For the UK, the relevant index is the Sterling Exchange Rate Index, and is set at 100 for Jan 2005. In 2007 the index stood at 104.07, in 2010 it fell to 80.67 and to 80.18 in 2011. This means that the pound's value fell by about 23% against all its trading partners currencies, reflecting an overall devaluation of the currency. This is sometimes called the effective exchange rate, because it reflects the currency's value against all of its trading partners.

Between 1945 and 1971 most world economies operated a fixed exchange rate system. Under these arrangements, each country's currency was given a par value, which was guaranteed by the central bank within a band of 2.5% either side. The central bank thus needed to intervene to maintain this rate. Suppose there is a greater supply of sterling onto the foreign exchange market than there is demand for it at its current par value. The central bank, in this case, the Bank of England, would intervene by buying its own currency from traders, which it would finance by running down reserves of gold and foreign currencies held for that purpose. If there was an excess demand for sterling, it would sell its own currency and purchase dollars, yen etc. to be placed back into its reserves.

Providing that there was, over time, a broad balance of demand and supply, this kind of arrangement worked quite well. But if there is a persistent excess supply of sterling, there would be a persistent drain on reserves. This cannot be sustained indefinitely, so the government would have to intervene to try to eliminate the cause of the problem. There is therefore scope for government policy action of the sort discussed in the next section.

One major disadvantage of the above system was that par values were not changed to reflect differences in the underlying economic performance of the major trading economies. The rise of Japan and the decline of the UK as economic powers were not reflected in the relative values of the two currencies. The UK, in particular, found it had persistent problems on its balance of payments at the par value of £1=$2.40, a rate which persisted from 1949 until 1967.

One way of understanding the arise of such problems is to follow the model below. Assume for the moment that all currency flows are driven by trade. Portfolio and direct investment are set to zero. Suppose there are two trading countries, the UK and the USA. The UK exports goods and services to the USA and the USA does the same to the UK. Consider three different exchange rates. £1 = $1, £1 = $0.667c and £1 = $0.50c. This is equivalent to $1 = £1, $1 = £1.50, and $1 = £2.00. Thus the dollar is appreciating against sterling or sterling is depreciating against the dollar. A UK car costing £5,000 will sell at $5,000, $3,333, and $2,500 respectively. At the lower dollar price, more cars will be sold to the US. As a result, there is a greater demand for sterling from US exporters. This is shown as schedule DD in Figure 10.2. Now consider the effect of these exchange rates on the sterling price of a US export priced at $5,000. This translates into sterling prices of £5,000, £7,500 and £10,000 respectively. As the pound depreciates against the dollar, the sterling price of US dollar exports rises and demand will fall. This means that the supply of sterling onto the foreign exchange market will rise as the value of the pound rises. This relationship is drawn as S in Figure 10.2.

If the market is allowed to find its own level, an equilibrium rate of exchange is determined. In this example, it is £1 = $1.50. At this rate the demand for sterling from US exporters equals the supply of sterling from UK importers. Since they are both using the same rate, it follows that the value of exports to the US must equal the value of imports, at that rate of exchange. In other words, equilibrium in the foreign exchange market coincides with equilibrium in the value of international merchandise trade.

Now suppose the US manages to sell far more goods to the UK, as the result of launching a new product. There will be a sharp rise in the sales of US exports at every possible rate of exchange. This is shown by a rightward shift in the SS curve as UK importers supply more sterling at every possible exchange rate. In a free market, the value of the pound would fall against the dollar, to £1.00 = $1.00 in this example. At this new rate of exchange, UK exports are cheaper in dollar terms and imports from the US become more expensive in sterling terms. This will reduce US import volumes and increase UK export volumes, with a new equilibrium at point B.

If, on the other hand, the Government is unwilling to permit the pound to fall in value, it would have to step in. It does this by providing an additional source of demand, sufficient to maintain the rate at £1=$1.50. It would have to run down its reserves to fund this process. Note that if the problem persisted next year, it would again have to run down its reserves. This solution is only temporary in nature; there are limits to the degree of support.

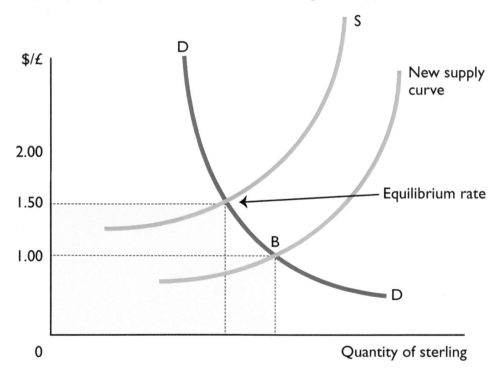

Fig 10.1 Free market equilibrium in the foreign exchange market

After 1971, this kind of intervention became less necessary. Exchange rates have now been left to find their own levels, that is, they have been permitted to float. The Government can still influence the free market rate, but the intervention is usually achieved via the manipulation of interest rates. The reason for this is that a very large proportion of currency movements are now driven by portfolio investments, which are not directly related to trade. Indeed, a large part of modern financial derivatives trading has evolved as a means of profiting from risk in various forms, including currency risk. These currency flows are affected by the rates of return earned, which itself is driven by levels of interest rates. In the context of the above example, the UK government can raise the rate of interest, which has the effect of increasing the demand for sterling from abroad. Such rate rises also reduce domestic demand, so governments have to use them with care.

An example may help to illustrate the ideas mentioned above. In the late 1980s, the UK was shadowing the German currency, the Deutsche Mark (DM), with a target rate of £1 = DM2.95, as part of its anti-inflation strategy. During 1991 and 1992, US interest rates fell and German rates rose, as reunification was financed. As a result, a large amount of portfolio funds and banking assets, were moved to Germany. This caused a wave of selling of the pound, which the UK authorities met by raising domestic interest rates. A wave of speculative selling then triggered several currency re-alignments in Europe. The UK borrowed £7.25 billion in foreign currency to assist its defence of sterling. By the 16th September the currency was trading at its floor level. On that day, two successive rises in interest rates were announced, from 10 to 12, and then from 12 to 15%. Neither had any effect on the selling wave of sterling, so the pound was allowed to float, it fell from 2.95 to 2.36DM in one month, a devaluation of about 20%, against that currency.

In this case, neither interest rate increases nor government announcements were sufficient to prevent a change in the value of the currency against the German mark.

Figure 10.3 shows the development of the spot exchange rate between sterling and the US dollar over the period 1995 to 2010, together with the associated trade balance, in £bn, over the same period. It is clear that there is some association between the rising value of sterling in the period 2001 to 2005 and the rising UK trade surplus in that period. The relationship is not very strong, because other factors drive the currency as well, as has been discussed.

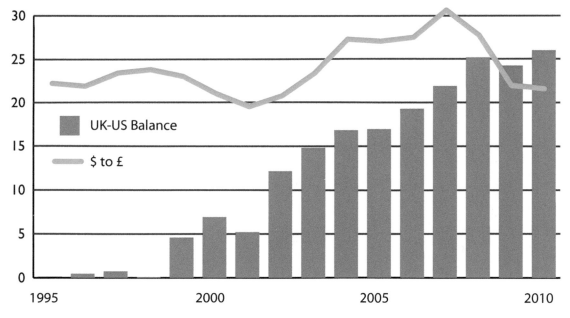

Fig 10.2 UK-US trade balance and the spot exchange rate, 1994-2006 (Source: Derived by the Author from IMF Direction of Trade Statistics, MIMAS 2007)

10.4 DEALING WITH A BALANCE OF PAYMENTS DEFICIT: FIXED EXCHANGE RATES

The way in which a balance of payments deficit is dealt with by a government will depend to a large extent on the cause of the deficit and whether it is a long or short term trend.

A deficit may arise on the part of the private transactions recorded in either the current or capital account of the balance of payments. In effect, this creates an excess supply of the domestic currency on the foreign exchange markets, since the demand for, say, sterling, generated by its credits, is less than the supply of sterling generated by private sector debits. If a government is committed to maintaining the present rate of exchange, it will have to find a means of supplying the difference between these two amounts, in order to maintain the target exchange rate.

It may do this by running down its stock of reserves of foreign exchange. In effect, it enters the foreign exchange market and buys back its own currency, creating an additional source of demand. But it can only do this as long as there is a positive stock of reserve currencies. Persistent deficits will drain these reserves and so their use can only be a temporary device. Alternatively, the government may try to reduce the deficit by the use of domestic monetary policy, namely, raising domestic rates of interest. This has two effects; it encourages an increase in holdings of portfolio investments of UK assets from abroad and it reduces domestic demand, thus slowing the growth of imports. Both these effects will reduce the size of the private sector deficit.

In extreme circumstances, additional financial support may be obtained from the IMF or other international banks, primarily to back up the official reserves. The price of such arrangements often means that national governments have to run their economic policies in line with IMF recommendations and these may not be very comfortable.

In addition to intervening in the foreign currency markets or using interest rate policy, governments may use the following policy instruments to try to reduce the deficit:

- Raise tariff barriers;
- grant export subsidies;
- impose exchange controls;
- impose quotas on imports.

Many of these alternative strategies are now more difficult to apply on a unilateral basis under WTO rules. For example, in 2001 the USA created an international row by unilaterally raising tariffs on steel imports, ostensibly because its traditional steel producers were facing unfair competition from Japanese, European and Indian producers. After a number of years, the issue was resolved, with the WTO finding that the USA had breached the agreed trade rules.

Note that many countries now recognise that these devices do not cure the underlying reason for exchange rate re-alignments, which are driven by changes in the relative economic competitiveness of the world's economies. The only way of ensuring a strong currency is to have a strong economy. In the long run, policies designed to ensure that the economy remains competitive are far more likely to be successful than those designed to deal with what is a symptom, not a cause, of a problem. But political expediency, as in the 2001 case of President Bush and US steel imports, is often a very strong driver.

The vast trade surplus generated by China has to be reinvested abroad in the form of overseas investments to help prevent an accumulation of large amounts of foreign currency in its reserves. Under a fixed rate scheme, the trade surplus currency will be in excess demand, and foreign currency can be purchased in exchange for Chinese currency needed to fund the trade. But accumulating reserves does not help the economy to grow. The Chinese economy has grown rapidly. In which case the revaluation, by making Chinese exports slightly more expensive in dollar terms, might help slow down Chinese export growth slightly. It would also lower the domestic price of imported goods in China, thus marginally encouraging more imports and helping to reduce the trade imbalance.

In March 2012 the Chinese government announced that it would allow the Yuan to float more freely. This is in line with previous appreciations of the Yuan against the Dollar. In the period 2011-2012 the Yuan has risen by 8% in value compared to the Dollar.

10.5 DEALING WITH A BALANCE OF PAYMENTS DEFICIT: FLOATING EXCHANGE RATES

Under a regime of floating exchange rates, government intervention should not be required, at least in theory. This is because any private sector deficit will generate economic forces that will help to restore equilibrium to the account. Two examples are given here.

Firstly, suppose there is a deficit in trade in goods and services on the current account and a balance on the private transactions of the capital account. There will be an excess supply of sterling at the present rate of exchange as a result. If sterling's value is determined by supply and demand, its price will fall against other countries' currencies. This will make exports become cheaper in overseas markets and imports dearer in the UK. Provided that certain conditions are satisfied exports will rise, generating an increase in demand for sterling and imports will fall, reducing its supply. Both of these processes will lead to a reduction in the excess supply of sterling. Therefore, the rate falls until it finds its equilibrium level, at which point exports and imports are also rebalanced.

Alternatively, the deficit may be on the capital account. But this means the same process will evolve. The difference being that lower currency values raise rates of return to outside holders of currency and start to make sterling look more attractive as a home for portfolio investment.

10.6 EXCHANGE RATES AND SHIPPING

One of the most obvious examples of the potential influence of exchange rates in shipping is that of brokers who earn their commission in US Dollars. This is the currency in which their business is done, but their expenses must be met in their home currency, so as the exchange rate alters so does their income. For example, sometime in mid 2007 the £ was worth US $1.97, whereas at the end of 2010 it was worth US $1.54. Therefore an income of US $100,000 is worth only £50,761 in 2007, but £64,935 in 2010. The fall in the value of the dollar generates a sterling capital loss in this case.

As you may imagine this could create problems as all the UK brokers' own expenses will normally have to be met in sterling and not US dollars. For this reason, brokers may very well opt for a US dollar rather than a sterling mortgage when buying a house. They also hire staff to manage their risk exposure to currency fluctuations.

We can look very simply at the business side for a moment and consider the cost of bunkering a vessel. This is a dollar cost. Let us say that in late 2010 the price in Rotterdam of 1,000 tons of bunkers would be US $600,000 ($600 per ton) giving a total of £387,000, using the current exchange rate. 3 months previously the exchange rate was such that the cost would have been £379,075 (assuming the dollar cost was the same).

This volatility in exchange rates can be dealt with in a number of ways:

- Measure all transactions in Dollars, where possible.

- Hedge some of the currency risk by using the forward exchange market. This works by entering into contract to buy Dollars, at a rate fixed today, for three months forward delivery. If a UK importer had a contract to settle with a US trader three months forward, they could hedge against currency risk in this fashion. There is of course, a cost to the hedge.

The increased volatility of exchange rates has led to the development of sophisticated financial products that are designed to permit shipowners and ship charterers to limit their degree of currency risk exposure. These are called financial derivatives or options. An analysis of this market is beyond the scope of this chapter.

10.7   CONCLUSION

The rate of exchange evidently has a strong influence on the balance of payments and is vital in considering prices in international trade.

The individual and the company in international trade and related services must understand what is happening on the exchange market and the balance of payments of their country.